AF673280

CHILD TRAFFICKING
An Unconscious Phenomenon

CHILD TRAFFICKING

An Unconscious Phenomenon

S K Bhagat

MD PUBLICATIONS PVT LTD
NEW DELHI
www.mdppl.com

Copyright © 2009 by MD Publications Pvt Ltd.

All rights reserved. No part of this book may be reproduced or utilized in any form or by any means, electronically or mechanically, including photocopying, recording, or by any information storage and retrieval system, without the prior permission in writing from the publisher.

Published by :

MD Publications Pvt Ltd
"MD House", 11, Darya Ganj,
New Delhi - 110 002
Phone : +91-11-41563325 (Customer Service)
+91-11-41562846 (Editorial)
E-mail (orders): order@mdppl.com
Website: www.mdppl.com

ISBN: 978-81-7533-214-0

Published and Printed by Mr. Pranav Gupta on behalf of **MD Publications Pvt Ltd** at Mohit Enterprises, Delhi.

PREFACE

Child trafficking is both a result and a cause of violation of child rights. This is because it is the children who are poor and marginalised, whose basic rights are violated that are most vulnerable to child trafficking. Children are trafficked for numerous purposes including labour, sexual exploitation (prostitution), sports and entertainment, adoption, marriage or illegal activities like begging, drug peddling etc.

Children are trafficked for several reasons including sexual exploitation; adoption; entertainment and sports (for example, acrobatics in circus, dance troupes, beer bars; as camel jockeys); marriage; labour; begging, organ trade (though only anecdotal evidence of this is available); drug peddling and smuggling. Trafficking of children usually happens through well organized networks. Family, relatives, friends, community leaders, brokers, the pimps and owners of brothels, the police, political connections and the criminal nexus: all or any of these have been found to be involved in the process of child trafficking.

Trafficking in children is a global problem affecting large numbers of children. Child trafficking across the region is not only committed by organized criminal networks. It may involve friends, relatives and even parents of children. There are push and pull factors that draw children into being trafficked and poverty is generally recognized as the most visible and widespread cause but, while further research is needed into the root causes, it is well documented that violence and abuse at home and in the community and indeed the lure of a better life means that children and young people can fall prey to traffickers.

Child trafficking is lucrative and linked with criminal activity and corruption. It is often hidden and hard to address. Trafficking always violates the child's right to grow up in a family environment. In addition, children who have been trafficked face a range of dangers, including violence and sexual abuse. Trafficked children are even arrested and detained as illegal aliens.

Child trafficking is a ghastly reality that stares in the face of the civilized global community. India is not free from the clutches of this social vice. Child trafficking is rampant in India and the Indian government despite undertaking several measures has not been able to root out this horrible social menace completely. Every year thousands of children are trafficked and are forced to serve as bonded labourers and slaves. The girl children fall prey to the prostitution rackets and land in the brothels or end up being sex slaves. Some of them are forced to work as domestic servants.

I am very grateful to Mr. Pranav Gupta, Director of MD Publications Pvt Ltd, New Delhi, for his cooperation and support for this book.

S K Bhagat

CONTENTS

1

Child Trafficking

An Introduction

EXPLOITATION OF CHILDREN

Unaccompanied children outside of care have to fend for themselves. Children who have not applied for asylum do not have a regular status and as such are barred from legal employment. In contrast, children who have filed an asylum application and are over the age of 15 are, in theory, permitted to work in non-hazardous jobs; however, due to the dysfunctional guardianship system, they are often unable to secure the necessary guardian's consent to obtain a work permit. As a result unaccompanied children who live outside of state-sponsored care arrangements-most unaccompanied children-find themselves in a daily struggle for survival, compelled to accept any type of work they find. Operating outside the legislative framework, many end up performing exploitative and hazardous work.

Children interviewed were paid wages below and sometimes far below the minimum wage, and they worked for extensive hours. Work under such conditions amounts to exploitation that may reach the level of forced labour. Although Human Rights Watch's research did not focus on trafficking, some children whose testimonies are documented in this report may have been trafficked, as defined in international law. It is too often reported that rural and urban

India has pervasive practices of child labor, juvenile servitude, domestic juvenile servitude and trafficking of juvenile girls. Despite enactment of the Juvenile Justice Act 1986 and 2000, and in spite of several positive provisions embodied into the Indian Constitution and the Universal Human Rights Declaration aimed at safeguarding the rights of children leisure, learning and play - the social reality continues to be grim. We find a large segment of children outside the school portals and equally a large number engaged either in work or in delinquent activities.

There is a need to identify potential risk factors for baby battering, child labor, child sexual abuse etc., so as to better understand the problem, improve the treatment of the victim as well as perpetrator and take preventive steps to restrict the incidence of child abuse. Announcements of new legislation, commissions or programs by the respective governments in the absence of the will to implement the same have nothing more than politically motivated ornamental values. A societal awareness to boldly report the cases of child abuse, honest and scientific investigation by the Investigating Agencies and speedy delivery of justice by the Courts is all that is required in addition to a change in the attitude of the community towards the children. It must be remembered that rights and duties are two sides of being human. A child can achieve his rights only if others perform their duties. Proper performance of duties by the parents, teachers, and government officials of the various departments associated with child welfare and community at large is necessary for fulfilling the rights of children and here comes the role of forensic medicine also.

CHILD LABOUR

The Constitution of Greece prohibits any form of compulsory work. In the context of protection of the family and citizen's health care, the state is obliged to adopt special measures for the protection of childhood and youth. Children from the ages of 15 to 17 who are employed are entit-led to special labour protection relating to work hours and must be paid at least the minimum wage. Greek law reflects international standards and prohibits employment of children below age 18 in occupations that may harm their health, security or morals. Human Rights Watch found unaccompanied children who were mainly working in the agriculture and construction sectors and some in garment manufacturing-all working without legal protection in situations that violated Greek law.

Interviews with both children and adults suggest that a large part of the workforce during orange, olive, and onion harvests consists of children. "There were a lot of children working there. Out of 15 persons... only five or six were adults," said 16-year-old Hafez S. about the orange harvest in Argos. Children were recruited from Athens or Patras, typically through fellow nationals and lived next to the plantation during the harvest. In contrast, unaccompanied children who worked in construction found such work around Athens, on short notice, and often for a few days only. Not surprisingly, children said it is more difficult to find jobs without a work permit.

Fifteen-year-old Nurullah F. told Human Rights Watch: "I found three jobs but because I don't have a work permit I can't work. The person I had to work for told me I could not get a work permit until I'm 18. He told me to go back to the police to say that I'm 18 and to have my birthday changed". Similarly, 17-year-old Musa M. told us: "They tell me that I'm underage so they don't want to keep me". Human Rights Watch visited a square in Athens where dozens of migrants and asylum seekers wait for jobs every morning. We encountered several young boys standing in a group. Although some of them seemed clearly younger than 18, when we asked them about their age, they were firm that they were not underage.

Children employed in farm work and on construction sites perform labour that exposes them to a combination of health and safety risks: the lifting of heavy loads, the risk of falling from height, cold temperatures over long hours, and substandard and unhygienic accommodation. None of the children interviewed performed such work under the exceptions permissible in national law, and the required safeguards and protection were not applied. Health and safety risks make such work prohibited forms of child labour and bring them into the category of worst form of child labour, as defined by article 3 of the Worst Forms of Child Labour Convention. While this is also in violation of Greek law, there was little evidence that the Greek authorities take steps to enforce the law and protect children.

All children who worked in the construction sector told us that they had to lift heavy loads and almost all had to mix cement and carry it up several floors for other workers. Fourteen-year-old Wali P. said he wasn't able to find any lighter work on construction sites: "carrying up the cement is the hardest. Always the young [boys] carry up the cement", adding, "I can't find any other work". Nurullah F., age 15, reported: "I had to carry cement up to the fourth floor.... They cut plastic containers and put cement inside and I had to carry those containers up to the fourth floor. They weighed about 18 kg". Children working outside the construction sector also ended up carrying heavy loads. Fifteen-year-old Nurullah F. told us: "I worked for 20 days in a factory.... We took boxes from the container and carried them into the shop. The boxes were sometimes one meter large, sometimes half a meter.... They were very heavy.... They weighed about 20-25 kilos".

Some children carried their heavy loads on concrete stairs; others, however, had to balance their loads on scaffolds and unfinished stairs without safety measures to prevent them from falling. Several children reported work injuries that resulted from falling off scaffolds and unfinished stairs. Wali P. told about his work and the fate of a friend:

> I walk up on wooden beams, as high as five floors. The [scaffold] is dangerous to walk up on and it's difficult to keep the balance with one big bucket on a small beam. My friend fell down from the second floor onto the scaffold [underneath]. He

> injured his hand.... He went to the hospital and was in hospital for two weeks.

Hazards were not limited to work in the construction sector. The risk of falling was also a risk for children employed in agriculture, a majority of whom harvested oranges. Boys climbed on ladders that stood on soft ground and reached out to pick oranges from the tops of trees. They told us how they and others frequently fell from these ladders. Hafez S, 16 years old, had harvested oranges:

> We had ladders and a bucket. We sometimes fell from the ladder. I fell down four times in one month. It wasn't very high so I wasn't injured. The soil was soft so the ladder wasn't very stable.

Ghulam S., aged 15, also spoke of the consequences of falling:

> Some trees were big. Two persons collected [from below] as far as hands could reach, and two climbed on a ladder to pick [from the top]. Sometimes people fell down from the ladder. My friend fell down and was unconscious for 30 minutes. Once he fell down and broke his finger.

Agricultural labourers are typically paid by the amount of fruit they harvest. Such schemes lead to competitive work environments in which every person tries to harvest as fast as he possibly can. This increases the likelihood of accidents as workers are less likely to take precautions. Twenty-five-year-old Yusuf K. described the competitive work environment during the olive harvest in Sparti: "We had to climb onto the tree to collect the olives. It was dangerous and many people fell down. Everybody tried to work fast to fill their boxes. It was very competitive.... I fell down many times".

In garment manufacturing, children typically have to work for 10-12 hours per day over a period of several months. Although the work itself is not subject to hazards, the excessively long work hours, coupled with the fact that they have to perform repeated tasks over prolonged periods in the same physical position, pose a health risk. Zahir B. told us: "The work was very hard, especially to sit in a chair for so many hours. It was an easy job that didn't require special knowledge but it was hard. I had back pain and shoulder pain; because I always had to lean forward I now have pain in my neck".

Seventeen-year-old Musa M. has a history of child labour and has been sewing clothes for years. He describes the impact of the long working hours on his health: "When I was in Iran I worked as a tailor and in Turkey as well. The doctor said I should change the job because I'm sitting for many hours without moving.... If I work too much I have pain in my kidneys.... If I work hard I feel a lot of pain. Then I take medicine". The orange harvest takes place during the winter months, in the cold and rainy season. Children who harvested oranges told us they had to start their work day as early as 4 a.m., in freezing temperatures, and the oranges they collected were covered in frost. Children did not have sufficiently warm clothing. Some fell ill as a result from working in such conditions. Sixteen-year-old Hafez S. said: "In the morning the trees were full of ice; we made a fire in the plantation; after a few minutes [of harvesting] we went back to the fire to warm our hands; we didn't have warm clothes".

An adult, Yusuf K., recalled how workers who harvested oranges in Arta, among them children aged 14 and 15, fell ill: "It was very hard and very cold. At 4am there was frost and we had to put our hands under our armpits to warm them.... When we went to work without water we were compelled to eat oranges. These oranges were frozen so people got sick. Some people also forgot to bring water and one bottle was finished very quickly and then they had no more water". Children who work on con-struction sites risk damage to their health from working unprotected under the sun. Fourteen-year-old Wali P. compared his work on construction to work in a green-house: "It's better to work in a greenhouse.... It's hot in the greenhouse but work outside is almost always under the sun".

Arif L. told us how he got sick after working unprotected under the sun: "One day I got sick. On that day I worked to carry bricks up to the third floor. When I got home suddenly my nose started bleeding. It was a very sunny day and I worked in the sun all day.... There was no protection against the sun". Living in substandard, over-crowded, poorly heated and unhygienic conditions jointly with adults, poses security and health risks for unaccompanied children. Unaccompanied children interviewed by Human Rights Watch who were employed on plantations stayed with other workers in often filthy accommodation provided by their employers, in some cases paying excessive rents. Yusuf K. described how 30 persons had to share a single toilet and as many as 60 persons stayed in one room, where they slept, ate, and stayed whenever weather conditions didn't permit outdoor work.

For that place, the owner collected 90 Euros monthly rent from each person, which adds up to around 5,000 Euros. All persons interviewed by Human Rights Watch said that numerous underage boys were living and working in such conditions. Fifteen-year-old Aktar P. recalled picking oranges in Argos:

> They kept in each room 10 persons together. The room was.... about 12 square meters. We paid one Euro per night. There was a mattress but no blanket and no sheet. My friend had a blanket and we slept the two of us under one blanket.... The room was not clean because there was no place for shoes and we ate and slept in the same room. We had one toilet for all [37 persons]. The toilet was in the garden, without roof and no running water.

WORK HOURS AND PAYMENT

Work hours and payment for children interviewed by Human Rights Watch varied on the type of sector they worked in. Common to all children was that wages were below the minimum wages prescribed by law. Sometimes children were paid as little as 30 percent of the minimum salary for a day's work. In the construction sector, where children are often recruited on a day-to-day basis, work lasts from early morning to around 3 or 4 p.m. Wages, children told us, are around 25 Euros per day: "I worked from 7 a.m. until 4 or 5 p.m. and got 20, 25 or 30 Euros," 16-year-old Mohammed W. told us.

Children in agriculture and garment manufacturing regularly worked for 12 hours and more. In garment manufacturing, they were paid between two Euro fifty and three Euros per hour. In agriculture they were paid per amount of harvested fruit, around 15 Euros for one ton of harvested oranges. This meant that in plantations with less fruit, children ended up working longer hours for the same wage-a day wage could be as low as ten Euros. Children employed in agriculture additionally had to pay for the often substandard accommodation provided by their employers from their salary. Sixteen-year-old Hafez S. recalled:

> For one ton of oranges we got 15 Euros. We tried to collect as much as possible. We collected four persons in one group. I earned about ten to fifteen Euros [per day]. One day I managed to earn 20 Euros.... I worked for 19 days and.... after I paid food and rent I got 150 Euros.

Children did not receive sufficient hours of rest in-between work days; breaks during the day were forbidden or very short. They got up as early as 3:30 a.m. either to travel to a distant work place or to queue for morning hygiene in overcrowded shared accommodation. In one case, a boy who was 17 told us that during his 12 hour work day in a garment sweatshop "I wasn't allowed to stop for one minute; otherwise I would have been fired".

Without a guardian who acts in their best interest, with no regular status or work permit, children are forced to make a living without any means to protect themselves from exploitative work conditions and conditions that are akin to forced labour. Being dependent on such income they become easy targets for exploitation. Fifteen-year-old Nurullah F., who unloaded heavy cargo from trucks in a factory, told:

> At the beginning the owner told me if I got a work permit I would get 29 Euros a day. After 20 days

> [he said] 400 Euros was sufficient and that I should leave. Because I worked overtime he owed me 300 Euros more. When I asked about overtime the owner told me if I needed more time to do [the same job] it was my choice.

Exploitation of children at their workplace in some cases may reach the level of forced labour. Wali N. arrived to Greece in 2004 at the age of 14. He traveled to Athens on his own, trusted in a stranger he managed to communicate with and was put to work for seven months:

> [In Athens] I recognized a person... who spoke Bangla... so I made friends with that person. He said we would go to a factory to sew clothes, to work and stay there. I worked in that place and slept in that place. I worked for 12 hours a day and I slept on a table there. I worked every day and I never went outside. I had the red card but the guy told me that this was not good and that the police would arrest me. He told me for my own safety I should stay inside.... I stayed there for about 7 months. The boss told me that he deducted from my salary the fees for sleeping and for food. For one month I received 50 Euros.

LEGAL STANDARDS GOVERNING CHILD LABOUR

International law does not prohibit all work carried out by children. However, International Labour Organization (ILO) conventions prohibit work that deprives children of their childhood, interferes with their schooling, their potential, their dignity and is harmful for their physical, mental and social development. Greece is a state party to some of the key conventions prohibiting child labour, such as the Convention on the Rights of the Child, but also the ILO Convention No. 182 concerning the Prohibition and Immediate Action for the Elimination of the Worst Forms of Child Labour (Worst Forms of Child Labour Convention), and ILO

Convention No. 138 concerning the Minimum Age for Admission to Employment (Minimum Age Convention).

Greece has, however, not ratified ILO Convention 184 concerning Safety and Health in Agriculture. The European Social Charter contains additional protective provisions including the child's right to a fair wage and the necessity to limit work hours in accordance with the child's development. International conventions to which Greece is a state party form an integral part of domestic law and prevail over any contrary domestic provision. Sanctions are provided for by both immigration and labour legislation. Immigration legislation forbids employers to hire aliens without residence permits. If an employer violates the prohibition of child labour, he or she faces imprisonment of up to two years, a fine and administrative penalties that may include the closing of business. Both provisions extend the same sanctions to the child's guardian. Despite these legal provisions, employers' who violate them face a low risk of being sanctioned.

Upon Greece's ratification of the Worst Forms of Child Labour Convention in 2001, labour inspectors were tasked to take targeted action to protect children. The Greek government reported for the year 2004 that labour inspectors detected a total of 35 children in prohibited forms of employment. Thirty-three employers were fined and charges were brought against two. In 2005, five employers were charged for the illegal employment of children and 29 fined; two of the cases were in the construction sector. In 2006, charges were brought against two employers and 17 fines were issued, none of them in the construction sector. In 2007, a total of nine employers were charged for the illegal employ-ment of children and 18 were fined, none of them in the construction sector.

These figures appear low in comparison to the numbers of children believed to be working, based on the testimony of 14 persons interviewed by Human Rights Watch who performed or witnessed prohibited forms of child labour.

TRAFFICKING

As the authorities assess vulnerability, one of the issues they need to be alert to is the possibility that unaccompanied children are victims of trafficking. The reality is that if not already in hands of traffickers bringing them into Greece, the failure of the protection system means unaccompanied children are at high risk of falling into their hands once they are in the country. The inadequate procedures followed by police-or perhaps, more accurately, the lack of proce-duresmean that trafficking victims are not identified. The inadequate provision of care makes it easy for trafficking gangs to operate. According to the International Organi-zation for Migration (IOM), the authorities have not adapted to the new forms of trafficking that involve child victims and various forms of exploitation, not just sexual. Instead, we were told, in the minds of officials trafficking is still largely associated with women from Eastern European countries trafficked for sexual exploitation.

UNACCOMPANIED GIRLS

Sexual exploitation is, of course, one of a range of significant risks. The United Nations Special Rapporteur on the sale of children, child prostitution and child porno-graphy noted as early as 2005 that the trafficking of unaccompanied girls from Africa into Greece for sexual exploitation could be a new trend in the country. Currently, very little is known about the fate of unaccompanied girls. There are no specialized shelters for girl victims of trafficking (that provide higher level of security and address specific needs these girls face) nor for unaccompanied girls in general. Rigorous in depth research is needed to document their situation. In the course of researching this report, Human Rights Watch collected only anecdotal stories about their fate. However, practitioners who work within NGOs and are familiar with the phenomenon of child trafficking in Greece state that girls end up in sexual exploitation, including working as prostitutes in Athens.

Human Rights Watch interviewed three unaccompanied girl children in detention who were possible trafficking victims. A 16-year-old girl from the Philippines said to us she was going to join "her aunt" in Athens to take up a job as a domestic worker. She later absconded from a care center jointly with a younger Somali girl. Both told staff that they had "husbands" in Athens. Ten-year-old Fatime S., an unaccompanied Somali girl, told us that she had been detained for 15 days at the Petru Ralli detention center in Athens when we met her. It was her fourth time in detention:

> My name is Fatime. I am 10 years old. I told the police how old I am, but they haven't had another place for me. I was arrested at the border. I got a paper to leave in one month. I've been in this jail for 15 days. But before I was arrested in the airport twice and released. I am alone. I have nobody here. If they release me, I'll just go to Omonia square. I have no one. I have been in Greece for six months. I came from the airport.

The girl had not been seen by any specialized organization since she was detained. When we asked staff at the detention center about the procedures in place for a girl like her, they were unable to explain to us the course of action to protect her from harm or refer her to specialized services.

UNACCOMPANIED BOYS

Human Rights Watch interviewed a dozen unaccompanied boys shortly after their release from the detention center in Mitilini, Lesvos Island. They all had been taken to the port after their release, given a ticket for the Athens-bound ferry and were left to fend for themselves without further information or assistance. Among them was Shakib K., a 15-year-old Afghan boy. Based on his description about his migration from Pakistan, he appeared to have been trafficked and to remain at imminent risk:

> My uncle told me I should go to Greece and that my life would be better. My father didn't accept but my uncle said I had to go. My uncle has to pay about 6,000 USD.... He told me that I would

> work and pay him back.... There are two smugglers, one is in Pakistan and one in Athens. They said they will take me like a prisoner unless they are given the money. I think my uncle will pay them.... The smuggler knows that I'm on the ferry. When I arrive the smuggler waits for me and will take me to a house to call Pakistan. If [my uncle] doesn't give the money they will keep me.

Shakib K. had been released from detention that day with a large number of adults and children. He had been given a deportation order, which required him to leave the country within 30 days. There was no interpreter in the Mitilini detention center on Lesvos Island and authorities did not conduct an interview with him.

Once the ferry arrived, Human Rights Watch stood close by and watched the boys disembark. Shakib K., together with other boys, was swiftly approached by a contact. The Human Rights Watch interpreter was a young-looking Afghan and mingled with the boys from the ferry. He was promptly approached by a stranger who offered him a place to stay. The price for the accommodation, he was told, would be discussed once they get there. Several police officers stood 15 meters away from this scene and took no interest in where these boys were going next.

FAIL TO IDENTIFY TRAFFICKING

Indeed, officials appear to remain blind to the inadequacy of their procedures which mean that trafficking-and the risks that children of becoming trafficking victims-may not be recognized. Visiting the Kyprinou immigration detention facility in Fylakio, Human Rights Watch asked the senior official in charge (the chief of police in Orestiada, in the Evros border region) whether there might be trafficking victims among half a dozen women of Eastern European origin and a number of unaccompanied children, among them a 12-year-old girl, at the center. He responded: "we don't have trafficking victims. I'm trained on this matter and we can identify them." Despite his assurances, Human Rights Watch noted that there was no interpreter among the staff in the detention center. Furthermore, the Afghan girl who traveled with her underage brother and cousin told Human Rights Watch that neither she nor her brother had been interviewed since their arrival. They were only told they would be detained for three months, and their presence was dealt with as if they were adults.

Human Rights Watch was unable to further investigate whether other children with special needs were present in the center because the authorities did not grant permission to speak to all detainees. Human Rights Watch received credible information that on one of the Aegean islands, girls who were possible trafficking victims had been detained together with their presumed trafficker. Although the police were alerted about the presence of the presumed trafficker, the police released them together. "For the police, it's too much trouble to protect these girls," we were told.

The Samos chief of police described to Human Rights Watch how unaccompanied children were released from the Samos detention center: "If the next day a relative comes and asks for the child's release we release the child-even the next day". When we questioned further how the identity of the relative was verified, he reconsidered his statement and said they would not hand over the child if they are not sure that the person is indeed a relative. He added that children rarely possessed documents. His answers strongly suggest that no standard procedures are followed when persons who claim to be children's relatives or care-givers seek their release.

The chief of police in Orestiada, where unaccompanied children go after their release, told Human Rights Watch: "unaccompanied children stay up to three months [in detention]. Relatives or friends come to pick them up.... Normally somebody comes to pick them up. They don't travel alone". We were told, however, that in practice children are released with a deportation order and no further assistance. The lack of safeguards leaves the way wide open for traffickers to exploit the desperate situation in which many unaccompanied children find themselves. Gangs recruit children for labour exploitation from places such as Athens and Patras. They also operate in public places where children can be easily approached and lure them with the promise to take them to another country.

Fourteen-year-old Wali P. told us:

> One person told me he could take children to Europethat was in Monastiraki. He was an Afghan. He told me there is a lady from another European country and she wants to bring children to another country. That lady would come and bring other children abroad if they didn't have their fingerprints taken. They asked me if I wanted to go. He told me it would not cost anything.... They only want children who are alone. He told me that lady was from a refugee organization, maybe UNICEF.

The Convention on the Rights of the Child obliges states parties to take all appropriate measures to prevent the abduction of, the sale of or traffic in children for any purpose or any form. The Convention's Optional Protocol on the Sale of Children, Child Prostitution and Child Pornography recognizes that particularly vulnerable groups, including girl children, are at greater risk of sexual exploitation and it calls on states parties to pay particular attention to the protection of such children.

Both Amnesty International and the US Department of State have criticized authorities' failure to correctly identify trafficking victims. Furthermore, Greek legislation only recognizes and protects trafficking victims from expulsion if the victim has "shown a clear intention to cooperate". Victims are given a 30-day reflection period to decide whether they will cooperate in the investigation of traffickers. Only if they agree to cooperate are they granted victim status and entitled to temporary residence. There are no provisions that would balance this requirement to cooperate with the risk of reprisal victims or their families may face. Only few victims are granted trafficking victim status. Human Rights Watch asked the Ministry of Justice to provide us the number of children who had been recognized as trafficking victims and eligible for temporary residence. As of the time of writing we have not received a reply.

The definition of trafficking in children in Greek legislation is not as far-reaching as those in international treaties and European law. A trafficker in Greece can be convicted if he or she exploits a person by using violence, threat or coercion, exercise of control or abuse of power, deceit, or takes advantage of a person's vulnerability. The Trafficking Protocol makes trafficking of a child a crime even if none of these means are used. Among the key international treaties combating trafficking in human beings, Greece has ratified only the Optional Protocol to the Convention on the Rights of the Child on the Sale of Children, Child Prostitution and Child Pornography.

It has signed but not ratified the United Nations Convention on Combating Transnational Organized Crime and its supplementing Protocol to prevent, suppress and punish trafficking in persons, especially women and children. Greece has signed but not ratified the Council of Europe Convention on Action against Trafficking in Human Beings and it is among the signatories of the Council of Europe Convention on the Protection of Children against Sexual Exploitation and Sexual Abuse. Gender based violence is quite common in almost all the developing countries. Though mostly identical, yet, some of the customs, which are reflected in the culture of each of the particular societies differently, create important distinctions.

The opponents to these customs have failed time and again to evoke the desired response despite the customs being reiterated again and again in many written works. In the present paper, some of the customs, prevalent for years in India, have been identified to reveal the gender-based violence in addition to the day to day harassment being faced by the women. Some recommendations that are always in the discussion at policy level but with no fruitful result have also been reviewed and an attempt has been made to put forward some simple suggestions to check gender-based violence, particularly, in the developing world.

It is a harsh reality that the woman in India has been ill-treated for ages in our male dominated society. She is deprived of her independent identity and is looked upon as a commodity. She is not only robbed of her dignity and pride by way of seduction by the men outside, but also, may become a victim of cruelty by her saviors, within the four walls of her own house. However, her trauma does not end here, it may even go up to the extent of forcing her to commit suicide or she may be burnt to death for various reasons including that of dowry. This type of violence transgresses the boundaries of caste, class, region or religion and is prevalent in almost all societies.

The atrocities committed on women can be divided into various groups: Physical violence may include assault, battery, serious injuries or burns etc. Sexual violence, which means robbing the dignity of woman not only by indecent behavior but it, may take the extreme form of rape. Female genital mutilation (FGM) removal of clitoris and other parts of a woman or girl child is often practiced in African countries. Verbal violence, which means indecency or use of abusive and filthy language against a woman or her near and dear ones. Social violence, which includes demeaning, disparaging and humiliating a woman or her parental relatives and friends. Emotional violence, leading to internal deprivation of love and affection, concern, sympathy and care, it also includes depriving her custody of children. Financial violence, which means depriving her of financial means and bare necessities of daily life, it also includes taking away the assets, which a woman possesses or earns. Intellectual violence, means denial of rights to take part in decision making and discussion for pressing issues. Other forms of violence, which may include denial of education, access to health facilities, reproductive rights, etc.

GLOBAL SCENARIO

Gender based violence that threatens the well being, rights and dignity of women has only recently emerged as a global issue extending across regional, social, cultural and economic boundaries. According to state statistics, about 18% of women are being sexually abused in the U.S. According to the UN Report on violence against women, the condition in other developed countries such as Denmark, Germany, Spain, Switzerland and the United Kingdom etc. is no better. In the U.S., the Department of Justice reported that, every year 3-4 million women are battered by their husbands or partners. Even in Sweden, which ranks high in the gender-related index, 66% of the 18650 reported cases of violence on women in 1996 were of domestic assault. Further 45% of 681 offences of homicide recorded in England and Wales in 1996 involved women killed by their spouses or lovers.

The data from developing countries like Antigua, Barbados, Columbia, Chile, Ecuador, Guatemala, Sri Lanka and others reveals widespread prevalence of physical and sexual abuse on women. In a study of 796 women from Japan carried out by Domestic Violence Group (1993) 59% reported physical abuse, 66% emotional abuse and 60% reported sexual abuse. Studies from African countries, Kenya, Uganda and Tanzania reveal that 42% women are subjected to physical abuse at their homes. In China, a conclusive evidence of wife battering has been reported among 57% women. The Universal Declaration of Human Rights and Convention on Elimination of all forms of Discrimination against Women (CEDAW) do enforce certain special rights and privileges for women. But it is amazing that only 44 countries have laws against domestic violence. Only 17 countries have made marital rape a criminal offence & only 27 countries have passed laws on sexual harassment.

THE INDIAN SCENARIO

The cherished womanhood, which has been extolled since long, had been eroded away with the influx of foreign and modern culture. Over the years, worldly pursuits have occupied maximized proportions because of which the traditional culture is withering away. The happiness and solace in the family have been snatched away by heart breaking acts like bride burning, dowry deaths, torture, cruelty and so forth. Even the female embryo is subjected to homicidal torture. The right of the female child is always staked to peril. For having born as a female child itself is considered as a curse by some sections of the society. A look at the turn of century census reveals that there were 972 females per 1000 males in 1901 whereas the figure is 933 females per 1000 males in 2001. Still more significant is that in the 0 – 6 age group there are only 927 girls per 1000 boys. In some Indian states like Punjab the ratio is as low as 793 girls per 1000 boys.

Placed on the wrong side of power and hierarchies, in their homes and work places, women, often face the brunt of violence. Records of the police provide details of reported cases of crime against women, but much of the violence goes unreported. In fact, women face violence at the hands of their protectors. The recorded data during the 90's reveals that crime against women in 1999 registered an increase of nearly 102% over the year 1989. In absolute terms an increase of 68699 cases was reported during the decade. The available data indicates an increasing trend during the last three years for cases registered under Indian Penal Code and under special laws such as Immoral Traffic (Prevention) Act and Indecent Representation of Women (Prevention) Act. Among the crimes against women, torture recorded as high as 278% increase, while the incidence of rape increased by 69% followed by molestation 24%. Sexual harassment recorded a consistent growth of 86% during the period 1995 to 1999.

There has been a steep rise in rape cases from 9150 in 1989 to 15468 in 1999 but the more disturbing feature of this finding is that 27% of the victims were minors. The figures, in spite of the fact that sexual offences against children are one of the most under-reported crimes in the country, speak for themselves. It has been argued that for every case reported against children there are a hundred, which are not reported. In 1997, the Supreme Court of India laid down five factors that qualify as sexual harassment. These are physical contact or advances, a demand or request for sexual favors, sexually colored remarks, showing pornography and other unwelcome physical and verbal or non-verbal sexual conduct. Recently the Supreme Court has recorded its strong disapproval against the practice of doctors in government hospitals, especially in rural areas, not to examine rape victims unless the police forwarded the case to them. It has observed that this attitude of the doctors delays examination of the victim resulting in the evidence being either washed away or lost.

The phenomenon of violence against women within the family in India is complex and deeply embedded. In India, marriage establishes a network of interacting indivi-duals and is rarely only a highly personal relationship between a man and a woman. An important part of the power relationship between spouses and indeed their families relates to dowry and its ramifications (Sharma 2002a). According to National Crime Records Bureau report 1998, 2371 cases of suicides were related to dowry disputes. A study of dowry victims in Delhi reports that in a sample of 150 dowry victims, one fourth were murdered or driven to commit suicide and more than half (61%) were thrown out of their husband's house after a long drawn period of harassment and torture. The study, reports Dowry related killings, to follow two patterns, first, the young brides were either murdered or forced to commit suicide (18.4%) when their parents refused to concede to continuing demands of dowry and second, the murders were committed on the pretext of 'complex family relations' or extra-marital relations (52.6%).

A critical analysis reveals that the crime situation has worsened over the years but the large number of cases that are registered may reflect that the hesitation regarding reporting these crimes is perhaps breaking down. May be today more women are mustering up courage to report cases of crime against themselves and seeking redressal. However, studies indicate that the statistics conceal rather than reveal the extent of the problem. The All India crime rate *i.e.* number of crimes per 100,000 population for crimes against women reported to the police worked out to be 13.8 during 1999. The Crime in India Report 1999, itself acknowledges that this rate of crime may be reviewed with caution, as a sizeable number of crimes against women go unreported due to the social stigma attached and the lengthy court procedures. According to a report out of every 100 rape cases in India, only 10 are reported and out of every 100 reported cases only 5 offenders are convicted. According to another report, in 1999, every day in India, 42 women were raped, 18 cases of dowry deaths occurred every hour, 5 women faced cruelty at home and 4 molestation cases were reported. According to yet another study, crimes against women increased from 123 to 127 cases per million persons, during the period 1998 to 1999, while total cognizable crime rate declined from 1837 to 1823 over the same period.

Post independence period in India, has witnessed a marked increase in women literacy, resulting into a vast number of women involved in the work place in all the vital sectors of the countries economy, whether out of choice or out of compulsion. However, they mostly fall in the unorganized sector, where they are ill paid but need to cling on to the jobs due to ever increasing unemployment. This need for survival drives women into what has been referred to as 'rape situations'. Harassment at work place is real and pervasive. Jokes with sexual undertones. Obscene behavior with sexual overtures, direct advances etc. combine to make the atmosphere at work place discriminatory to women. The phenomenon of violence against women arises from patriarchal notions of ownership over women's bodies, sexuality, labour, reproductive rights, mobility and level of autonomy. Deep-rooted ideas about male superiority enable men to freely exercise unlimited power over women's lives and effectively legitimize it too. Violence is thus a tool that men use constantly to control women as a result of highly internalized patriarchal conditioning coupled with legitimacy for coercion to enforce compliance and increasing aspirations, frustrations and 'might is right' becoming a legitimate view and increasing need for assertion of individual egos and control. Within this context, several developments serve as a backdrop to the discussion and analysis of increased violence against women. In the wake of liberalization, new modes of living are being introduced.

Consumerism, unreal aspirations incited by the barrage of the advertising industry and 'get rich quick' schemes has been increasingly influencing the thinking and behavior. An increasingly growing gap is being witnessed between the aspirations and their fulfillment, which is reflected in an increased violence in human interactions. The deluge of private companies into the electronic media has led to a spate of programs based on sex and violence. In the contemporary scenario almost all channels are running programs, which stress on bigamy or extramarital relation-ships. Advertisements use women's bodies to sell any thing ranging from cars to soap. A substantial population is being influenced by underlying philosophy of instant self-gratification, trying to actualize their sexual fantasies. Increasing contractualization and casualization of the female work force as a part of liberalization policies has increased their vulnerability at the work place.

The status of girls in the labour market is different than the boys and they are considered to be more productive in the household activities. The deep routed gender bias in the minds of people also leads to more female child labour. Lately the trend of teenaged commercial sex workers among girls has been reported to be on rise. According to a report, there are about 10 million commercially sexually exploited women in India, of which one fifth are under the age of 18 years. Wife battering is the commonest form of abuse worldwide irrespective of class, religion and community. Studies have correlated childhood abuse, alcoholism, unemployment and poverty with the growth of this malaise. In India, there is a tendency to club marital violence under the overall heads of dowry, dowry deaths and dowry violence. However, oppression of wives for bringing inadequate dowry may only be another excuse for using violence against them.

The problem of violence against women has to be visualized in a wider context and cannot be viewed in isolation from the status of women in the society. The practice among the Indian women of ending their lives by setting themselves ablaze with the pyre of their deceased husbands or being forced to do so, in the yesteryears—the "SATI PRATHA" though banned now, reflects the extent of dependence of women on their men. However, legislation alone cannot by itself solve deep-rooted social problems, one has to approach them in other ways too. Therefore, what is required is not only a strong legal support network but also opportunities for economic independence, essential education and awareness, alternative accommodation and a change in attitude and mindset of society, judiciary, legislature, executive, men and the most important woman herself. Restructuring society in terms of power and role relationship while emphasizing the egalitarian values is the need of the hour.

The Parliament of India has passed a bill proposing death penalty for convicted rapists, but the women organizations argue that this will be another pretext for courts to give the benefit of doubt to the accused. In this entire scenario, the women's organizations are indeed a strong platform. However, policy level reforms in response to gender based violence will be able to succeed only when such organizations are able to convince policy makers that responding to violence is both necessary and achievable. Law can be ahead of public opinion in matters of social policy, but if the gulf is too wide, there is every likelihood of its non-observance either unconsciously or deliberately. This is tragically true of the Dowry Prohibition Law, which is flouted by one and all in the Indian Society, irrespective of their caste, creed and religion. Even the law enforcing agencies, believe it to be an ornamental legislation, not seriously intended for implementation. The offenders do not consider themselves guilty and the victims do not perceive the conduct immoral like in other offences.

The prevailing evil of dowry system in this part of the world, despite the existing stringent laws (Sec. 498A, 304B Indian Penal Code) to curb the menace, has shown an upward trend. There has also been some feminist movement in the society and at present, one finds women's organi-zations struggling for their rights and protesting against the atrocities on them. For awakening of social conscience and providing justice and opportunity to the women, the following recommendations are often made:

- Promoting education among the general public is necessary to annul many myths and superstitions, which lead to helplessness and frustrations in them. Educating the society about the equal status of a girl child is the utmost requirement.
- Popularizing vocational courses, as per the caliber of the individuals, will go a long way in decreasing the insecurity of the unemployed, thereby boosting their self-confidence and will power.
- Marriage counseling, discouraging and banning costly and ostentatious marriage rituals, strict implementation of anti-dowry laws, may help in decreasing or preventing the tensions of day to day married life.
- Society should work towards protecting the rights of women. In this regard, effective cooperation between Non Government Organizations (NGOs), voluntary and law enforcing agencies, is a must to enable women to enjoy equal rights, instill confidence and self respect in them and to make them economically independent.
- Promotion of the concept of 'Family Planning' in rural India, so that its principles are followed in letter and in spirit, all over the country. Social health workers, NGOs, Govt. Organizations and the society as a whole should strive towards bringing down the family size and its related problems, both in the rural and in the urban community etc., etc.

But these remain limited to policy level only on account of the lack of political will and sincere efforts towards their implementation; consequently, the all-important goal of women empowerment continues to be a distant dream for the women in many developing countries including India. The concept of women empowerment is not new and can be traced back from a story about King Arthur who was ambushed and imprisoned by the Monarch of a neighboring kingdom. The monarch could have killed him but was moved by Arthur's youthful happiness and offered him freedom if he could answer a difficult question within a specified period of one year. The question was "what do women really want"? Such a question would perplex even the most knowledgeable man, and, to young Arthur, it seemed an impossible query.

Since it was better than death, Arthur accepted the monarch's proposition to have an answer by year's end. He returned to his kingdom and sought the help of princesses, priests, the wise men, the court jesters and the prostitutes. No one could give him a satisfactory answer, but what most people did tell him was to consult the 'old witch'. The last month of the year arrived and Arthur had no alternative but to talk to the witch. She agreed to answer his question but he would have to accept her price first. The old witch wanted to marry Gawain, the most noble of the Knights of the Round Table and Arthur's closest friend. Young Arthur was horrified. She was hunchbacked and awfully hideous, had only one tooth, smelled like sewage water and often made obscene noises. He had never run across such a repugnant creature. Arthur refused to ask/force his friend to marry her and have to endure such a burden.

Gawain, upon learning of the proposal, spoke to Arthur. He told him that nothing was too big of a sacrifice compared to king's life that he had pledged to the monarch in the event of failing to give the right answer. Hence the wedding was announced and the witch answered Arthur's question: "What a woman really wants is to be able to be in charge of her own life". Everyone instantly knew that the witch had uttered a great truth and that Arthur's life would be spared. And so it went. The neighboring monarch spared Arthur's life and granted him total freedom. The answer was not the end, but the beginning of a lovely and lucid story on women empowerment. What a wedding Gawain and the witch had! Arthur was torn between relief and anguish.

The old witch put her worst manners on display, ate with her hands, belched and made everyone uncomfortable. The wedding night approached. Gawain, steeling himself for a horrible night entered the bedroom. What a sight awaited! The most beautiful woman he had ever seen lay before him.

The knight was astounded and asked what had happened. The beauty replied that since he had been so kind to her (when she'd been a witch) half the time she would be her horrible deformed self and the other half, she would be her beautiful maiden self. Which would he want her to be during the day and which during the night? During the day a beautiful woman to show off to his friends, but at night, in the privacy of his home, an old spooky witch. Or would he prefer having by day a hideous witch, but by night a beautiful woman to enjoy many intimate moments. What a cruel question! Gawain began to think of his predicament and then said that he would let her choose for herself. Upon hearing this, she announced that she would be beautiful all the time, because he had respected her and had let her be in charge of her own life. But really now what is the moral of this story?

If you don't respect women, things are going to get ugly! What is required is 'public awareness, mass education, financial and social independence and the will to safeguard and fight for their rights' among the Indian women. But above all, Indian women need to remove a deep-rooted malady that has sapped the very roots of our so-called civilized society— disparity between a male and female child. We recommend the following corrective measures:

- Change in the perception of society towards the dignity of women treating them at par with their male counterparts, because threat to male authority is the main cause of domestic violence not only in the developing world but also the developed.
- Awareness about gender biases because violence against women is primarily a gender issue. Non Government Organizations and government agencies such as National Commission for women may play an important role in sensitizing the society about gender rights.
- Imparting legal education to the girls at high school or secondary school level, enabling them to fight for their rights.
- Educating the women about their rights as well as the

agency to be approached in case of a particular problem, keeping in mind the present educational status of the majority of Indian women.

- Motivation of women from poor and backward families to utilize the schemes started by the government for their welfare in general and the economic empowerment in particular.
- Strict implementation of the legal provisions of the legislation, which are meant for the protection of women.
- Developing programs to make the women morally strong or empowered because, bestowing judicial rights or making women literate alone can never end the violence against them.
- Setting up Family Counseling Centers and ensuring their proper functioning with the objective to streng-then the families and not breaking them apart. They need to propagate the concept—"family is the prime unit of society" and provide a platform where men, women, old and young can share their problems and receive good counseling. At present 500 voluntary organizations are running Family Counseling Centers all over the country with aid from the Central Social Welfare Board.
- The electronic and the print media have already made a dent by bringing out the atrocities towards women in the open but they need to stress more.

2

Designing Trafficking Study

Methodology

There is a dearth of information about violence against children, including trafficking, that actually comes from children. This gap has resulted in the development of responses that have often been ad hoc and sometimes even counterproductive. Historically, this has been true in the discourse around child labour and other forms of exploitation, though in the last decade child labour research that is child-centred and engages children themselves has grown in scope and number.

The study builds on a broad UNICEF IRC research agenda on child trafficking that began with an analysis of the situation in Africa, was followed by research in Europe and Central Asia, and will continue with a currently under-way study on child trafficking in South Asia. This report presents information and quotations from 31 children. It recognizes that the participation of all children, especially those with concrete experience of trafficking situations, is crucial to the prevention, early identification and elimination of child trafficking. It is hoped that this initiative will stimulate further research and, in a modest way, provide some guidance for policy and practice.

TERMINOLOGY AND DEFINITIONS

The Protocol to Prevent, Suppress and Punish Trafficking in Persons, Especially Women and Children, (the 'Palermo

Protocol') contains the most widely accepted international definitions of trafficking in human beings and child trafficking. It was adopted in November 2000 by the United Nations General Assembly to supplement the United Nations Convention against Transnational Organized Crime.

Article 3 on 'Use of Terms' states:

(a.) "Trafficking in persons" shall mean the recruitment, transportation, transfer, harbouring or receipt of persons, by means of the threat or use of force or other forms of coercion, of abduction, of fraud, of deception, of the abuse of power or of a position of vulnerability or of the giving or receiving of payments or benefits to achieve the consent of a person having control over another person, for the purpose of exploitation. Exploitation shall include, at a minimum, the exploitation of the prostitution of others or other forms of sexual exploitation, forced labour or services, slavery or practices similar to slavery, servitude or the removal of organs;

(b.) The consent of a victim of trafficking in persons to the intended exploitation set forth in subparagraph (a) of this article shall be irrelevant where any of the means set forth in subparagraph (a) have been used;

(c.) The recruitment, transportation, transfer, harbouring or receipt of a child for the purpose of exploitation shall be considered "trafficking in persons" even if this does not involve any of the means set forth in subparagraph (a) of this article;

(d.) "Child" shall mean any person under eighteen years of age.

Even though the Palermo Protocol was developed specifically for transnational cases of human trafficking, the definition itself does not include reference to border crossing. It applies therefore also to cases that take place within the same country. Victims of trafficking are often forced, threatened, coerced or deceived during the trafficking process. However, the definition of trafficking in the Palermo Protocol establishes the trafficking of children as a special case. Any child recruited and transported for the purpose of exploitation is considered to be a trafficking victim whether or not the child has been forced or deceived in any way. Some children are trafficked directly from their family home or place of residence, while others leave home first and come under the control of a trafficker later on, sometimes after they have already arrived in another country.

A number of the young people interviewed for this report left home in search of better opportunities, either within their own country or abroad. In this report, the term 'migrant' is not restricted to individuals who travel outside of their own countries. Those who make money from the commercial sexual exploitation of children (or adults) are generally referred to as 'pimps'. Since there is no similar term that can be applied to employers or others who make money from trafficked children, the term 'trafficker' is used generically. It refers both to the individuals who recruit and transport children with an intention to subsequently exploit them, and those who make money out of the children's activities while they are being exploited.

METHODOLOGY

THE QUESTIONNAIRE

Consultations with the children and young people participating in this study took the form of one-on-one interviews using a standard questionnaire. The ques-tionnaire was designed to collect information that could help improve existing efforts to prevent child trafficking, including re-trafficking of the same victims, and to assist trafficked children in their recovery. A number of resources were used in developing the questionnaire, including the experiences of shelter staff who had interviewed trafficked children and health professionals who had assessed the medical issues and other practical needs of child victims of trafficking. A handbook for professionals working with child victims of abuse and human trafficking published by UNICEF and other relevant research guidelines were also consulted while the questionnaire was prepared.

Early in the process, it became clear that information routinely collected by professionals did not provide a complete picture of children's trafficking experience. The concerns of police to identify and investigate crimes, and of health professionals and social workers to assess the children's immediate needs, explain the focus of the inter-views. There is also a tendency to focus on the abuse experi-enced during the trafficking episodes. Most interviews of trafficked children, therefore, do not look at a child's situation before being trafficked. Such investigation may reveal the reasons (direct or indirect) a child may have ended up under the control of a trafficker, or shed light on the child's subsequent recovery. Understanding what happens to a child after exploitation can help determine whether the procedures followed and assistance provided were appropriate, and whether due consideration was given to the child's views, mindful of the child's best interests.

The questionnaire was designed to fill in these gaps. Part 1 contains basic questions about the child's experiences while being trafficked. These were to be answered by a professional who had been involved in providing care or assistance to the child in a shelter in the child's home country after the trafficking experience. Part 2 focused on the child's experiences before and after being trafficked and was to be answered by the children themselves. The questionnaire contained some 150 questions – one third directed to the person providing care to the young person (Part 1) and two thirds addressed directly to the young person interviewed (Part 2). Dividing the questionnaire into two parts had ethical and practical implications. First, it was crucial to avoid any risk of asking the children to repeat details about abusive personal experiences, which they had already recounted in detail to health professionals and, in some cases, also to police. It was felt that this could open up old wounds and create further trauma. Second, it was important to avoid lengthy interviews to avoid overburdening the respondents. Keeping the interviews focused on particular periods of the trafficking process helped to ensure that questions were thoroughly answered, particularly questions asked towards the end of the interview about the young person's experience after being trafficked.

Informed Consent

All the children and young people were asked whether they would like to participate in the research. Interviewers were instructed to read a standard explanation to them before asking questions and adjust it to fit the respondent's apparent maturity. Interviews began with the following statement:

We would like to ask you some questions to help find out whether recent attempts to prevent children from being abused affected you at all, and also want to find out whether the assistance provided to you and other children/young people who have been abused is as appropriate as possible.

There was also an explanation about how the information provided would be used, which specified that the child's name or any personal details that might identify the child would not be made publicly available or used in any reports for publication. After this explanation, the interviewers stated:

> You do not have to answer these questions, or you can decide not to answer a particular question. Are you happy to listen to the questions and to try and answer them?

The participants were also informed that additional information would be provided by a staff member who was well acquainted with their case. All participants were given an opportunity to object to this or to provide the information themselves, although none did. Neither, however, did any of the young respondents ask what type of information was being provided about them. While this might mean that they had confidence in their care staff, it also suggests that they may not have felt sufficiently empowered or in control of their lives to challenge people they perceived to be in a position of authority. If the respondents were 18 years or older at the time of the interview, they provided formal written consent to the interview and the use of the respondents' information by UNICEF.

For children under 18 years old, a person "with current responsibility for the child" was asked to give formal written consent for the child to be questioned. Initially it was intended that the person giving consent should be "legally responsible" for the child, (i.e., either a parent, permanent guardian or someone who had been given formal temporary guardianship of the child). However, in practice such legal appointments were not always made. This was particularly the case for children who had parents or a permanent guardian but were still living in a shelter and were reluctant to return home. In these cases, those who organized the interviews were instructed to obtain consent from the person temporarily in charge of the child's protection and care, such as the director of the shelter.

PROTECTING PRIVACY

Although the interviewee's real names were noted at the time of the interviews, each interview was promptly assigned a reference number, which ensured that any subsequent communications about the responses given in the course of interviews would not contain a reference to the child or young person's real name. It is important to note that many of the respondents indicated that they wanted to provide information and did not necessarily want their identity hidden. Several spoke out as proud survivors of painful experiences survivors who wanted their voices to be heard both to influence government policy and give hope to other child victims.

THE INTERVIEWS

The interviews were conducted in the interviewee's native language and were structured as an informal conver-sation between two people (interviewee and interviewer) with no third party present. Notes were taken during the interviews and the responses were transcribed in the language in which the interview had been conducted. The responses were subsequently translated into English. None of the interviews was tape recorded. All interviews were conducted by women, including the interview with the one boy who participated in the study. In Kosovo and the Republic of Moldova, staff who had worked in the shelters where the respondents had received care (and where some were still living), interviewed the children. In Romania, where respondents had been identified in different parts of the country, UNICEF arranged to have the children interviewed by one person, a sociologist who visited each location and met each of the respondents for the first time. This eliminated the need to train several different care staff. A similar approach was taken by UNICEF Albania, which assigned a psychologist to interview young people in different shelters throughout the country.

It was assumed that interviews conducted by staff the children and young people knew and those conducted by persons whom they did not know would illicit different types of information. It was considered that the participating children and young people might be more inclined to talk openly with someone they knew and trusted than with an interviewer who was meeting the child for the first time, although this hypothesis was not shown to be true. It was also reasonable to expect that an interviewer who was already familiar with the child's experience would be able to obtain more detailed information about sensitive episodes than a stranger. In a few cases, care staff did in fact provide valuable details that a child had omitted, both deliberately and unconsciously. However, in many cases, independent interviewers were able to identify significant, previously unidentified factors, which helped professionals to better understand a child's situation.

THE CHILDREN AND YOUNG PEOPLE INTERVIEWED

"Thirty-one children and young people – 30 girls and 1 boy " were interviewed in Albania, Kosovo, Republic of Moldova and Romania between September 2005 and June 2006. Two of the 31 respondents were identified as belonging to the Roma minority and were nationals of two different countries. The children and young people interviewed were

10 to 17 years old when they were trafficked and 13 to 24 years old when interviewed. More than one third of the respondents had turned 18 by the time they were interviewed. While some children had been under the control of traffickers for only a few days, others had remained under their control for extended periods of months or years. For one girl (A1), the trafficking experience continued for seven years.

Half of the children had been trafficked within their own countries. The other half had been trafficked to destinations in seven other European countries: Belgium, Denmark, France, Greece, Italy, Russian Federation and Turkey. Several of the children were not trafficked directly from their home country but had already been living in a European Union (EU) country at the time they were recruited for trafficking. The participating children and young people were all nationals of the countries in which they were assisted. Their stories reflect the following trafficking patterns of children who were:

- trafficked within their own countries;
- recruited in their own country and were destined to be taken abroad, but had escaped or were intercepted before they could be trafficked abroad;
- trafficked abroad and subsequently repatriated under official government-to-government protocols;
- trafficked abroad and had returned to their own country under their own steam, but had subsequently come to the attention of the authorities or decided on their own to seek assistance; or
- residing outside their own country (with or without legal travel documents) at the time a trafficker took control of them and subsequently trafficked either within the same country or to a third country.

THE SELECTION OF RESPONDENTS

For the selection of respondents, UNICEF Country Offices worked closely with agencies providing assistance to trafficked children in each of the four countries. These agencies provide residential care for victims of trafficking (mainly women and girls) and one of them also cares for children who had experienced other forms of abuse.

Three key criteria were used for selecting respondents:

- they were trafficked before reaching the age of 18;
- they had received assistance or care in a shelter operated either by the government, an international organization or a non-governmental organization (NGO) in one of the four countries; and
- they had expressed willingness to talk about their experience and to participate in this study.

LIMITATIONS OF THE DATA

The aim of this report is not to identify regional trends or patterns or presume that the experience of the interviewed 31 children represents the experiences of all trafficked children in the region. Rather, the report is intended to stimulate research and new policy approaches, and to inform action that is based on the active participation of children and young people. It also provides individual children a platform to describe their experiences and perceptions. This study has intrinsic limitations that are common to any other study on trafficking. The complex, dynamic and clandestine nature of the phenomenon poses enormous challenges to collecting good quality, up-to-date, reliable and comparable data. In addition, the study has a number of inherent characteristics that strictly prevent the generalization of its findings.

ILLUSTRATIVE AND INDIVIDUAL, NOT REPRESENTATIVE

The 31 children and young people who were interviewed are a very small sample of those trafficked under the age of 18. They are not assumed to be a represen-tative sample, either of children identified as victims of trafficking and who have received assistance in these countries, or of the wider and undefined group of all children who have been trafficked from those countries. For the same reason, no attempt was made to compare or contrast the data from these interviews with patterns and trends of child trafficking reported for the

South Eastern European region and beyond. Furthermore, the study is oriented towards children who received institutional assistance during their recovery.

This selection through shelters means that certain groups of trafficked children were not included in the interview process, notably:

- Children who have been trafficked but have not been identified as such, and as a result, have not sought or received assistance from child protection agencies. The experiences of those children and young people might be very different, particularly in the process of recovery and reintegration.
- Children who are known to have been trafficked but who have been assisted in ways other than through residential care or who have not been included in any other formal assistance programme.
- Children who have gone abroad, been trafficked and exploited, and who either remain there in a situation of exploitation or who have, after escaping or coming to the attention of the authorities, remained in the country to which they were trafficked.

SERVICES REFLECT SOCIAL BIASES

Why is residential care for victims of trafficking usually tailored to meet the needs of women and girls who have been trafficked for the purpose of sexual exploitation? One reason may be that police and other professionals often assume that 'human trafficking' is always linked to forced prostitution and that mostly women and girls are affected. As a result, women and girls trafficked into sexual exploi-tation are more likely than boys and men to be identified as victims of trafficking and referred to shelters and other services. There is also often a social denial of the sexual exploitation of boys due to perceptions of masculinity. This explains why many shelters are not suitable for boys or girls who have experienced other forms of exploitation or abuse.

Given that residential care for victims of trafficking is

generally focused on sexually exploited women and girls, the decision to restrict the study to children who received assistance in a shelter increased the likelihood that the respondents had been trafficked for sexual exploitation. Due to a strong gender biases in existing victim assistance structures, boys who are trafficked for sexual exploitation or other forms of exploitation are hardly referred to those shelters. In fact, all but one of the young people participating in this study were girls trafficked for the purpose of sexual exploitation. Another important limitation to note is that the questionnaire and interview process were designed for use with young people who had been trafficked between ages 15 and 17.

Although this was not stated explicitly in the questionnaire, it was not surprising that it was mainly children in this age group who were considered suitable to be interviewed. This means that certain forms of trafficking to which younger children are more vulnerable, such as trafficking for the purpose of begging, are not discussed in the context of this study. Finally, the study did not include a control group. This means that the risk factors revealed in the interviews with trafficked children can neither be confirmed nor denied.

LIMITATIONS IN THE ACCURACY AND DETAIL OF THE INFORMATION

This study has the inherent limitations of any study based on interviews. The interviews reflect the children's subjective reality, which in some cases differed from information from various other sources (*e.g.* case managers and law enforcement files). This was particularly the case with regard to their recollection of dates and numbers. Reasons for these discrepancies are diverse: they may reflect a conscious decision made by the child, interview fatigue or even forgetfulness. They may have something to do with the child's relationship with the interviewer, the conditions of the interview, the child's interpretation of past experiences, as well as her or his physical and psychological condition. Trauma, taboos or shame can all influence how a child responds.

Furthermore, any interview is a presentation of self, and people select to disclose information that they feel is more relevant or desirable. The fact that some respondents were much younger when they were trafficked is likely to have further influenced their perception of events. This may be the case because they did not fully understand the complexity of what was happening to them, were not involved in the decision-making process, or because the information they received from adults (*e.g.* parents, teachers and police officers) or peers was misunderstood, incomplete or simplified. Because traffickers often rely on deceit and threats to control children, a child's understanding of what is happening may be further distorted. Information be-comes especially ambiguous in cases of cross-border traf-ficking, when children end up in a country with a different culture and language. There may also have been flaws in the information received from various other sources.

A number of young people who were interviewed made serious allegations about the corruption or inefficiency of agencies that had a duty to protect them (police, immigration services and social services). However, no effort was made to follow these up or to obtain comments from the services concerned. Any allegations were consequently reported as they were made. Despite the study's limitations, the young respondents' experiences and comments provide a wealth of information about what happens to children before, during and after they are trafficked information that is often not revealed by reports analysing trafficking patterns, thus also failing to inform the development of relevant laws and policies in the region.

CASE HISTORIES

LIFE BEFORE BEING TRAFFICKED

Family Situation

The children and young people interviewed came from very different backgrounds: about half lived in small village communities; the other half lived in small towns or larger cities. About 50 per cent of the respondents had been living with both birth parents, seven had been living in families with a step-parent and eight were in single parent families, living with their biological mother or father. Only one child had been living for many years in a residential institution. The vast majority of children and young people (22) reported coming from families that experienced domestic violence and abuse. Less than half of the children (14) described their families as 'poor'. More than half of the children (17) also stated that one or both of their parents were addicted to alcohol. Parental alcohol addiction was always connected to domestic violence and abuse and was reported mainly by the children in the Republic of Moldova and Romania. But the children living in these households were not always poor. In fact, alcohol and violence dominated family life in about half of the non-poor families of the children interviewed. There were also some res-pondents who were trafficked from families that were neither violent nor poor. These children had not made the decision themselves to leave but had been abducted or deceived into leaving their homes. In the interviews, the children and young people described what poverty, work, violence and abuse, and their parents' addiction to alcohol meant in their daily lives.

Poverty

Most children who identified their families as poor (14 children) in the interview said their families relied on social assistance, including social welfare income (e.g. disability pension or child allowance), borrowing and irregular income earned from unskilled jobs in the informal sector. We were accumulating debts to the State (for payment of the utilities) and we had to keep moving to worse and worse apartments. But by selling the apartments we were making money, and yes, we did not have enough room but we had money to buy clothes every month. I did not have anything to eat or to wear and did not attend school. I had no money either for food or anything else or for clothes. I wanted to earn money.

Working Children

Many of the children reported they had to take on various household chores or felt compelled to contribute to the family income. Some also reported they were sent out by a parent or guardian to borrow, beg or make money in other ways, including through commercial sex. In some extreme cases, children became the main breadwinner or took on the role as head of the household. In 2002, my older sister married and moved to her own home and I was left alone with my parents. It was very hard for me. I had to keep the house by myself because my mother is an alcoholic and used to go away from home for days. My father is very strict and I had to learn how to cook, to wash, to do everything in the household, while my father worked in the field. Starting with the age of 16 my life turned to disaster. We had no money for bread but a lot of small debts to neighbours. My mother started pressuring me to go to the city and ask friends for money. Meanwhile, I met another girl who, at the disco, intro-duced me to all kinds of boys. All the money I earned was brought home and the entire family lived on it. My mother pretended to know nothing. But she did not ask me where the money was coming from, when should it be paid back, etc.

And instead, she put pressure on me to bring more. I've been working since I was a little girl and I've tried to do everything for my parents to love me. At 12 years old I was doing everything that needs to be done in the house, I was taking care of my brothers and sisters. My mother was ill. She had a caesarean operation and didn't do anything anymore. My youngest brother was ill and my mother stayed with him in the hospital, so I cooked, I washed the clothes and the children, I cleaned. Even the neighbours in the apartment building noticed and wondered how I could keep the house for the entire family. My father would call them (business owners) on the phone and I had to go and collect the money. Or, my father would call the priests and they allowed me to beg in front of the church... I also did all the chores in the household because my mother came tired from work and all she did was cook. I was doing all the rest and I was taking care of the little one, too.

And when I came with the money, my father used to give me a beating and say that it was short, that I had stolen some for sure. And my mother would let him. She was just like him. If he didn't start a fight, she would start it. [While living in a Western country] My mother said she was ill, my father [an invalid] was begging sometimes and I was working selling newspapers. We found all kinds of supplies in garbage cans. My mother went to the cans only when my father made her... Life was so bad...Until one evening when my father told me to go and make money, to walk the street. I refused and my mother said to me to come to my senses and they both trashed me with a crowbar.

Domestic Violence and Abuse

A significant number of the children interviewed (22) reported that they had experienced some form of domestic violence and abuse or neglect. In many cases, the violence was directed by male family members against the mother and child or by both parents towards the child. Domestic violence took the form of physical or psychological violence and/or sexual abuse. In some extreme cases, children were raped and in one instance, a child's mother was murdered by her father.

My father caught me hanging around with some guys in a bar so he beat me badly and burned my hair and then I ran away from home. Later on, I woke up again because my father was trying to rape me, but since I refused he beat me up and raped me. He would shut my mouth with his socks and he threatened me that if I tell anybody about this he would kill my mother and sister. He didn't rape me again but he beat me up many times. My father used to hit my mother frequently. He used to hit me as well. My mother joined a sect and started to beat us up. She said she was taking the devils out of us. She was giving me the worst beatings, because she said I had more devils in me. My stepfather couldn't stand me, my real father believed all the rubbish about me and was saying that I was not his daughter, and my mother... maybe I've made mistakes too, but I say she is the one to be blamed, because she has taught me nothing, she didn't take care of me, she wanted to sell me for 500 Euro to a man.

Alcohol Addiction

Of the children and young people interviewed, 17 reported that alcoholic parents or other family members had threatened their safety and well-being. The testimonies indicated that alcohol addiction was linked to domestic violence and abuse.

I had troubles with my parents as they drank alcohol and told me to earn money.... My father hit my mother, sometimes it was *vice versa*. My mother died when I was 10 years old. I lived with my father and my elder brother. Often my father got drunk and everything they earned was spent on drinking. My father treated me badly very often. He called me bad names and sometimes beat me. Until I was 6 my life was happy. I was living with my grandparents in an apartment building, in a two- room apartment. My mother was coming and going and making a lot of trouble for my grandmother, especially when she got drunk and needed money.

In these homes, children reported experiences of chaos, fear, abandonment, denial, abuse and real or potential violence, inflicted by the very people who were supposed to care for them. Early in life they learned not to depend on their parents to meet their needs but instead to rely on themselves.

Education, Information and Awareness

School Attendance

The children and young people interviewed had varying levels of education at the time they were trafficked. Some were still attending school, others had completed compulsory education, still others had dropped out of school or had never attended school. All six respondents who had completed compulsory schooling and continued with their education had not left home on their own initiative, but were abducted by traffickers or others who abused them. Three of these children came from 'better off' households, while two others came from 'poor' families according to the respondents' own assessments of their household's income level. Only one of these six children came from a household marred by domestic violence.

> As a child, I lived with my family and I was very happy and my family always supported me. I went to school and I was an excellent student so my father was proud of me.

Nine of the children and young people interviewed had dropped out of school before completing compulsory education, and nearly all of them reported they had come from households characterized by the children themselves as poor and violent. Two of the children had never attended school.

The children reported leaving school for a variety of reasons. In most cases, their decisions were directly linked to insufficient household income.

> I did not regularly attend school because I didn't have clothes, notebooks and shoes. I dropped out of school because there was no money for anything. I was ashamed in front of my schoolmates. I would have liked to go on with my studies at a high school but my parents said they would not have money to support me.

Some of the respondents reported other reasons for not wishing to remain in school.

> I was addicted to computer games, to the Internet. I was wasting days and nights. I was missing school until they failed to promote me. From that point on I didn't want to go to school anymore. I started the ninth grade and two weeks later I asked my father for some money and he refused. So I didn't go to school any more and instead I just hung around in [city] where I met [boy's name] and I dated him for a year and a half without the knowledge of my family. The teachers were getting on my nerves.

Only one child who had dropped out indicated that there was any official follow up by the school.

School representatives came to ask why I do not study. My mother said I didn't have anything to study.

Several children had been sent to schools for 'children with special needs where, regardless of how well they performed, they would not be able to obtain a degree that would enable them to continue on to higher education. The children's perception of such schools was that they labelled students as abnormal or learning-disabled and that it was better not to attend them at all.

Information, Knowledge and Awareness

The children and young people were asked whether they had received any advice or information before being trafficked that might have helped them to protect themselves from exploitation and abuse, including trafficking. The questions focused on whether they had received specific information about sexual abuse or trafficking, information about working in another country or advice about precautions to take when going abroad. While some had heard vague stories about trafficking or even knew of other young people who had been trafficked, others had received general information about the risks of sexual assault or harassment in the context of their home cities or communities.

Most of the children and young people felt strongly that they knew little about trafficking before leaving home. They felt they had been left on their own to find information or get advice that could have helped them. Furthermore, they indicated that the little information that was available was often based on hearsay and was therefore inaccurate and incomplete. All children indicated that schools did little to provide relevant information to protect them from trafficking.

I never had any information from anyone. Nobody told us anything. Before? Before I had not a clue. I've been through a lot and I've learned a lot. Everything I know now I've learned at my own expense.

Information on Risks of Sexual Abuse

A vast majority of the young respondents said that at

the time they were trafficked, they did not know how to recognize the risks of exploitation and abuse, including trafficking, or how to control these risks. For all of these children, the trafficking experience represented a painful learning process.

Only 11 children had received any information on the risks of sexual abuse, nearly all through informal networks (peers, mothers or other female relatives or neighbours). Only six of these children had a vague understanding of how to protect themselves from sexual abuse and what to do if they were abused.

Of course I knew I could be raped if I walk at night or go with unknown boys to apartments. I was careful not to do something stupid.... I knew one must hit the violator on the testicles if he attacks you, to throw something into his eyes, as well as to tell to the police. Our teacher talked to girls from our class about sexual issues, she told us not to walk at night as we might get into trouble. Sometimes my mother told me to be careful not to be raped by somebody. Only what my sister (23 years old) told me, that is: to be a good girl and be careful not to get pregnant. I heard from my cousin who is a teacher but I didn't pay attention to her words, thinking that she does not love me, but later on I realized the importance of her words, but it was too late.

Taboos related to sexuality and feelings of shame associated with sexual exploitation, appear to also have played a role in keeping some of the young respondents uninformed.

I declared everything, both at the police and at home. I cannot say I have problems, but I feel they have grown colder to me. It would have been better to keep my mouth shut and everything would be fine now. Like about my cousin who sold me. Nobody had told me she was a prostitute, that she was recruiting girls.... In the village, my grandmother was saying that this cousin was alright, a good girl and she was going to school. After what happened they were asking me why I left with her, like I did know!... Well no, I didn't know because they hadn't told me anything so I can be on my guard.

Of the children and young people interviewed, only 15 had received minimal information about sexually transmitted infections (including HIV and AIDS) and knew of ways to protect themselves. (Although using this information effectively is difficult, if not impossible, in a situation of sexual exploitation, it is a clear indication of just how uninformed these children were about the risks they faced.)

I knew only what we were taught in biology class at school plus the need to use a condom to avoid getting pregnant [not as protection against diseases]. At school, from the media, TV, movies. I was afraid of AIDS. I talked to clients about using condoms. Most of them refused, were insulting me.

Many children interviewed made a deliberate choice to leave home. Some of them had made concrete plans to go abroad for work or for other reasons. Their stories high-light the importance of ensuring that children have access to information about leaving home or migrating to another country in order to protect them from harm. Yet out of 31 interviewed children only 12 children had received some information before being trafficked about the risks associated with travelling abroad and living away from home. Most of this information came from informal networks (*e.g.*, siblings who had been abroad, neighbours, colleagues, friends) and from television. Only one of the children thought that the information she received had influenced how she behaved and reacted later on, although it was clearly not effective enough to prevent trafficking.

Of the 15 children who were trafficked across borders, no child reported receiving accurate information about life abroad, including from their parents and the majority had been presented with inaccurate rosy pictures about life abroad from the people who had trafficked them.

I had no warning information before leaving home. I had imagined that this foreign country would have been a marvellous place with flowers, trees and parks everywhere; with nice homes and good people dressed smart. Rich people. I wasn't given any information about the risks before travelling abroad, either at school or elsewhere. My mother provided some vague warnings, but without providing information about risks.

Two respondents mentioned that they had been advised to try and get a job abroad via an employment agency. But one explained: "I didn't try; I did not trust agencies. They demanded a lot of money".

Few of the children knew what basic precautions to take when travelling away from home or abroad: only three of the respondents had taken a telephone number with them in case of an emergency. None had taken a photocopy of their passport or identity document.

Insufficient and Incomplete Information on Trafficking

The children's responses indicated that the little information on trafficking they did have access to was incomplete, unclear and perpetuated myths about the phenomenon. In some cases, children lacked reliable information because their main source of information was their trafficker or others who were involved in exploiting them. Any information these children received was used to manipulate, influence or control. Other sources had not warned them of these potential risks.

I remember that once a neighbour of mine who had been in in a foreign country told me that she had seen girls standing underneath the bridge and being beaten by some others. In fact, I did not ask her for more details and I did not understand quite well why they had to stand under the bridge and why some people would beat them. It did not influence my decisions because I received too little information. My classmates talked about it, the girls from the factory spoke among themselves. They knew about the prostitution of our girls in a foreign country. However, they knew nothing of this kind about the capital. I knew for sure that I should not trust any promises if these were related to that foreign country. I would have never gone there. But I went to the capital ... I knew that girls are sold from TV and newspapers. But this time it was my cousin, I had never thought she would sell me. I thought that only strange people can sell, not your own relatives. My parents had some second thoughts that I could be sold, but my cousin swore everything would be all right.

Finally, many children and young people indicated that they simply dismissed the little information they did receive because they felt that they would know better than to allow themselves to be deceived in such ways.

I was so sure of myself. I never believed that something bad would happen to me though I have heard previously that bad things might happen. I read about this in papers, saw it on TV, but I have never thought that it is so simple to sell and cheat people. Yes, I have had information re-garding sexual abuse and STDs. I was informed in school and through some pamphlets, too. But I never took them seriously; I never thought these things would ever touch me.

Some children were aware of the risks of trafficking, but did not seek or receive any advice or information on what they could do to protect themselves, other than remaining at home. Yet many children felt that staying at home was not an option. Without alternatives, these children had no practical means to protect themselves.

I was given no advice nor did I try to get any. I knew I would be an illegal worker and I was counting on my girlfriend and her acquaintances to find work for a lot of money. But I did not have any information. I did not need any advice because I needed money quickly, clothes, telephones and money to buy a computer so everybody could see how well I could manage on my own. I had only two alternatives: to commit suicide by poisoning myself or to go abroad. I thought better work as prostitute than bearing the difficult situation I was in. Then, I was sure that if somebody would force me to work in the street, I would work only 2-3 days and I would have been able to run away from them because I am clever.

The 'Changing Point'

When children described their lives, many said, "My life

was good before..." or "I was a happy child until..." In these cases, a particular experience or event had precipitated a crisis that pushed the child into a situation that increased his or her risk of being trafficked. The types of changes that appear to have had the greatest impact include a change of residence or of family composition, or in the child's own interaction and relationship with friends and peers. Often, a series of such experiences and events occurred, which added to already challenging living conditions:

- Family moving from an urban to a rural area Life was good.

We were living in a house in the city. We had everything we needed. It was nice. In 2003, we moved to the countryside. Life is harder, duller, at school it is less fun. I got bored with this life and decided to go back to the city. My family sold their city apartment because too many debts had accumulated and they could not afford it any longer. We moved to a house in a village. After moving to the countryside, my parents did not cover the costs of my commuting to school and I dropped out after completing the 9th grade.

- Divorce or parental separation
- Parent or other family members migrate to work abroad

My mother went abroad. She was not getting along with my father. I had to do all the work around the house and wasn't happy.

- Death of one parent:

I had a normal life. At that time, I was 14 years old and I went to school and did sports. Also the economic situation of my family was good. Everything changed when my father died. My mother has mental problems and after my father passed away she became sicker. She yelled at me for no reason. She blamed me for not doing the housework and spending a lot of time outside the home. I used to get up very early every morning to do the cleaning until 8.30, the time that my mother would get up. Then she started to shout at me about the fact that I hadn't done anything and she used to hit me. When my older brother returned back from work he used to hit me too, as my mother complained to him about me. He would believe her rather than me.

- Introduction of a step-parent:

We were a happy family before the death of my father. Mom remarried. I felt I was betrayed for that man. The first two weeks were very good but later on things started to change, and I started feeling jealousy towards my step-mother .... So my father started treating me very bad, he would beat me and tell me that I must love my step-mother if I want to live with them as a family. My step-father tried to kick me out of the house.

- A relationship not accepted by the parents:

When my parents learned about my relationship, they forced me to break up with him, because he was from a family that used to have a lot of problems in the past. Because I resisted breaking up, both parents started to beat me and kept me closed inside a room tightly bound with a rope in my bed for about two months. They feared that I might run away with him.

- Peer violence:

At the placement centre, it was nice until I got fed up because there were some older girls who used to beat me up and swear at me all the time. My sister who also stayed there could not take my side because they would have given her a thrashing too. My sister ran away from the centre and a few days after, I ran away, too. I only told a girl who we got along well with that I was leaving to look for my sister. At the age of 15, I met through my schoolmates a gang of men. They were fierce, ugly, full of scars, pock- marked and were swarming around the school where they were recruiting girls. I was afraid and refused all their advances. I was scared of their threats. I did not file a complaint with the police and was ashamed to tell my parents. My mother realized something was not right because I was not going out anymore; I was making a detour to go to school. Still, I couldn't believe and she couldn't believe that anything bad might happen to me if I ignored them. But two boys from the gang kidnapped me.

It is obvious from the children's testimonies that most of them did not realize the risks they were facing once these major changes affected their lives. This was in part due to a general lack of information, knowledge and awareness of the dangers of trafficking. But placing them at even greater risk was the fact that many of them were left on their own and did not have a person or institution to turn to for advice. Others consulted with siblings, friends or peers, which, in some cases, led them into even more risky situations. Lacking support in protecting themselves, they became rather easy prey for those who chose to deceive, exploit and eventually traffic them.

LEAVING HOME

Without support or safe alternatives, many of the children responded to family violence and other problems by leaving home. The age at which these children left home varied significantly and ranged from 10 to 17 years. More than half the respondents (17 out of 31) made a deliberate choice to leave home; a majority of them felt pressured to leave, to a varying extent, by their situation at home. Once they left, some had no place to go and stayed on the street for a while. Others made plans to migrate to a specific destination and still others were hosted by friends, peers or extended family members. In many cases, the first contacts made in the initial phase after leaving home led them into exploitation and abuse, including trafficking.

Leaving Home to Escape Domestic Violence and Abuse

Of the children and young people interviewed, 12 left home to escape from domestic violence and abuse. The circumstances in which children left home varied. Some left home after a period of neglect, abuse or being forced to work hard to earn money. Others were fleeing direct threats and violence.

The situation at my home was unbearable. The step-father continued to abuse me sexually and this was the reason I decided to leave home. When I left home, I was around 14-15 years old. A neighbour of mine proposed me to go with him abroad. There we could get married. He would work while I had to take care of the house, cook and clean. At the time I decided to leave home, I was just happy to do that and I couldn't think of anything else. Life at my home was impossible. In fact, I have been thinking a lot to run away from home, but sometimes I felt sorry about my step- mother, sometimes she was good with us. That night, I was very nervous.... But I was very afraid of the 'lover' of my step-mother. I hadn't thought of anything, I just wanted to go away, I had nothing to lose. One afternoon, I went to have something to drink with a friend of mine and her fiancé. Her fiancé was a drug dealer. It was her birthday, so we stayed long together, until 8pm. While getting back home, my brother saw me and followed me. He stopped me and started beating me in the street. After he left, I wanted to get back home but was afraid that he would keep hitting me, so I decided not to return home. I stayed for nearly two weeks at the house of a friend of mine. Then I went to the capital to stay at the house of my cousin. There I met two friends of mine, one 23 years old and the other 19 years old. They promised to send me to Greece. I have a lot of relatives there. So I decided to go with them, since I couldn't get back home anymore. In Greece I thought at least I would go to school. I was 14 years old. I fell in love with him...when my family learned about that and also of the fact that I had sexual relationships with him, they wanted to kill me. My parents very often started to say to me "we will poison you, like [an acquaintance] did to his daughter" or "we will drown you in the well and will say to others that our daughter has run away from home". Finally, they decided to lock me inside home. I remained locked inside for about four months and one month I was bound in the bed. One day while my father was in hospital, I was alone at home with my grandmother. She helped me. She cut the rope with which I was bound in the bed. I decided to run away from home. My life was in danger. My parents were ready to kill me. I didn't think of anything, I just wanted to go far away from home. I went to a cousin of mine and I remained at his apartment in the city for about ten days. Then, he brought me to a bar-restaurant in the capital. The owner of the bar provided me a job. There were other girls working there. I was about 16-17 years old at that time.

The departure was not always clean cut and, sometimes, particularly in the case of younger children, involved repeated returns and departures:

> I ran away from home when I was 12 years old.... I stayed on the street for a week. While I was out on the street many people abused me sexually and physically. After a while I went back home and my father tried to beat me again but I didn't let him. Than I ran away a few other times and I stayed on the street for a while, and then I went back home again. But my father continued beating me so I would run away again and this lasted for a while.

Leaving Home for Work or for Other Reasons

Some children and young people said they left home because they wanted to earn money and believed their prospects would be better somewhere else either in their own country or abroad. In the cases of older adolescents, departure was relatively well planned but turned out badly.

I left to work as a housekeeper and earn 500 dollars a month. I was going to earn money by working in a bar. I was promised that I would be selling at the market and earn 50 dollars. My friend promised me that [an acquaintance] would find us a job. I thought I was going to work as a cook or do the dishes at a restaurant in [the capital city of a nearby country]. I had a boyfriend five years older than me. He suggested we should marry. I worked as a seamstress at a clothes factory in [a town]. I wanted to earn money for the wedding and foolishly I left for [the capital city of a nearby country]. I wanted to earn money as a cook in [that city], as I was promised. I met a friend who said he could arrange for us to leave, to make money fast. He had been abroad before (to visit his mother in [an EU country]) and knew what's what. I was curious to know how things were outside, I wanted to go see how it is, to buy a computer and designer clothes, not like these ones here from the flea market and come back.

Some convinced themselves that they were just taking some time away from home and embarking on a journey for some fun or even a holiday.

The only reason why I left home for the first time was to have fun and didn't think anything else. My cousin told me she would give me a pleasant vacation.

These children clearly stated that they felt they were making their own decisions and acting independently. Yet given the difficult circumstances that many of them faced at home, the lines between voluntary and forced or coerced are easily blurred. Many types of coercion, some quite subtle, and force influenced their decision-making process. A decision that might appear to be voluntary under a particular circumstance might have not been made at all or been different had circumstances been different.

POLICY RECOMMENDATIONS

What can be done to Prevent Child Trafficking

These recommendations are based on the broad body of UNICEF IRC studies on child trafficking and reconfirmed through the voices of the children and young people quoted in this study.

The vast majority of children and young people (22) reported coming from families that experienced domestic violence and abuse. More than half of the children (17) also stated that one or both of their parents were addicted to alcohol. Without support or safe alternatives, many of the children responded to family violence and other problems by leaving home.

National child protection systems should be developed and made operational by the Government at the national and community level, framed by and based on children's rights. At local level (*e.g.*, at the level of a small town or municipality or a group of villages) authorities should ensure that systems are in place so that social workers, teachers, police officers and others with information or responsibilities for children work together, exchange information on a systematic basis and have standardized responses whenever there are signs that a child might be experiencing abuse or is in danger of being abused. Such systems must ensure that the child's best interests are a primary consideration in every decision and action and professionals need to be held accountable for dereliction of duty. These professionals also need to be trained in how to consult with girls and boys of various ages and back-grounds.

National child protection systems need to address the root causes of child trafficking, such as gender discrimi-nation, patriarchal structures, and other social, economic and structural factors. They need to recognize the inter-linkages between various forms of violence, abuse and exploitation, as violence in the family makes children parti-cularly vulnerable. Support needs to be given to families and communities through livelihood opportunities, family counseling, drug and alcohol prevention and rehabilitation, parental education (for fathers and mothers) including positive discipline, and information about child rights and child protection issues. Child sensitive and child- friendly reporting mechanisms (including help lines) need to be made available and accessible for children.

Safe alternatives should be developed by state social services in association with civil society and non-governmental organisations, for adolescents who chose to leave home or who are unwilling to return home due to a history of ill-treatment, including as witnesses of domestic violence. Residential institutions should always be an option of last resort.

Children and young people need to be consulted and meaningfully involved in the design of the various components of the child protection system, as well as in the monitoring of its effectiveness.

Of the 15 children who were trafficked across borders, no child reported having received accurate information about migration and the majority had been presented with inaccurate rosy pictures about life abroad from the people who had trafficked them.

The danger of being trafficked by relatives, peers or someone the child is already acquainted with is real and must not be underestimated when raising awareness about the risks of trafficking. Information and awareness-raising about the risks of sexual abuse and exploitation and trafficking should therefore also aim to dismantle the myth of 'stranger – danger'. Information campaigns about human trafficking need to reflect the complexity of trafficking and raise awareness in the broadest possible manner. Information also needs to target the buyers of sexual services to inform them that sexual exploitation of children is a violation of human rights.

Child-friendly and age-specific information, in local languages, needs to be made available and accessible for children. It needs to be developed together with children and young people who have experience on the issues. This can include, for example, safety booklets, radio programmes and community theatre.

Nine of the children and young people interviewed had dropped out of school before completing compulsory education, and nearly all of them described their family environment as poor and violent. Two of the children had never attended school. The decisions for leaving school were directly linked to insufficient household income. Some of the respondents reported that they saw little benefit in remaining in school.

Inclusive systems are needed to ensure that all children are registered and do attend school, including children belonging to minorities and marginalised groups. Similarly, these systems must respond if girls and boys drop out early, not simply by penalizing the children or their parents, but by interviewing the child and investigating the household's circumstances and determining what type of support they might need, including livelihood options. Standards and mechanisms should be in place to ensure that children do not experience violence and abuse in the classroom or school environment.

Life skills should be taught in every school, including information and discussions about gender, sexuality, HIV and AIDS. At a suitable age, children should also be given information about the different forms of abuse, the responses that may be appropriate, and where they can turn to for help. Teachers should be trained in child participatory methods and children should be given the possibility to influence the school environment. Alongside conventional career advice, schoolchildren and graduates in countries with high rates of emigration should be given guidance on how to check whether offers of jobs abroad are genuine and safe to accept, and what practical pre-cautions they can take to protect themselves.

The Trafficking Experience

Characteristics of Trafficking Cases

Roughly half of the respondents had been exploited abroad and half within their own countries: In Kosovo, all children and young people interviewed had been exploited internally; in the Republic of Moldova, all respondents had been exploited abroad; in Albania and Romania, half the children had been exploited abroad, the other half within their own countries. Due to the selection process, which restricted the study to children who had received assistance or care in a shelter, nearly all respondents had been sexually exploited , while some reported multiple or changing forms of exploitation, including commercial sexual exploitation, begging and petty crime.

Differing definitions

All children and young people who participated in this study were classified as victims of trafficking in their home countries and were consequently referred to shelters for assistance. From the interviews, it is not fully clear if all 31 children met the three major criteria highlighted in the international legal definition of child trafficking. Some children described situations where they were sexually exploited for commercial purposes rather than trafficked. Not always was there a third person involved in recruiting and moving these children for the purpose of exploitation: Some children left home and started working in a bar, where they were subsequently sexually abused and exploited.

The case of the only boy who was interviewed illustrates how national authorities in both origin and destination countries apply different definitions when identifying and classifying children: The boy had travelled with a young adult, slightly older than himself, to a Western European country to earn money by stealing. He had accepted a loan from his companion to finance the trip and was supposed to repay the costs from his earnings. When he came in contact with the authorities of the destination country, he was arrested as a juvenile delinquent and spent time in prison. Upon return to his home country, however, he was identified as a victim of trafficking and referred to a shelter.

These 31 children's experiences illustrate that reality does not always fit neatly into the definition of child traf-ficking provided by the Palermo Protocol. The real situation of these children is much more complex. Their subjective perception of exploitation and abuse often varies, making it a particular challenge to fully understand the dynamics of exploitation and abuse when children are moving from one place to another.

THE BEGINNING OF THE TRAFFICKING PROCESS

Although each child's personal and family circum-stances differed, recurrent patterns emerged as children described how and where the trafficking process started, how they had met their trafficker, and what role the trafficker had in the children's departure from home. The majority of the respondents left home on their own initiative or was convinced to leave by the trafficker. Some children were abducted by force.

Children left home on their own initiative for various reasons – to escape abuse, to travel, to look for work or seek adventure. Among those children who left home on their own, some fell under the control of a trafficker almost immediately, while others were on their own for while. I got bored with life at home and I decided to go to a nearby town. I walked and hitch-hiked there, then to another city where I slept in the marketplace and ate walnuts directly from the tree. Then I decided to go further. I went to another city and yet another one, where I met [*the trafficker*]. I told my mother that it would be all right that I was going to wash dishes, to work as a cleaning woman or as a waitress, that I could do all these things. I knew how to keep house, I was resourceful and I could cook by myself. But I knew it wasn't true and instead, together with my girlfriend that we would be dancers, like my sister. I wanted to visit other towns. I met a friend and went to her flat and I spent 10 days there. She was 33 years old and she was bringing her boyfriends in her flat, but she didn't allow them to touch me, saying that I was too young. They took my friend by force to work in a bar. She advised them to take me as well, which is what happened. *Left home after being deceived or enticed away by a trafficker.*Thirteen children were deceived or otherwise enticed by a trafficker to leave their homes. These were mostly children who were eager to find work for a short period so that they could earn money quickly for very concrete purposes, including to pay for a wedding, designer clothes, a computer or school equip-ment. All these children reported that their families were experiencing some financial difficulties, and were especially susceptible to deceptive traffickers who lied about job offers and opportunities.

I thought that I was grown up and could earn money to support myself. A woman from the village called me and suggested I should go to the capital. Her husband was there and could help me find a job. I knew that the capital was a very rich city. Many people from our village had been working there. So, yes, I believed her. She promised they would find a job for me, to do repairs in apartments. I wanted to earn money for the wedding and I foolishly left for [the capital of a neighbouring country]. My friend promised me that an acquaintance would find us a job there. I wanted to earn money as a cook. I left to work as a house-keeper and earn 500 dollars a month. I was promised that I would be selling at the market and earn 50 dollars. I was given only good promises. I was promised work as a salesgirl at the market. I was supposed to sell citrus plants. I was happy that I could earn a lot of money and be able to ensure my own living. I was worried only by the fact that I had to give back my debts for the identity card, train ticket, pocket money. After I had been in [an EU country] with my parents for a while, I had enough of their beatings and wanted to go back to [*the home country*], to my grandmother. I knew I needed a passport, but my parents had my passport, they were keeping it under their head. I believed the good neighbour, a nice and understanding man. He had seen how my parents were treating me and I believed he wanted to save me and take me back to my grandmother. But instead he sold me to a pimp who made money out of me [in another Western country].

Involuntary Departure and Abduction

Five children were abducted and soon after came under the control of the trafficker. In a vast majority of these cases, the persons who abducted these children were not strangers but acquaintances, friends of friends or someone from the same community. Most of these abducted children came from families that were not affected by domestic violence.

One day while I was in the town, a man kidnapped me and took me to a village where he raped me and he kept me there. One day, I was standing next to the school gate with my friend when some guys came in a van and they kidnapped us and took us to another village and in the basement of a house. They beat me up there and then I realized that my friend was their friend too and this was all organized. The relation between my mother and my father was not good, but I was not intending to run away from home. I was deceived and kidnapped, when I accepted a ride in the car of a friend. When I was 17, a [female] cousin of mine came and picked me up from home and for two hours she pretended we were going to visit our aunt who was sick. My cousin hurried me along and persuaded me to get into a taxi without waiting for my father.

Organization of the Trip and Travel Modes

Fifteen interviewed children were trafficked across a national border. With one exception, all of these children knew where they were going. However, less than half of them informed someone in the family about their destination. Those who did inform someone usually told their mothers. Some offered only partial information, did not mention the purpose for which or the date when they were leaving, and others kept silent because the traffickers had told them not to say anything or because the family opposed their departure. In nearly all cases, the trafficker organized and paid for the travel, including documents (sometimes forged), tickets or transportation and made arrangements for pick up at the destination. The travel- related costs became the children's debts to the trafficker and were used to restrain and control the children. In nearly all cases, the children were accompanied on their trip by a friend or acquaintance.

Most children crossed the border through border posts and interacted with train conductors and customers. Some children were intercepted by border guards who took the children away from the traffickers. In other cases, border controls did not end the trafficking process, even though some children had incomplete or forged documents. In some cases, the testimonies from children indicate that corruption seemed to facilitate the border crossing.

I travelled together with my friend [a 20-year-old female[. We crossed the border legally, with documents, in a car driven by a driver [hired by the traffickers] and two other boys who were going to 'work'. The traffickers had organized everything, also our passports. A customs officer noticed that I was 'a child', but the driver told him that I was going for a trip with them. I did not have my parents' written consent, but the customs officer did not insist and did not intervene either. The trip was paid and organized by my friend.We crossed the border legally, in a car with a driver. Although my father was wanted by the police, nobody asked anything. We travelled with a minibus. I did not have my parents' written consent, so when the customs officer asked the question I lied saying that I was accompanied by my aunt [a lady in the minibus] who was taking me to her mother in [an EU country]. I crossed the border without any problem. A customs officer asked only if we had the amount of money according to regulations, and we showed the 2000 Euro that the driver had given us. We paid the conductor to hide us in his compartment. The train conductor took money, he made sure to talk to all frontier guards.

THE TRAFFICKERSN

Only eight children were trafficked by a 'stranger', someone they had not met before.

A stranger offered to help me get work abroad. He said he would give me money for the train ticket and for the identity card. I was promised work in the market. He advised me not to tell the rest of my family where I was going.

Most of the children interviewed (21), knew their traffickers. In some cases the exploiter was identified as a boyfriend or lover; in three cases it was a neighbour; in three others, a cousin. My cousin asked my parents to let me go with her and I wanted to go on holidays with her because I trusted her.

My cousin told me she could offer me a pleasant holiday.... My parents were against the idea, but later they accepted it. They went to a notary office for a paper from a lawyer, got me an identity card and a passport and I left to [name of the country]. There [her cousin's husband] told me I was going to be a prostitute; he locked me up and took away my identity documents.

The interviews highlight that exploiters were often among the adolescents' peer group, especially in the cases of those children who, after leaving home, relied on the support of relatives, friends or other peers for accommodation, work and joint travel.

I had a friend and she lived next to me and when she would invite friends over, I would often join them.... One day she took me with her and we went in an apartment with lots of guys. They all sexually abused us and at the end I saw that they gave some money to my friend. This lasted for three weeks, every night after midnight she would come and get me and then we would return early in the morning. This all happened with my approval, until my father caught me and he beat me up badly.... Later I got married and after a month my husband started doing the same thing as my friend, every night he would bring clients home.

Traffickers were both, women and men, mostly adults, but in some cases they were under 18 years of age or even much younger.

One day, while I was staying at the doorstep, a neighbour, called Ariana [original name changed], came up to me and said: "Come with me, you will be my little sister, you will stay some time with me; we will have a lot to eat and then we will come back again". But she cheated me. I was 10 years old when I left with Ariana. She was older than me; she was 13 to 14 years old. We also took with us my little sister. We went to a city. I was very afraid of Ariana. She used to beat me and said very often: "I will drown you in the sea". She introduced me to a lot of boys.... I was forced to stay with them all day long.... They gave me money and she took everything from me. She used to buy a lot of things to eat for herself and gave me nothing. We also went to the capital. There, I used to beg in the street or knock at the doors and ask for money and food.

Seven of the children were exploited by more than one trafficker. They were either sold from one trafficker to another or had periods in which they managed to break free from the control of traffickers, work independently or spent time in shelters. All of these children eventually came back under the control of a trafficker.

My boyfriend sent me to [an EU country] to make money as a prostitute. So one day, together with another girl, we travelled by plane with a false passport to [the EU country]. At the train station [in the capital] some guys were waiting for us. They took us to another city. There, I started working as a prostitute, I had to make money: I owed my boyfriend

3,500 of our local currency because he paid my journey. And I had to make 8,500 Euro in order to help him to buy drugs. After I made 12,000 Euro, he came to meet me and together we travelled to another country. He was a drug dealer and I helped him. One night, when I was out to have a drink by myself, a group of four guys from my country who were trafficking drugs, kidnapped me. They had beaten and threatened me. They had drugs and weapons inside the car. They said to me: "you will work for us". [In an EU country] At the beginning I begged and stole from shops. Afterwards, the trafficker put me out to make money in the street [commercial sexual exploitation] because I couldn't steal any longer because the entire police knew me. Because I made only small amounts of money the trafficker sold me to another trafficker. I began to know [the city]. I was repeatedly picked up by the police and learned how to get myself out of jail. I learned [the language] and I learned who the trafficker's friends were, who to beware of and my network of steady clients expanded. After all this, I managed to escape. I found a 'sponsor' [a married man who paid for her hotel] and started on my own.... There were better periods and worse periods, arguments and fights with the girls on the street. For various periods I had to work for other traffickers because they were threatening me. I had no papers. I was countless times picked up by the police for theft or for lack of documents. I was kidnapped by a network of traffickers who drugged me, raped me and locked me up, from where I managed to escape following a police intervention in force. I gave lots of statements, lots that I don't know how many and I helped in the arrest of this network. [After about one year] Since the traffickers had their eye on me again they had heard that I was making more than 500 Euro a night and they wanted me back I left everything I had made in the hotel in [the city] ... and I left with my best girlfriends [both over 20 years old] to another Western country. Coercion and control during the trafficking process The traffickers used various methods and strategies to keep the children under their control.

- Threats and intimidation?
- Beatings, rape and other forms of violence?

- Physical restraints, such as constant surveillance or keeping the child locked up?
- Depriving the child of identity papers?
- Keeping the child high on drugs or alcohol.?

As many as 23 children reported being subjected to two or more forms of coercion and restraint. However, there were also five children (the youngest of the group) who reported that they did not feel any form of active coercion or restraint. Some of these children felt they did not have any alternative but to stay, or felt dependent on their exploiters because they felt they had nowhere else to go.

I was sold by my cousin and her pimp to a network of traffickers who intended to make money in [an EU country]. They locked me up, for the period needed to prepare the trip, in a house on the outskirts of the town. I was guarded permanently by a fierce man in his forties. I was forced to do all the house work. They beat me up and raped me repeatedly. I was kept there unconscious since I was forced to have alcoholic drinks and during that time they abused me badly. I could not even think about escaping since it was a basement and they were all around. I was in this situation for two weeks until they took me to [a town] and left me at a playground.

I lived with 20 girls in the trafficker's apartment. I was beaten many times. They told me if I ran away they would find and kill me, would come to my village and kill my mother.... Then he sold me to a woman. They took us by maxi taxi to the place where we were sold. We were sold to the clients, three to four girls per night. A woman took the money. We were always supervised. We were beaten for any little thing. We ate only pasta. Several girls ran away, the trafficker caught them and beat them hard in front of us. They told us that the same will happen to us if we run away. During my time there, the owner of the bar and a friend of his used me and one day the owner had to leave because his son was sick, so he left me with his friend, who sexually used me and when I would refuse or I would try to get out they would keep me locked in the basement. They threatened me saying that there was nothing I could do, that everybody had seen me with them and nobody would believe me, that they would set fire to my house, that they would kill my mother and my child, that they would rape my sisters. They threatened me saying that if I would not work for them, they would make me the laughing stock of the village.

Some traffickers used threats, violence and other forms of coercion from the moment they recruited or abducted their victims. In other cases, the relationship between the child and the trafficker changed. The exploiter began by earning the child's trust and making the child feel he/she was a friend. Yet once the exploiter controlled the child, the relationship quickly turned violent. In some cases, traffickers used relatively sophisticated forms of emotional manipulation, convincing the girls that they loved them. All adolescent girls who fell victim to this strategy had previously experienced abuse at home.

In the beginning, it was nice. He kept me for himself, he bought me clothes, cosmetics, he was treating me nicely. Then, an ex-girlfriend of his arrived and, for the time, this one stayed with him and he sent me to produce [make money]. My sister was jealous of me because she was making money together with the other girls and I was kept only for him. At that time, we patched things up as I went to make money, too. When his ex-girlfriend left, he kept me for himself again. He was rather old but nice. Only that he used to hit me, to curse me if I didn't obey him and I didn't go fetch something (for instance beer from the fridge). I had to be obedient and do the work around the house. I fell in love with a guy from another city. I loved him so much. He said to me: "Our future is abroad . You have to go there, to work as a prostitute, just for a short period of time. With the money you will gain, you will pay my journey to that foreign country. And we will live there". He had money to pay only for my journey. At first I cried, I didn't want to, but since I loved him very much, I decided to do what he suggested me.

The Way Trafficking Episodes Came to an End

The ways in which the trafficking and exploitation process came to an end varied widely. Of the 31 children and young people interviewed, 18 actively escaped from their situation of exploitation, alone or with the help of others; one third of these children approached the police for help. The other 13 respondents were either not able or not trying to escape but were taken out of the exploitative situation by third persons, most frequently the police. The police identified these children either during the movement process or at destination. Often these 'main actors' had support from others: friends, relatives and frequently, the police.

The information provided by the children who tried to escape reveals that their escape was a process rather than a single event. In each case, it took time, knowledge, imagination, courage and luck. They needed to understand the strategies of the traffickers and identify persons they could rely on. Escaping also required overcoming fear, both the routine fear that some felt and the fear of additional punishment they would be subjected to if they were recaptured. Five children managed to escape without any help.

The house was far away from the road, on the outskirts of the town. Even if I made motions from the window, the passers-by could not see me and could not hear me. The windows were nailed shut, I tried them all. The windows had roller blinds always rolled down. Whenever I tried to roll them up he would catch me and beat me up. He [the traffickers' accomplice] was staying in the house all the time and was watching me day and night.... Since I was making him coffee, I was looking in the cupboard for a cup and that is how I noticed there were some keys hidden there. I took them and, one night when he left me alone in the room, I managed to escape and I found the road to the centre of the town, to the police. While we were walking through the woods they stopped near an old house and they forced me in there. It was four of them. I stayed there for three days without food or water, being raped by all of them and also beaten by them. One day we all left that old house and I remained with one of them, while the others went to look for something. I was freed to have some water and while he was drinking the water I got a piece of wood and I hit him on the head and ran away.

Other children's accounts revealed that the child's social network in the place of exploitation and people they had stayed in contact with back home played an important role in planning the escape. Most children who developed an escape strategy relied upon the help of a relative, a friend, another trafficked woman or girl, an NGO worker, or a 'client' paying for sex or various combinations of all four. These contacts helped to organize the escape and the initial phase after the children had gotten away from the traffickers.

I tried to escape, but they beat me cruelly. I managed to run away together with another 14-year-old girl to a family where we lived for two weeks. One day, when I went to buy some bread, I was detained by the police and sent to a temporary shelter. I spoke with a girl who also wanted to run away. We did not speak openly about that in order not to be denounced. I ran away with that girl, who had the key to an apartment of a friend of hers who lived in the suburbs of the city. We stayed there around two weeks in order to be convinced that no one was chasing us. Then we phoned some relatives at home. I tried to run away three times. Two times I was caught and beaten severely. I succeeded in running away only the third time. I got acquainted with a woman from my country who took me to her place and we lived together. One month later she helped me to get work as a waitress. It was she who advised me to go to the police. When I caught on how things stood, I started coming out on the street earlier than the other girls, so they don't see me and I made some money to call my grandmother and tell her what I was doing.... I asked my grandmother how I could get away. She talked to the police in our village and they told her that if I went to the police and said that I was a minor, they would help me come back home. There was also another girl belonging to the same pimp who had told me the same thing. But she had advised me that it would be better to wait for a police patrol car to pass by in the area so I could tell them and they could take me away from there. Otherwise, I might not be able to reach the police station, as we were being watched. So this is what I did. I tried to escape but they locked me in and beat me. When I found out that I was pregnant, the pimps threatened me with an abortion. So once, when they took me to a client, I jumped from the second floor. I hid myself, but some girls helped me to find my friend with whom I had departed in the beginning and who worked for another pimp. She took me to an apartment, gave me money and took me to the train. It was impossible to escape as they watched me day and night. A client who was also a lawyer put pressure on the trafficker to buy me a return ticket to my country. I told three clients that I had been kidnapped from home and that I'm a minor. But they told the owner about it, because they didn't care. But one of the clients said that he would save me from the club.... Then, I gave him the telephone number of a school-mate and asked him to convey the message "[name] is expecting you in [city]". Following this call, my school friend understood that something bad was happening and called my parents. My mother immediately notified the police.

The fact that men paying for commercial sex were among the people who helped children to escape suggests that such men do not simply create demand for commercial sex but can also play an important role in identifying trafficking cases. Raising awareness among men who pay for sex about the predicament of victims of trafficking and the possibility that a woman they see as a sex worker may in fact be a child and a victim of trafficking can contribute to the identification of victims, in particular those under 18 years of age. Relying on a client for help, however, can be risky for victims of trafficking since they have no way of knowing how the client will use the information or whether the client is complicit with the trafficker.

Organizing and preparing the escape also relied upon understanding the traffickers' strategies. Some of the children found out that their traffickers operated a network that helped them to control the children and prevent escapes. In a few cases, understanding the traffickers' strategies involved suspecting corruption of officials. In the cases of two children with similar experiences, police officers and traffickers came from the same town and were complicit.

I worked out which client might help me and I managed to save about 500 Euro to travel home. But I cut my hair and dyed it, to change my looks so they would not recognise me. I knew that pimps caught girls who were running away at one of the railway stations where the trains to my country left. So I did not go to that one but to a different station.

Escape did not always mean the end of trafficking for the child. As was illustrated earlier, children can return under the control of the same traffickers or be recruited or abducted by different traffickers.

The Children's Experience with the Police

In about half of the cases (15), the police played a major role in getting the child out of the exploitative situation. In six of these cases, it was the child who took the initiative to contact the police in order to seek assistance. In the other cases, the police identified children as victims of trafficking during raids, at the border or in some circumstances, when checking the child's identity. During the interviews, the children and young people expressed mixed feelings about the police. Some trusted the police and in general, felt they had been supported and assisted by them, ("The policemen had been very good with me"). Others felt extreme mistrust. Some children never tried contacting the police because they felt guilty about what the traffickers had forced them to do and were afraid of legal consequences. More often, however, fears and mistrust were grounded in warnings by traffickers and threats to children who cooperated with the police. Some children also suspected that the police were corrupt and complicit with traffickers.

I didn't try to contact the police. All policemen were bought. I gave hundreds of statements, lists of names and amounts and dates and so on. They are still free! The police did nothing because they are hand in hand. I was afraid that if I talked to the police, they [the traffickers] would find me and hurt me. I was so scared. One girl in [the destination country] had told me that in our country centres for women and girls who return from abroad have been set up and that police treat them very badly and force them to make reports. I contacted the police six months after I ran away from the traffickers. I was afraid of the foreign country's police. I did not have identity documents and did not know if they would help me. However, I went to the police but I did not tell them that I was forced to prostitute. I told them that my documents were stolen and I could not return to my country. I did not tell them that I was trafficked but they helped me to come back to my country. I wanted to leave them [the traffickers], but I was afraid. I wanted to report them to the police, but I felt unsafe doing that in my country, so I decided to postpone it until we arrived in [the destination country]. Many times, the police caught us and kept us at the police station just for verifications, but I had never told them about my situation as I was so afraid. The police asked me to report about persons I had met, but I didn't accept to do that because I was very afraid.

Some children who had been trafficked came repeat-edly in contact with police in their own country, at borders or abroad. These contacts happened on the streets, when the children were suspected of theft or having an identity document that was not 'in order' and in raids on apartments serving as brothels. However, this apparently did not automatically lead to the child being referred to assistance.

The police sent us to the police station. He [the trafficker] told to me not to tell the truth. I was so happy that the police had caught us, but in the same time I was so afraid of him.... All the time in the police station I was with him. He told the police that I was his sister and that we had come to [the destination country] to meet our father who was working there. He showed the police the family certificate (the false one). The police handed us over to the police [of our home country] in the customs post. The police [in our home country] questioned us and he told them the same story, that "I was his sister". I couldn't talk; I couldn't tell them the truth. Afterwards, they set us free. We took a taxi and in a city on our way home, we were stopped by some other policemen. I think they had doubts about us, that's why they stopped us. I told them the truth. At that moment the guy called his father and his father communicated with the police too. He gave to the police money and they set us 'free'.

One day, a friend of mine helped me. He gave me money in order to get away from Ariana, but I wasn't able to get away from her. I was afraid of her.... If I would return home my mother would treat me the same.... I have contacted the police several times. They sent me home. When I turned back home...the friends of my mother continued to pay visits to us every night, I remember that my uncle shouted and beat my mother because of me.... Then, after some time, I met again Ariana. I continued begging and meeting different boys and men.... One day, while Ariana was sleeping, I together with my sister went away and met a policeman in the street. We asked him for help and he returned us home again.... My mother didn't want us back, I continued to meet with the friends of my mother...but not very often, because my mother was afraid of my uncle.

Furthermore, in many cases, there were no individual case assessments to determine the best interests of the child. Instead, children were facing standard procedures that did not succeed in identifying and responding to their specific situation and needs. This lack of flexibility in the options and services offered to children may sometimes have increased their risk of exploitation and abuse. The police told me that if I was a minor, they could not send me back home.

They had to place me in a juvenile shelter. Only if I wanted to be recorded as an adult, they could send me directly to my country. So I said I was adult and they sent me to [the capital of her home country]. I travelled in a group of adults who were also sent back to my country. Two of them helped me to find my way in the capital and get to the railway station. I got on a train. Then I called my grandmother and she told me what buses I had to take to get home. The police informed me about the two alternatives I had: either to return to my country or to go to a centre there [in the destination country]. I wanted neither to return to my country nor to go to the centre. I just wanted to get in touch again with my boyfriend. I cried and screamed at the police station and they decided to let me free, to go anywhere I wanted. At the police station, a colonel gave me [the equivalent of about one Euro] for a soda and a pretzel and also a note to the attention of the railway police to send me back to my hometown. He said, "You go to the police in your town and solve your problems there". I knew I could turn to a foundation in that city that had helped us with the school. But all they could have done was to take me and send me to a shelter, not home to grandmother. And I was sorry to leave my brother alone, I always helped him with his maths homework.

PANEL

The children's testimonies shed light on the complex factors that characterize the trafficking process. There are many different patterns of trafficking and exploitation, different factors that are interrelated in a variety of ways, and multiple phases involved in the trafficking process. Two examples provide some insight into these complex dynamics. They demonstrate how children can fall in and out of the control of multiple traffickers and highlight how institutional actors who came in contact with the children "in many cases the police" did not exercise their full responsibilities to protect them and thereby may have put children at a greater risk of abuse.

GIRL #1 I met a friend and went to her flat and I spent 10 days there. She was 33 year old and she was bringing her boyfriends in her flat, but she didn't allow them to touch me, saying that I was too young. They took my friend by force to work in a bar. She advised them to take me as well, which is what happened. In that café, we stayed for two days and afterwards the police came there and since we didn't possess any documents, they sent us to the police station. They sent us to a shelter. And then, we were sent to the court, where we testified against the owner of the bar. In the shelter, I met one of my friends who told me that she had a boutique of clothes and she could employ me there. But in the meantime, she left the shelter. I disliked everything in that shelter and I made the request to the custodians to leave that place. They told me if I want to leave, the only thing I had to do is to sign a paper. I did so and left the shelter. I was 16 at that time. After leaving the shelter, I paid a visit to a café and met the girl whom I knew from the shelter. She was accompanied by two men. They took us with them saying that they got me a job in a shop, but when we arrived there I saw that it was a bar. One week after, the owner of the bar started to beat me and bring the clients to me. He was selling me for money. This lasted for one month and a half, until my brother - in - law visited that place and saw me. He informed the police. The police came and got me out and sent me to a shelter. This time I did not make a statement against the bar owner because I was afraid of him.

GIRL #2 (In an EU country.) At the beginning I begged and stole from shops. Afterwards, the trafficker put me out to make money in the street (prostitution) because I couldn't steal any longer because the entire police knew me. Because I made only small amounts of money the trafficker sold me to another trafficker. They made me work as a prostitute. I began to know [the city]. I was repeatedly picked up by the police and learned how to get myself out of jail. I learned [the language] and I learned who the trafficker's friends were, who to beware of, and my network of steady clients expanded. After all this, I managed to escape. I found a 'sponsor' [a married man who paid for her hotel] and started on my own, with a girl that I taught to forget about riding the high horses. I told her, shut up and get to work yourself, so we can live. There were better periods and worse periods, arguments and fights with the girls on the street. For various periods I had to work for other traffickers because they were threatening me. I had no papers. I was countless times picked up by the police for theft or for lack of documents. I was kidnapped by a network of traffickers who drugged me, raped me and locked me up, from where I managed to escape following a police intervention in force. I gave lots of statements, lots that I don't know how many and I helped in the arrest of this network. (After about one year) Since the traffickers had their eye on me again they had heard that I was making more than 500 Euro a night and they wanted me back - I left everything I had made in the hotel in [the city] ... and I left with my best girlfriends [both over 20 years old] to another Western country.

POLICY RECOMMENDATIONS

What can be done to protect and assist children in situations of trafficking and exploitation? These recommendations are based on the broad body of UNICEF IRC studies on child trafficking 16 and reconfirmed through the voices of the children and young people quoted in this study.

There are many different patterns of trafficking and exploitation, different factors that are interrelated in a variety of ways, and multiple phases involved in the trafficking process. Most children interviewed, knew their traffickers. In some cases the exploiter was identified as a boyfriend or lover; in three cases it was a neighbour; in three others a cousin. Traffickers were both women and men, mostly adults, but in some cases they were under 18 years of age or even much younger.

Responses should recognize and take into consideration that the trafficker is often a relative, a peer or someone with whom the child is already acquainted, and he/she may therefore be reluctant to report due to attachment, shame or fear or both. Special measures should be taken when the trafficker is a child. Actions should be taken to avoid the risk of re-trafficking.

The protection of the rights of trafficked children and a victim-oriented approach should be central in any anti-trafficking law enforcement and identification process. Special measures (*e.g.* diversion) should be taken when the trafficker is a juvenile to avoid the child's entry into the criminal justice system.

Some children were intercepted by border guards who took the children away from the traffickers. In other cases, border controls did not end the trafficking process, even though some children had incomplete or forged documents.

In some cases, corruption seemed to facilitate the border crossing. Some children also suspected that the police were corrupt and complicit with the traffickers.

Governments should assess what measures are in place at the borders to identify and protect children being trafficked. Existing measures may be either inadequate or not fully enforced or simply ignored. All actors who may interact with children who are being trafficked should be trained regarding the special risks, vulnerabilities and rights of trafficked children. The establishment of a Europe-wide referral system, with clear procedures and communication protocols, could facilitate this. Child migrants need better access to information on their rights and how to get access to assistance once they leave home, both in their own country and abroad.

Most children who developed an escape strategy relied upon the help of a relative, a friend, another trafficked woman or girl, an NGO worker, a 'client' paying for sexual services or various combinations of all of these.

Governments should provide outreach services, hotlines, free telephone advice including on legal issues, drop-in centres and child-friendly information/material. These services should be developed in a consultative process with children and young people, including those belonging to marginalised groups, migrants and victims of exploi-tation and trafficking. Identification procedures should be developed aimed at detecting indicators of trafficking and referral to services. Further research on identification processes may be necessary.

Partnership should be developed with agencies with a labour protection mandate to monitor and provide support to exploited children. In the specific context of the sex industry, imaginative schemes should be designed to encourage men who pay for sex to identify victims of trafficking, particularly those under 18 years of age. They should also know who to contact in order to ensure that a victim of trafficking receives appropriate assistance. Support should be given to encourage initiatives of boys and men who work with peers on gender and sexuality to prevent and combat sexual exploitation.

The experience of the 31 children who participated in this study illustrate that reality does not always fit neatly into the definition of child trafficking provided by the Palermo Protocol. The real situation of these children is much more complex. Their subjective perception of exploitation and abuse often varies, making it a particular challenge to fully understand the dynamics of exploitation and abuse when children are moving from one place to another.

Children migrating to seek work within their own country or abroad need more effective protection. This involves protection measures at home, to give them opportunities to find out about employment opportunities and to find out if those they hear about are genuine and safe; and measures abroad, to prevent forced labour in the informal economy as well as exploitation in formal employment. This also means discarding the assumption those adolescents (especially 15- to 17-year-olds) do not or should not migrate to work away from home. Children should be given the opportunity to acquire skills (e.g. language and technical skills) that will help them gain access to the labour market in accordance with international standards and national labour regulations.

Further research is needed concerning children's motives for migrating and their experiences once they do, including on the forms of abuse they experience, the degree to which they are informed of the risks involved and their suggested actions in terms of policy and programme response. Children and young people could also be involved in designing the research and be associated with its development, when safe and appropriate.

REPATRIATION AND RECOVERY

The Repatriation Process

Among the 16 children who were trafficked abroad, 12 were repatriated by the police of the destination country; the other four children made their way home alone or with the help of their social network. In some of these cases, once the child had escaped, it took several months and in one instance, a full year, before the child was referred for assistance. The children spent this period either in the destination country, travelling to other countries or in their home country. Repatriations organized by the children alone or with the help of their social network, sometimes exposed the children to additional risks or continued abuse and exploitation.

I ran out of money before getting home and had to bribe myself across the last border by having sex with a train controller.

Once back in their home country, it was the police who eventually referred these children to a shelter. Only one girl called a telephone hotline to contact service providers.

Of the 12 children who made contact with the police in the destination country, only four were referred to a shelter in the destination country. Four children were repatriated immediately and another four children were detained by the police: two were kept in a police station for a few days and two in a detention centre where one stayed for six weeks, the other for about three months. Only a few of these children reported having received assistance, in particular medical treatment. The children's responses suggest that once they were under the responsibility of authorities in the destination country, they were given little information about their legal status and rights, what types of services they could access, or any other relevant information about their situation. Most children interviewed said that their views, wishes and concerns with regard to repatriation were hardly taken into account and many of the children had no idea what was going to happen to them.

Conducting a risk assessment prior to repatriation and identifying a family member or other guardian to take responsibility for the child upon return are basic safeguards to protect the rights of repatriated children. They should be conducted routinely. However, in the majority of cases when the repatriation process was organized by the authorities of a destination country, the child's parents or family were not officially contacted by the authorities of either the destination country or home country in preparation for repatriation, according to information provided by the child. This suggests that in these specific cases, no risk assessment was conducted to find out if it was safe for the child to return home and to identify, for those who at the time of repatriation were still under 18, a family member or other guardian to take responsibility for the child. Many of the children were not able to contact their families prior to repatriation. As soon as we reached the first city in [the destination country] we were captured by the police and arrested. I was in the police station for five days. They didn't permit us to contact anyone. So I did not contact my family. I had no chance to do it.

While still abroad, few of the children had a temporary guardian appointed or had the opportunity to talk to a lawyer. Several children were asked whether they wanted to return to their own country. Two girls reported that they were offered only two alternatives, which depended upon whether or not they self-declared to be under or above 18 years of age. As under-18s, they could remain in the country and be referred to a shelter; as adults they could be returned to their home country.

The police told me that if I was a minor, they could not send me back home. They had to place me in a juvenile shelter. Only if I wanted to be recorded as an adult, they could send me directly to my country. So I said I was adult and they sent me to [the capital of her home country]. I travelled in a group of adults who were also sent back to my country. Two of them helped me to find my way in the capital and get to the railway station. I got on a train. Then I called my grandmother and she told me what buses I had to take to get home.

The boy who was convicted of theft in an EU country reported that, while being held in juvenile detention in that country, he was told he had three choices: he could serve his sentence in detention and stay in the country where he was being held until he reached 18 years of age; he could be adopted by a local family and remain permanently in that country; or he could return to his home country. That was a very good life [in the juvenile detention centre], I had everything I wanted: excellent food, computers, but missing home was the worst. To have no one to talk to except in that English of theirs, to have no father, no brother, to have no friends... it was agony. His choice was to return to his home country, where his passport was stamped with an instruction that he should not be allowed abroad again before reaching age 18. Two thirds of the children who had been trafficked across borders wanted to return to their home country.

I was so happy when I got back to my country. I got in my knees and thanked God for bringing me back. I did not want to stay there [the destination country]. I was not afraid to come back home. I have parents.

The others were fearful of what would happen once they returned home; many of them still feared the traffickers. These very different experiences highlight once again the critical importance of conducting an individual case and risk assessment for each child, taking into account the views of the child, in order to determine if repatriation is in the best interests of the child or not. I was afraid of going back home because of the traffickers.

They got interested in me. They had looked for me at home. The police was also there. I'd like to go abroad again because here [in her home country] I have problems of security. My life is in danger as I have reported a lot of persons to the police. My family would not accept me back. I was terrified by the idea that I was going to come back. I am in the witness protection programme. I cried a lot, I had no place where to go and I did not know what was going to happen to me.

RESIDENTIAL CARE IN HOME COUNTRY

All the respondents had spent some time in a shelter in their own country, so all had experiences with residential assistance for victims of trafficking. In most cases, it was the police who referred the children to the shelters, independent of whether they had been trafficked abroad or within their own countries. While most children had stayed in only one shelter, some had transited through multiple facilities. The maximum number of shelters one girl had been to was four. Periods spent in care varied from a number of days to many months. One respondent spent two and a half years in a residential care centre, after being repatriated as an adult. She was still looking for a long-term solution at the time she was interviewed.

Most of the children and young people considered the assistance they received while in residential care to be "very helpful".

> I liked the way they treat a child. I have learned a lot of things and I have started to see the world in a different light. I had the opportunity to meet other people who suffered. We became friends.

> I liked it very much. It was a great help with accommodation, food and especially advice. I've learned a lot of things about abuse, about diseases, about how to protect myself. The ladies took care of me, helped me find employment and a low rent apartment. It has been very helpful for the life I'm leading now. I've learned a lot of things. Had I only known all of these things before.... My mother came too [to the shelter] to see the film [*Lilia For Ever*] and she read with me the booklet *Myths and Realities about Trafficking*. And my mother said that she could not have even imagined. Now I know how to protect myself. I have agreed with my family on certain passwords in case of emergency. I have realized that the trafficker can be nice too, not necessarily fierce, he can be kind. Both my mother and me understand things better. They have helped me a lot to recover morally and psychologically. Also, me and my little boy were offered healthcare assistance and humanitarian aid. I get 60 dollars monthly to raise my child. I managed to solve my gynaecological and kidney problems, I consulted the psychologist and the psychiatrist many times.

In their home country, nearly all the young people were provided with health care. Their physical and psychological health was assessed soon after their arrival and the treatment prescribed was made available. Most mentioned that they consulted with a psychologist and felt this had helped them reduce their anxiety, although a majority also stated when they were interviewed that they were still disturbed by their experiences.

- I'm not at all scared anymore.
- The psychologist helped me to see the positive side and to be able to move on.
- I talked and, especially with the lady psychologist, I've learned solutions to my problems.
- I am still worried, only that now I know how to protect myself better. I'm still worried. When I see a group of boys or a tipsy man they scare me to death. I can't even go to the shop by myself. I'm afraid of men when I'm alone.

The most common negative comment about living in a residential facility was that the children felt isolated and homesick.

They offered me everything but I missed my family more than anything else.

The only boy who participated in this study and who had been in juvenile detention in an EU country felt that conditions in detention had been preferable to the residential facility.

This period [in a shelter] did not help me at all. They kept me there, far from my parents, in their shabby homeless guy clothes. Had they not released me sooner I had a plan to run away through a window, but I thought the police would catch me again and I could hardly wait to go back home and show off my clothes to everybody and give my father and my brother the clothes I had bought [in an EU country] for them.

Most of the respondents reported that they had

participated in the preparation of a 'reintegration plan' drawn up by a care professional. The plans focused on com-pleting or restarting education for the child or young person, helping them finding a job, solving accommodation problems and identifying additional assistance that could help them once they left the residential facility. These were important steps to help the young people plan their future in both the short- and the medium-term.

ACCESS TO EDUCATION, TRAINING AND JOBS

Many of the respondents said their reintegration plans put a special emphasis on education and training in order to increase their potential to get a job. The majority either returned to school (to complete their period of compulsory schooling) or attended a vocational training course. The latter group included courses in fields that are conventionally considered to be women's work (hairdressing, manicuring, house-keeping, dress-making and cooking) and courses for less conventional jobs, such as construction industry training. Some respondents opted to also learn technical skills (drawing or computer courses) or a language, most often English.

Some children decided not to attend courses or dropped out after a while. There were individual reasons for this. In some instances, it was evident that the child did not think the course was suitable. In others, children encountered difficulties that forced them to stop the course.

While I was taking the hairdressers course, a guy told to the girls what had happened to me. The girls started to say things to me and I quit going there again.

I attended a course to be a hair stylist but I missed a few days because I got sick and the owner expelled me, so I would like to continue with the course and also to continue my schooling.

I wanted to attend a vocational training course for waiters/waitresses, but I had no money. The course was free but I would not have been able to work during that time and I would not have had money to pay my rent.

A minority of the respondents got a job immediately, even though the job openings did not always meet their expectations. Given general challenges that young people often face in finding employment in the countries covered by this study, the assistance given by social workers was often considered crucial.

SEEKING A DURABLE SOLUTION

After they got away from the traffickers, the children and young people who participated in this study resorted to different living situations with family friends, independent of the family, or in shelters. For some, this period was characterized by constant change. Moving from place to place, they lived with different family members, friends and partners. None of the respondents reported being pushed out of a shelter before they wanted to leave. Nonetheless, one "regretted" having left a shelter and said she wished she had stayed longer to take full advantage of the facilities. Thirteen children and young people were still living in a shelter at the time they were interviewed; the other 18 children had left the shelter to live with their parents, other relatives, friends or a partner.

After leaving the shelter, I lived for 1-2 months at my aunt's [who took her away from her abusive parents] and another two months in a rented apartment. Afterwards I moved in with the family of my boyfriend. He has gone to work in [another country] to make some money for us. I do not pay rent but I contribute to the expenses of the household. My current family loves me, respects me. They have even proved that they care for me and about me.

While some children successfully returned to their family or community, others faced major difficulties, including stigmatization and rejection, and even danger. Aware of these risks, many children were careful about how they talked to family, friends and peers and what kind of information they shared.

Talking to Family and Friends

Irrespective of where the children and young people

lived, most of them were in contact with their families at the time they were interviewed.

The children were very strategic with regard to choosing the persons they spoke to about their experiences, the type of information they shared and what information they preferred to keep to themselves. Most of the interviewed children had told other family members something about their experiences. Given the fact that nearly all cases were associated with sexual exploitation and rape, the informed family member was usually the mother or another female family member. Some children felt their father or brother blamed them for the exploitation or did not understand them. In most cases, siblings, particularly younger ones, were not informed in order to be protected from information that was considered dangerous or potentially harmful. Very few children spoke about their experiences with friends or other persons beyond the direct family.

My mother only knows some of it, because I cannot tell her. I know she would suffer. The pain would be too much for her.

I cannot tell my grandmother everything because I'd cause her too much pain and she has a heart condition. She suspects, but I cannot tell her everything I've been through. But my aunt knows everything, everything.

My father and older brother know only what I declared to the police. My older sister knows a bit less. I keep everything in me. I don't want to talk.

I work in the city and rent a room. I go home more seldom; I stay more often with my aunt. My sister knows, maybe she told to my brother as well. But I told neither him nor my father.

My mother knows everything that happened. My sisters know just part of it. The family has always helped me and they are helping me now, too.

I told my parents about what happened to me. I went to the police to denounce the trafficker. They were very helpful during the investigation. I was accompanied by my parents to the court, especially by my mother. She supported me morally. Sometimes my father is upset and reproaches me that I went to [another country]. This happens when he gets drunk.

My father and brother know everything that happened to me. My mother and grandparents know only part of it. Both my father and my brother have been helpful, they have not scolded me, instead they have tried to understand why I left, what went wrong, what we could do differently now.

Stigmatization and Rejection

According to the children's statements, some families were very supportive, while in other families only individual relatives showed sympathy. In other cases, no family member offered support. Many children encountered parents or other family members or both who had difficulty accepting what had happened to the children.

I had difficulties with my uncle and his wife who are our neighbours. They keep mentioning that I am a bar girl.

In the village where my parents and my siblings live, everybody talks and treats me very badly, including my mother.

They know what happened to me. My mother, my brother and my sister understand me, but my father blames me.

I have good relations with everybody in the village, except for a girl who tells everybody that she's heard I am a prostitute.

The girls also reported experiencing varying degrees of difficulty in rebuilding their relationships with peers and with boys and men. When I came back home I had two marriage offers but after they found out [about] my past they never came again.

Out of fear of rejection and stigmatization, some children thought it was better not to talk about their experiences or even to return home.

I don't want to tell, they would only laugh at me. I went

to the priest and I confessed all my sins. For the others I am smart, I tell them I have money, I don't want them to know anything. I told them just that I've been abroad and girls come to borrow my clothes because they are cool. But I don't want to give them, let them go make their own clothes.

I declared everything, both at the police and at home. I cannot say I have problems, but I can feel they have grown colder to me. It would have been better to keep my mouth shut and everything would be fine now. My mother, when she's drunk, she flaps her mouth and spreads the rumour in the entire village that they kidnapped me and they raped me and ever since, both the old ones and the young ones behave like I was eating people. At the disco, they all shun me, our neighbours don't even drink water in our house because they say it turns their stomach. The boys laugh at me.

Some respondents felt there was no way they could create a normal life back home and were eager to leave for another city or country.

When I came back home, of course I had difficulties, especially with my father, who many times reminded me what had happened, *e.g.*, when I served him a drink he used to tell me "Take it easy, you're not in the café anymore", and there were occasions when he mentioned the same things in front of our guests...I can clearly see that there is no future for me here. I don't see any future here, because when I went out with a guy, as soon as he understood the things from my past he left me.... I would like somebody to help me to go somewhere in Western countries because I don't see any future for me here. The café owner [who had exploited her and against whom she had given evidence] threatened me and I'm also afraid that people will continue to talk about my past. They will not understand me, and I will not have the chance to create my own family here or to have a normal life.

Follow-up Contacts with Shelter Staff and Social Workers

After leaving the shelter, nearly all the respondents were told that a social worker or member of the staff at the facility where they had received treatment would be available to them for follow-up advice and support. The frequency of follow-up contacts varied. Where children still faced domestic violence after returning home, social workers faced a particular challenge in maintaining contact with the children. The majority of the respondents, however, reported being satisfied with the help they received.

It is fine that I can call the shelter anytime I need support and they do not refuse me. The staff of the shelter inquired about me all the time, and we talk on the phone several times a month. When my fiancé beat me up, the police here [in her home city] again didn't do anything. I talked to the shelter coordinator who called [the regional administration] and with a simple telephone call, the police came to help me. Without the ladies from the shelter it would be much more difficult.

During my period at home, I had support from social services and [an organization]. They helped us with two beds and the generator necessary for my father's work. I had regular visits from the social worker and from one psychiatrist.

In just a few isolated cases, children felt they did not need any further follow-up by service providers and social workers.

I don't want to feel as if I'm being followed by the police. I have had enough advice, I need money, not advice.

Access to Justice

Only 11 children reported that they had been able to consult a lawyer/attorney while they were in an assistance programme. Most of those respondents who provided evidence to the police, however, were not represented by a lawyer/attorney (15 children). Some of these children had been told by the police that they could contact a lawyer/attorney, but had no financial means to do so. Many therefore perceived justice to be a matter of money. Justice is not served and you need a lot of money.

There is no money to contact a lawyer/attorney or to seek justice. In another case, the parents, wanting to put their child's perpetrator behind bars, had contacted a lawyer/attorney, but the respondent said she did not want to go through the whole procedure of testifying and reliving her experiences. I don't want to hear anything more about statements, police, lawyers and trials. I want to forget.

One girl felt the police were more interested in prosecuting the traffickers than in protecting the victims and was still worried that the traffickers would come after her. I was questioned twice by the police while I was abroad. They were not concerned about me; they were more concerned about how to catch others…who were behind me…. I am still afraid of those guys that I reported in the police station in [the capital of an EU country]… maybe when they are freed they will come and look for me.

In only 4 of the 31 cases the children reported that their trafficker had been sentenced and imprisoned. Because only a few of the cases had gone to trial, the children had little information to offer about the way police investigation, prosecution procedures and the trial had impacted them. In the case where traffickers had been convicted, the respondents had not benefited materially. None was paid compensation of any sort. The interviews therefore suggest that for the majority of these 31 children, the criminal justice system was not effective, either abroad or in their own countries. In the four cases in which traffickers were convicted, sentences ranged from six months to 10 years' imprisonment. In one of these cases, a pimp who had been arrested and convicted had already been freed by the time of the interview. The risks and difficulties of returning home, therefore, go beyond stigmatization and include con-crete threats by traffickers and the danger of being re-trafficked.

I don't feel well and I don't have any plans for the future since the guys that kidnapped me were in prison for two and a half years after I testified against them and now they are out of prison. I heard from others that they said that if they ever get me they will kill me. I used to go out with a guy for a while and I told him the whole story and we wanted to get engaged, but those guys that got out of the prison beat him up badly and he left me. So this is the reason why I don't have a future here.

The risk of reprisals appears particularly serious in cases where traffickers come from the same community or region as their victims. One of the two girls who had been trafficked by her female cousin testified against the relative. In consequence, her cousin was convicted and sentenced to imprisonment. This led to divisions in the family, which continued to cause problems for the girl who testified. She observed that others in her village had grown cold towards her and concluded that, "It would have been better to keep my mouth shut and everything would be fine now".

In another case, a child reported, "The trafficker's mother says she wants revenge on my family because her daughter was sentenced to 10 years' imprisonment because of me". In this case the respondent was not represented by a lawyer in court: "The police told me that justice was on my side", she said. One girl, based on her experience with giving testimony against her first trafficker, drew the conclusion that it would be too dangerous for her to provide evidence against her second trafficker: The first café owner [who was sentenced to six months' imprisonment] told people that if he meets me he will kill me, because I caused his imprisonment, and therefore I'm very much afraid.

Another 17-year-old reported that she was living back in her home village, where she had seen the traffickers, still unpunished. They glare at me, but they are afraid of the police in [the local provincial capital, *i.e.* police from the Organized Crime Unit]. Yet another girl had been under the control of traffickers for six years but none of the traffickers had been prosecuted for any of the offences committed against her, despite the fact that she had given evidence to the police in her own country. At the time of the interview, she still hoped they might make an arrest. After having spent more than two years in a secure shelter, with her own movements restricted, she remarked, "Sometimes I feel sorry for reporting them to the police".

BEYOND ABUSE

Despite the fact that most of these children and young people had endured violence and abuse, the majority were optimistic about their future and anticipated it as "a success", "very happy", and "very beautiful". Their dreams included: having a good job, their own family (to be married and have children), their own house or apartment, and a particular level of education or qualification. Several of the girls wanted to become policewomen, and one wanted a husband who was a police officer as well. One of these girls said, "I want to help everyone in need". The two young people with children of their own both emphasized the importance of protecting and creating a safe environment for their children.

The girls were also optimistic about marriage. One girl who had returned home to a community with a tradition of arranged marriage hoped that her aunts would find her a good husband. She still didn't trust herself to make such an important decision. "I am afraid of finding my future husband by myself, I might make mistakes". Many wanted to stay in their home country. Only six of them mentioned plans to work abroad. The two who reported that they were not currently entitled to use their passports to travel abroad obviously resented this. They were planning to leave for another country as soon as they turned 18 and travel restrictions that had been imposed on them as child victims of trafficking would be lifted.

What can be done to better support children after they have been trafficked? These recommendations are based on the broad body of UNICEF IRC studies on child trafficking and reconfirmed through the voices of the children and young people quoted in this study. Of the 12 children who made contact with the police in the destination country, only four were referred to a shelter in the destination country. Four children were repatriated imme-diately and another four children were detained by the police; two children were kept in a police station for a few days and two in a detention centre where one stayed for six weeks and the other for about three months. The children's responses suggest that once they were under the responsibility of authorities in the destination country, they were given little information about their legal status and fundamental rights, what types of services they could access, their options or any other relevant information about their situation. In most of the cases, the child's parents or family were not officially contacted by the authorities of the destination country or their home country in preparation for repatriation.

Individual case management for each child identified as a victim of trafficking must be ensured. This includes an individual needs and risk assessment, the determination of the best interests of each individual child in all actions concerning the child and taking into account the child's views. Governments need to ensure that child victims of trafficking are never placed in law enforcement detention facilities or otherwise deprived of liberty and that they are provided with temporary humanitarian visas. Conducting a risk assessment prior to repatriation is of critical importance in order to determine if repatriation is in the best interests of the child or not is key. Identifying a family member or other guardian to take responsibility for the child upon return is a basic safeguard to protect the rights of repatriated children and should be conducted routinely. Children need to be informed and consulted when deter-mining the types and forms of assistance they will receive. These consultations need to take place before the child is referred to assistance and when the child is received in a shelter or other forms of assistance. Regularly revisiting the child's views and opinions during the assistance process is particularly important in order to evaluate its effectiveness to support the child and its ability to meet the child's best interests and needs.

Only 11 children reported that they had been able to consult a lawyer while they were in an assistance pro-gramme. Most of those respondents who provided evidence to the police, however, were not represented by a lawyer.

Governments need to ensure that every child has access to legal counselling and representation regardless of whether he or she is willing to testify. A legal guardian should be immediately appointed to represent the best interests of the child and the child should be provided with free legal assistance and counselling. Law enforcement agencies and judicial authorities should take particular care to protect the rights of the child victim and avoid unnecessary questioning, repetition of testimony and visual contact with the defendant. Governments need to develop child- and age-specific material on relevant judicial procedures, in-cluding on children's rights in such situations.

Once back in their home country, nearly all the young people were provided with health care. Their physical and psychological health was assessed soon after their arrival and the treatment prescribed was made available. According to the children's statements, some families were very supportive, while in other families only individual relatives showed sympathy. In other cases, no family mem-ber offered support. Many children encountered parents and/or other family members who had difficulty accepting what had happened to their children. Some children felt there was no way they could create a normal life back home and were eager to leave for another city or country.

Governments should put in place appropriate measures to ensure the physical and psychosocial recovery of the child after the trafficking experience (with a focus on resilience building), including appropriate accommodation, coun-selling, legal assistance, health care, psychological and material assistance, interpretation services, education, vocational training, employment opportunities and other relevant protective measures, where necessary also for the family members at risk in countries of origin. Long-term support services should be made available at the local and community levels through counselling and other mechanisms to support programmes.

Educational opportunities offered to children who have been trafficked need to consider the fact that the child may come from a family that does not or cannot, for financial reasons, support the child staying in school. Seeking and taking into account the views of the child with regard to education and vocational training is critical. Further measures are needed to ensure that young people who have been trafficked are prepared to meet the challenges of an independent and self-determined life and find productive employment so they can break the cycle of poverty and dependence. Parents and other members of households to which children who have been trafficked return should be given advice (prior to family reunification) on how to prevent secondary victimization and stigmatization, both within the family and by other members of the community. The level of detail of information that the parents or others are given about the child's experiences must be guided by the child's best interests and determined primarily by the child, in consultation with the social worker or caregivers overseeing the reunification process. Family members should also be given information on symptoms of post-traumatic stress and on how to respond to these appropriately.

Awareness-raising and mobilization of community members is necessary to counteract stigmatization of girls and boys who have been sexually exploited. Efforts should be taken to mobilize boys and men to take action against gender discrimination and sexual exploitation. The promotion of a child-friendly environment is particularly important. There is a need to evaluate which of the services, information and skills provided in shelters the children consider most useful. This information can inform the development of the general school curriculum and support the strengthening of the overall child protection system. Additional research with children who have been trafficked is needed to get a better understanding of their long-term needs.

A HUMAN RIGHTS-BASED APPROACH TO CHILD TRAFFICKING

KEY FINDINGS

Much of the information from the interviews with the 31 children confirms findings from previous research on child trafficking. It also gives new dimensions and insights into the lives of children who have been trafficked. The findings from these interviews indicate:

- Trafficking is not a single event but a highly complex and dynamic process, involving multiple actors. The experiences of the 31 children illustrate that reality does not always fit neatly into the definition of child trafficking provided by the Palermo Protocol. The com-plexity of child trafficking often makes it difficult, in practice, to distinguish between trafficking and other forms of exploitation and abuse of children.
- The experience of young people in this study indicates the linkages between various forms of neglect, violence, abuse and exploitation. The study acknowledges that children who have experienced violence in the home are at risk of being recruited by traffickers or they may choose to migrate and risk ending up in exploi-tative situations.
- The children's testimonies provide some indication of how institutional actors who came in contact with the children, in countries of origin and destination, before, during and after the period of exploitation, often failed to provide the necessary protection of children con-cerned. In some cases they may have put these children at a greater risk of abuse.
- The study also reveals that these children and young people were seldom given the opportunity to participate in decisions affecting their lives. Decisions were often taken without their involvement or full understanding of what was at stake and they were not always consul-ted in the development of their rehabilitation pro-grammes nor in evaluating services established to support them. Finally, this report shows that when children who have been trafficked are given the oppor-tunity to describe their experiences and express their views, this information sheds light onto those factors that make children vulnerable, their reasons for leaving home and their special needs regarding prevention, assistance and protection.

Children's participation plays an important role in helping to identify areas for additional research and to inform effective policy responses. Any interventions to prevent and combat trafficking must be grounded by an understanding of these factors and based on a child rights based approach. The children and young people interviewed for this study have helped to deepen this understanding

LESSONS TO INFORM POLICYMAKING

Prevention

A lesson to be learned from the experience of these children is that they could have been prevented from being trafficked in the first place. The fact that 12 of the 31 respondents said they left home to avoid some form of domestic abuse suggests that social services and other institutions in the children's home countries were not providing adequate protection for these children while they were still living at home. Other actors in the community (neighbours, teachers, law enforcement agencies, social workers and others) might have been aware of the hardships and problems experienced by the families concerned.

Nonetheless, the interviews do not indicate any direct contact between these actors and the children. At the same time, the children's accounts also confirm that the responsibility for preventing child trafficking rests not only with the children's home countries, but also with countries to which they migrate with or without their families. It is important that national child protection systems not only support children who have been abused, but also invest in prevention strategies by addressing the root causes of trafficking, such as gender discrimination and other social economic and structural factors, as well as the demand side of trafficking, meaning the demand for children from clients, brothel owners and factory owners.

Families and community members, including children themselves, play an important role in preventing child abuse and exploitation and in monitoring risk factors at the community level. Vulnerable families and other community members need support through the provision of livelihood options, family counselling, parenting education (for fathers and mothers), drug and alcohol prevention and rehabilitation and overall information about child protection issues and children's rights.

Protection

The testimonies provided by the 31 young people who participated in this study indicate that a full range of child protection initiatives is needed to protect children from abuse and exploitation. These initiatives must be imple-mented in the places where traffickers recruit children and in the destinations to which children are trafficked. For interventions to be effective, they must address the multiple factors that contribute to trafficking. Multidisciplinary teams need to be organized at the community level and should consist of all professionals who have a role to play in detecting and responding to cases of child abuse and exploitation, including health professionals (*e.g.* doctors, nurses and paramedics); educational professionals: (*e.g.* teachers, school directors, personnel responsible for responding to school dropouts): law enforcement officials (*e.g.* police, prosecutors and judges) and others. These professionals must be properly trained in the detection of incidents of child abuse and neglect and in identifying cases of child trafficking and of the exploitation associated with trafficking. Furthermore, in countries of origin and destination, standard procedures need to be developed to ensure that the best interests of the child and the child's right to have his or her views heard and taken into account are respected.

Information, Skills and Safe Places

Nearly all the children and young people who participated in this study indicated that they lacked access to quality information and skills that could have helped prevent them from being trafficked, protect themselves from harmful and abusive relationships, know where to turn to for advice and assistance and learn about the risks they might face when leaving home. These testimonies highlight the urgent need to ensure that all children have access to child rights education and benefit from child-friendly information about different forms of abuse and opportunities to develop skills to better protect themselves from such abuse.

From the children's stories it also became clear that information by itself is not enough. Beyond this, those children who felt that staying at home was no longer an option, had no concrete alternatives; no safe place to go. A framework needs to be in place to respond to children's concerns, offering a hotline or other contacts to call upon for advice and information, and safe places that provide shelter for children who suffer abuse and violence in the home. Child- friendly, aġe-appropriate and diversity sensitive information needs to be developed in close partnership with children and young people themselves.

The active participation of children

When children are trafficked, they suffer physical and psychological trauma and they are often limited, fully or in part, to make decisions for themselves. During the period that they were under the control of a trafficker, all 31 young people interviewed for this study were denied the right to make decisions about their lives. There is also some evi-dence that the children who remained under a trafficker's control for many years had lost a great deal of their 'agency', i.e. their capacity to make decisions and act on them. It is safe to conclude that part of the recovery process after being trafficked must ensure that victims are given an opportunity to regain confidence and life skills to take charge of their lives. Across the board, all children who were interviewed reported that once they were out of the control of the trafficker, they felt that their views were not sufficiently taken into account. Those who found themselves in foreign countries, in particular, continued to feel treated as objects, passive 'victims' whose fate was decided by others.

This does not mean that the institutions did not provide useful assistance, but rather that they did not always consider it necessary to consult the children about the solutions being envisaged or decided upon. As one girl put it, "Nobody talked to me, they do not care". It is critical to ensure respect for, and effective implementation of, the provisions of article 12 of the CRC, 22 in particular, children's rights to have their opinions heard and taken into account. A key moment for determining the 'best interests' of children who have been trafficked occurs when decisions are taken that affect them in the long-term The accounts of the 11 children who were repatriated by foreign govern-ments when still under 18 years of age provide no indication that any procedures were followed to ensure that their best interests were a primary consideration. In particular, the appointment of a temporary guardian was not followed in any of these cases.

OBSERVATIONS ON THE RESEARCH PROCESS

Although the group of children and young people interviewed was small, some observations can be made about the ways in which information is obtained from trafficked children, as well as conclusions made about how to better protect them from abuse. The interviews indicate that there is a risk of re-traumatization for the trafficked children. The experience of the young persons interviewed, however, suggests that re-traumatization can be avoided to some extent if appropriate methods are used, while valuable, in fact vital, information can be obtained for the development of evidenced-informed anti-trafficking and prevention efforts. *Was there evidence that this research caused any further harm to the respondents?* The respondents were all asked at the end of their interview whether the questions had been too intrusive. A relatively high number of respondents felt fine about the interview, although some found it intrusive. In one of the countries, the psychologist supervising the interviews reported that the individual interviewers had all noted that, "the girls were extremely affected by the questions raised in the interview" and that "this always happens when somebody reminds them of their past".

Many children commented that they appreciated the fact that the interview did not focus on details related to the trafficking process. It's fine that you didn't pester me with names and amounts and other stuff like this. I was worried that you would want details again, like at the police. Some children stated very clearly that they were selective about the types of information that they shared and with whom they shared it. I cannot tell everything because I'd cause too much pain [to others]. I'm ashamed to talk about it. I know how to talk, both to you [the inter-viewer] and others. I know what I should say and what not. More than a half of the children were still worried about their experiences when they were interviewed or said they were still frightened. Nevertheless, some presented their experiences in quite an objective way, highlighting how they took initiatives to improve their situation during or in between different trafficking experiences. They gave the impression that they had managed to cope with the trauma. Some recited their story placing themselves at the centre as a hero who endured hardships but eventually succeeded in triumphing over adversity, rather than portraying themselves as a victim.

This may have been due in part to an increase in their confidence and self-esteem on account of therapy they received while in residential care. Many respondents wanted to explain what they had learned from their experiences and ended the interview with comments such as: "I would like to send a message to all girls who have experienced what I did, that they should accept help" and "I would like to pass a message to young girls to be very careful. I don't know how this message will influence them because when I heard about this kind of risk myself, I didn't pay attention". Interview fatigue was an issue, even with those children who did not perceive the interview as intrusive.

Attaining the right balance between protecting these children from undergoing too many interviews, from the risks of re-traumatization or violation of their privacy on one side, and obtaining valuable information about their experiences to inform better prevention strategies in future on the other side, is bound to remain difficult. The balance needs to be determined by the best interests of the children involved, providing them with anticipated and full information about the process and scope of the interview, letting them take an informed decision on whether they want to participate or not and respecting their decisions. They should also be informed that they can always take a break or fully withdraw from the interview whenever they would like to do so.

Further Research Needs Revealed by the Findings of this Study

The feasibility of interviewing young people between three and six months after they have left residential care raises the possibility of tracking some children for much longer periods in order to assess the long-term impact, both of the abuse they experienced and the assistance they received. While it is important not to endlessly remind victims of their abuse or to intrude on their privacy, the information obtained from these respondents suggests that a great deal remains to be learned. It suggests that interviewing young people at periods of one, two or more years after they have left residential care would produce further valuable lessons. These interviews revealed relatively little about the relationships the children re-established with members of their home communities. It would be extre-mely useful to better understand whether stigmatization is a short- or long-term experience and whether some trafficking victims develop successful strategies for dealing with it.

Since this study was limited to the participation of children who had been identified and assisted in their home countries, it will be important to better understand the situation of other child victims of trafficking: children who have not been identified as victims of trafficking by official authorities, children who have not received any assistance and those who have not returned to their home country but received assistance abroad or otherwise sustained an independent life abroad. This will offer additional important information to better understand the complexity of child trafficking and to give children an effective opportunity to enjoy their fundamental human rights.

3

Child Trafficking and Movement

This chapter was conceived as a starting point for a discussion on the phenomenon of trafficking that is currently affecting communities in all countries across Europe, be they source, transit or recipient and the potential for RCRC response to the consequent vulnerabilities. It also aims to provide a snapshot analysis of relevant policy documents adopted by the Movement. The recommen-dations of this chapter cover those related to NS in Europe as well the Federation Secretariat/Europe Department. The phenomenon of trafficking in Europe has become increasingly an issue during recent years even though the phenomenon itself is not new. It has been highlighted as an aspect of transnational organized crime striking at the heart of national sovereignty referred to by some as the dark-side of globalization. The distinction between trafficking and smuggling is an important one.

Trafficking in persons is defined as the recruitment, transportation, transfer, harbouring or receipt of persons, by means of threat or use of force or other forms of coercion, of abduction, of fraud, of deception, of the abuse of power or of a position of vulnerability or of the giving or receiving of payments or benefits to achieve the consent of a person having control over another person, for the purpose of exploitation. Exploitation shall include, at a minimum, the exploitation of the prostitution of others or other forms of sexual exploitation, forced labour or services, slavery or practices similar to slavery, servitude or the removal of organs. In other words trafficking is a crime against the person trafficked as well as the state to which she/he is trafficked.

Smuggling of Migrants is defined as the procurement, in order to obtain, directly or indirectly, a financial or other material benefit, of the illegal entry of a person into a State Party of which the person is not national or permanent resident and thus is not a crime against the person but against the State to which the person is smuggled. The pur-pose of this chapter is to focus on trafficking but with the caveat that often a persons intention to be smuggled often ends in their being trafficked and possibly to a country other than their chosen destination. The root causes of trafficking include inter alia unemployment, poverty, gender inequalities (including the particular issues of girl children and adolescent males), social and cultural attitudes in countries of origin and the demand for sexual services, cheap labour and other forms of exploitation in the destination countries including the trafficking of persons as unwilling organ donors. Persons at risks are often already vulnerable in their home country.

In the same vein, conflicts, wars political and economic transition, have left societies with disrupted social structures and marginalized vulnerable groups and health and social services that are failing or inaccessible. There is a growing gap between the groups that benefit from transition and marginalised groups that do not. The lack of social structures, supplemented by unemployment and a general feeling of a future with no perspectives or opportunities creates a situation of hopelessness and moral degradation. The tendency of, especially, European Union and EFTA States to restrict and limit access to the asylum process is driving more and more people into the hands of traffickers. This is compounded by the way States are narrowing their application of the 1951 Convention Relating to the Status of Refugees by restricting its meaning to literal terms. This often leads to the denial of refugee status to certain persecuted groups such as women at risk from violence or genital mutilation or those fleeing persecution by non-state actors.

In addition the introduction of Schengen and other mechanisms has severely limited the opportunities for legal labour migration despite the demographic changes in Europe and the consequent rapidly diminishing labour forces. There are many routes used by smugglers and traffickers within, into and out of Europe but they can be grouped in a very general way as follows (these routes are sometimes combined):

- The Balkan routes?
- Central European routes?
- The Mediterranean routes?
- Northern-Baltic routes?
- The CIS routes.?

It is worthwhile to note that, even if EU/EFTA is the most frequent destination, there are a growing number of trafficked persons (especially women) taken into the Balkans itself. The EU Accession States have also become destination countries and there is also considerable intra-CIS trafficking. The latter is rather complex and deserves attention as such both in the CIS context as well as within its regions. It is important to bear in mind that trafficking in human beings is not only an Eastern or Central European problem. It should be viewed in an all-Europe context which severely affects source, transit and recipient countries. It must also be borne in mind that trafficking is not restricted by borders and occurs across continents and thus the global perspective must also be maintained. It is important for Europeans examining trafficking issues to remain abreast of the debates taking place in other regions and to strive to obtain global consensus on the best ways of devising solutions.

To address trafficking in Europe a comprehensive strategy is needed that addresses root causes, the trafficking chain and the consequent vulnerabilities. Governments and the EU must take a leading role in developing this strategy. However, the Movement has a substantial and comple-mentary role because of its concern for the vulnerability of those trafficked as well as the impact of public debate on host populations.

The Movement's principal entry point is vulnerability, based on the Fundamental Principles. Further we retain a global approach to vulnerability and are not motivated by any status or label that may be applied to a person or group of persons. This is articulated clearly in the background paper to Resolution 4/2001 of the Council of Delegates entitled the Movement Action in favour of Refugees and Internally Displaced Persons. Paragraph 10 - Development of Movement Strategy, further calls on the International Federation in consultation with National Societies to develop a proposal for a plan of action on other aspects of population movement. This plan of action will address, inter alia, migration and the resultant vulnerability, migrants in irregular situation.

Within the mandate of the Council of Delegates resolution and in the European context, the Berlin Conference, in its Plan of Action on migration calls upon National Societies in countries of origin, transit and destination to improve their co-operation ... in order to better protect, support and assist migrants and their families, regardless of status. Similarly, in the same plan of action, all European NS agree to act against all forms of exploitation and deception.

NATIONAL SOCIETIES ACTIVITIES

The Berlin Plan of Action is subdivided into four core responses to migration and it is useful to look at trafficking in the same way:

- Protection
- Humanitarian Response
- Integration
- Advocacy

Additionally, trafficking must be considered in relation to:

- Source countries
- Transit countries
- Destination countries

And by definition NS will have to very seriously consider partnerships and transnational programming. NS programming should be based on comparative advantages and focus on the areas where it has resources and can add value. The role of each NS needs to be clearly explained to all stakeholders and should aim for recognition as such. NS should also develop referral mechanisms for those activities which it feels cannot be undertaken efficiently within its own resources.

PREVENTION

Prevention can be considered along two general themes Protection and Advocacy. Protection activities include the provision of alternative income sources through training, provision of micro-credit and similar whilst advocacy will include provision of information to vulnerable and susceptible groups as to the dangers inherent in trafficking as well as the development of mutually supportive social networks. There also needs for Advocacy at the level of the general public and authorities to counter negative publicity which promotes discriminatory attitudes and intolerance. It is also important to encourage public and political acceptance of the need to differentiate between the criminal perpetrators and vulnerable victims of trafficking. A starting point for this could be the strengthening and supplementation of existing activities. All activities but particularly advocacy need to take account of the Fundamental Principles but particularly those of Humanity, Independence and Impartiality.

HUMANITARIAN RESPONSE/PROTECTION

The Berlin Plan of Action on Migration, adopted at the European National Societies Conference in April 2002 under the Operational Guidance theme calls upon NS to "develop innovative delivery mechanisms that take into account the circumstances including detention". In practice this would mean delivering a wide range of services, humanitarian assistance, psychological/psychosocial and medical care, legal assistance (either directly or through referrals), tracing and access to relevant information. This range of activities is by no means exhaustive, and it will vary from country to country as well as from National Society to National Society based on their priorities and expertise.

Two other issues are also of note:

(a.) A mechanism is currently in development whereby the three components of the Movement (NS, ICRC and the Federation) have, uniquely, come together to address the issue of detention, a serious issue in several countries.

(b.) Another issue of serious concern is that of the security of staff delivering assistance to or within so-called "Safe Houses" or high-risk shelters. Invariably these shelters are in clandestine locations and are sometimes guarded by armed law enforcement agencies. Therefore it is recommended that NS NOT accept management responsibilities for these shelters. NS can, if requested and/or based on their own decisions, provide services to persons in these kinds of shelters on a confidential basis. Special training for staff/volunteers working in these circumstances, including personal security should be mandatory.

Issues for consideration:

- The right of victims of trafficking to remain silent and not incriminate themselves through their own testi-mony is at risk in some countries needs to be supported and upheld. Experience has shown that victims who do give evidence are often subject to violence and retribution in both host countries and countries to which they are returned (violence is sometimes directed against their families) and this raises a further and serious protection issue. NS need to advocate for adequate protection of victims who do give evidence and where retribution either in the receiving country or in the country of return is an issue.
- *Mandatory HIV testing*: in some countries, due to the perceived or real health risks, victims of human trafficking are sometimes exposed to mandatory HIV testing. Such testing should be conducted with the full and informed consent of the concerned and discretion and confidentiality must be ensured.
- *Gender issues*: All actions, be they assistance or protection,

must take into account specific gender issues not only in the activities themselves but also as well as in the general approach

- *Confidentiality*: NS staff engaged in work with victims of trafficking are almost certain to come across facts and details that need to be kept confidential. Every effort should be made through advocacy to secure government and police agreement that information obtained in an atmosphere of confidentiality should remain protected and that this protection should be recognized in sending, receiving and transit countries. If this is not possible, the National Society should explain the situation in which it operates to victims, which should clearly understand that NS, unlike the ICRC, are local institutions and as such subject to national law and the potential of being forced to provide documented information (hard copies or electronic) to police forces or the government. NS policy should be to retain only that information or material absolutely essential to the maintenance of the case.
- *Safety of staff/volunteers*: as mentioned above, work related to trafficking is indeed "reaching out to those in the shadows" and to people who may be of interest to organized crime. Thus every effort must be made to ensure security of staff/volunteers through proper training (including security training), confidentiality, and clear distance and distinction from law enforcement by focusing on the humanitarian aspect and the maintenance of strict independence.

INTEGRATION/RE-INTEGRATION

In many countries of destination, programmes exist which are, by and large, handled by the authorities and law enforcement agencies (sometimes including change of identity). However, various integration programmes can be implemented by which are similar to the integration of displaced, refugees and migrants. In source countries, during the process of the reintegration of returned former victims of trafficking, the NS might consider to be engaged. It is important to note that if it is handled by IOM, per case funds exist to cover for a range of activities (such as medical check-up, psychosocial, skills or vocational training) in order that former victims can restart their life anew.

Specific issues for consideration:

- *Sometimes agents of trafficking are parents/relatives*: regrettably it is not uncommon that the initial agents of trafficking, especially of women and children, are parents or close friends and relatives who in hope of better future (consciously or unconsciously) are contributing to the trafficking chain.
- *Danger of re-trafficking*: When dealing with re-integration, the danger of re-trafficking is a real one.
- These cases often require maximum confidentiality, and advocacy to ensure confidentiality should be a priority in return countries.

ADVOCACY

The Berlin plan of Action for Migration states that advocacy must include all levels, including governments, the media and the public at large, thus:

- NS should advocate for the ratification by their government of the 2000 UN Convention on Trans-national Organized Crime and its additional Protocols on Trafficking (As yet there are insufficient ratifications for this treaty to enter into force). Other advocacy initiatives include humanitarian needs identified by NS (in addition to issues identified in this chapter) and the need for country level policies on this issue. Examples could include: training for law enforcement agencies.
- Participation in National Task Force Groups on Trafficking, representing particularly the humanitarian dimension often ignored by governments. The objective should be an integrated and permanent involvement in national actions.
- Building partnership with IOM, ILO and NGOs engaged in this field, following/principles, and advocating /

positions. Developing good relationships with the media, utilizing contacts to emphasize the humanitarian dimension and needs with a clear distance from law enforcement and migration management.

- Public awareness campaigns in various forms. Should be involved only in the humanitarian aspects. It should target age/gender groups at risk, or general public not only in the country of source but also in country of destination to address the demand-side (the unwilling or unconscious contributors to trafficking). Due to its extensive network that can be a very efficient in national public awareness campaigns.
- These campaigns should include efforts to build awareness of the issues among members of parliament as well as others more directly involved in imple-menting legislation.
- Societies normally have membership representing the broad mass of the population. Advocacy campaigns should ensure that all members of the NS have access to the facts about the victims of trafficking and NS/ Federation policy.
- To raise the issue at internal meetings in the respective countries, share the information with the NS network, advocating among volunteers and members, might be a first important step.

Issues for consideration:

- *Victims of trafficking must be recognized as victims not criminals*: regrettably in many countries victims of trafficking are perceived as criminals and treated as such by State agencies and others responsible for their welfare. It is vital that they are be treated, not as criminals but, as the victims they have become and are provided with the assistance and protection needed. NS have a role in providing education and information to those employed in such State agencies.
- *Humanitarian vulnerability Vs law enforcement*: while States tend to see the trafficking problem as border management

and law enforcement should clearly focus on the humanitarian dimension and the needs of the victims.

- *Principle of non-refoument(non-return)*: some persons fleeing "a well-founded fear of persecution" are lured into a trafficking network as the only way to escape from their country of origin. Therefore it is important to keep in mind the principle of non-return since persons might face serious harm in the country of origin. It should also be borne in mind that the Principle of Non-Refoulement is enshrined not only in the 1951 Refugee Convention but also in the 1987 Convention against Torture which requires States not to return anybody who risks any form of cruel or degrading treatment (regardless of their status). The Principle is generally accepted as forming customary international law. In other words all States are obliged to respect the Principle whether or not they have acceded to any particular treaty or convention.
- *Access to procedure for victims having a valid asylum case*: Those victims of trafficking with an asylum case should be informed of and allowed to access to the status determination procedure in the destination country. They also have the right to ask their country's diplomatic or consular representatives to be informed if they are detained.

FUNDING POSSIBILITIES

The EU CARDS programme for Balkans includes the fight against trafficking as a strategic objective. TACIS and PHARE programmes of the EU also give attention to the problem of trafficking in human beings. Other individual EU and non-EU governmental funding exists, likewise US funding in the form of joint US/EU info campaigns worthwhile noting. The Brussels Declaration mobili-zing EU instruments "used in co-operation with govern-ment authorities or in supporting NGOs and civil society should be further developed with all countries of origin, transit and destination".

The Federation Secretariat can give support in identi-fying possible funding sources for programmes. Further-more it can coordinate efforts by NS and broker new partnerships in the European and wider context.

What can the Federation do?

- On the basis of this chapter and other current initiatives both from the Secretariat and National Societies, the Secretariat has started comprehensive consultations with European NS towards developing a position on trafficking in Europe in line with Berlin and with the Council of Delegates Resolution 2001/4.
- Based on the feedback from European NSs, the Federation is currently mapping activities through an interactive database shortly to be available on DMIS, but more in- depth research is needed.
- Brokering partnerships that are consistent with existing policies and initiatives in the European context and beyond. Promoting awareness both "in house" as well as in the European context regarding trafficking.

In this respect PERCO is encouraged to develop its work on trafficking. Similarly the Reach-out Refugee Pro-tection Training Project is developing a module on trafficking.

- Continue the dialogue with ICRC regarding points of convergence on trafficking, assistance to detained irregular migrants and tracing. Engage with IOM in a dialogue on trafficking (both in the field and Gva), again our involvement based on our mandate, but points of common interest can be identified Engage with ILO in a dialogue on trafficking (both in the field and Gva), again our involvement based on our mandate, but points of common interest can be identified.
- The Federation represents European NSs at the international level (UN, OSCE, etc.,) and together with NSs, needs to be the "humanitarian voice" of those made vulnerable by trafficking. This should be based on an agreed advocacy platform and operational modalities. A focal point has been established in the Secretariat Europe Dept. for population movement issues, including migration and trafficking, to liaise with Senior Refugee

Officer and other relevant Departments of the Secretariat under the guidance of the Head of Europe Dept.

Trafficking is hard to define simply. The stereotypical image is of young women or girls sold into sexual slavery, but the reality is more complex. In international law, trafficking was first defined by the 2000 UN Protocol to Prevent, Suppress and Punish Trafficking in Persons Especially Women and Children, (known as the "Palermo protocol"). This does not restrict trafficking to cases of force or deception but also inculpates "the abuse of power or of a position of vulnerability". Thus, consent can never constitute a defence to a charge of trafficking. Deception or lack of consent may not be present at all stages. The victim may consent to be transferred for work or arranged marriage, but not to the actual nature or conditions of the work to be done. For instance, the victim may have agreed to work in the sex industry but not to be held in slavery-like conditions; or she may have agreed to work in a factory but not in a brothel, etc. Trafficking may include: child labour, including domestic work; begging; criminal work like selling drugs; servile marriage; illegal adoption; recruitment to serve in armed forces.

A much narrower definition of trafficking is offered by Article 240 of the Criminal Law of the PRC (1979, revised 1997). This outlaws the abduction, kidnapping, purchase, sale or transfer of women and children *for the purpose of selling*. The Article does not include deception or abduction of people with no intention to sell them but for direct services like forced labour or sexual exploitation. It also refers to children as people less than 14 years of age, rather than the UN's definition of children as those under 18. Finally, Chinese criminal law takes no account of men who are trafficked.

This narrow definition helps to explain the surprisingly low figures for human trafficking that Chinese officials give. The Ministry of Public Security reports that in 2006 police uncovered a total of 2,500 trafficking cases. But this refers only to cases cracked by the police and which fit China's definition. (For example, in May 2004 the Yunnan provincial government said 571 children had been abducted in the province between 2001 and 2004 and that the police had located and returned 537 of them. But parents were reported as saying that only very few children abducted from Kunming had been found.) In 2005, the UN Committee on the Rights of the Child expressed its concern that Chinese data gave no clear indication of the number of children trafficked.

Many cases are reported by Chinese media. In 2004 media reported arrests in a case where 76 baby boys were sold in Hohhot, Inner Mongolia and another where 200 children, mostly boys, were kidnapped in Kunming, Yunnan. In 2005, 16 people were arrested in connection with the kidnapping of 31 baby girls, aged from newborn to 3 months. Reports stated that they were to be sold to foreigners for CNY 800 to 4,000 each.

But there is no clarity over prices paid for trafficked children. In December 2004, about 40 parents petitioned central government to crack down on child trafficking and help find their missing children. They wanted Beijing to pressure local governments to report children suspected of being stolen. Most of the parents were migrant workers from Dongguan, Guangdong, and lost their children in that city. Most of the children abducted were boys, from newborns to 12 year olds. In an article reporting this incident, police were quoted as saying a baby boy can be sold for between CNY 10,000 and 20,000 on the mainland, whilst a girl generally fetches only a few thousand *yuan.*

Trafficking is a complex, multi-dimensional pheno-menon that may assume many forms which are probably determined more by demand than by supply. It can include slave marriage, sex work, sweatshops, domestic work, agricultural labour, child beggars and so on. Some cases are clear-cut "trafficking" whilst others may be better defined as illegal migrant labour. China is a source, transit and destination country for women, men and children trafficked for sexual exploitation and forced labour. Most trafficking in China is internal but there is also significant trafficking of Chinese citizens to many parts of the world, particularly women and girls into commercial sexual exploitation in Taiwan, Thailand, Malaysia and Japan.

In the 1980s and early 90s most women and girls were being trafficked for marriage. More recently employment is increasingly the dominant cause, with illegal adoption also on the rise. The lack of girls for marriage in eastern rural areas is fuelling demand for girl babies to be raised as future brides for the sons of better-off farmers. We know from our own research and other sources that many children and young people (or their parents) are enticed by promises of a better life or one which will enable them to support their families. Some children are kidnapped; others are sold or hired out to adult controllers who use them in different ways. Some are sold for adoption, but most are used to beg or to work on the street—selling flowers, singing, shining shoes. Some children disappear into sex work. Newspapers report deliberate maiming of children so that their begging brings in more money.

Families in east and central China want more children because it gives them more status and labour power. Better-off families appear not to mind being fined. They don't, however, want a disabled baby. Couples commonly believe that more children mean more income: an extra pair of hands to help on the land—even if they migrate, it will still mean more income. More children are thought to improve the adults' prospects of being looked after when they are old. As a result, it is believed that some communities in western China have become like "baby factories". There are also examples where remote, uneducated, illiterate women, threatened by an official with being fined for having an above-quota child, will be encouraged to hand over the baby in return for being let off the fine.

Demand may be growing because of rising infertility in urban areas. Some babies are clearly being trafficked to meet demand from childless couples. The distinction between voluntary migration and trafficking is often slight. Many victims leave their communities willingly in response to an offer of work outside. Some are duped and end up in exploitative or harmful employment or in the sex trade. The risk of contracting HIV/AIDS from paid sex, and male clients' growing awareness of this risk, may creating demand for younger girls in brothels. (There is certainly evidence of this pattern in Thailand).

A range of factors make some children particularly vulnerable. Among these are extreme poverty and debt; low levels of basic education; limited job opportunities; family dysfunction; a community's ignorance of risks associated with migration and ignorance of the law and poor law enforcement. Young people separated from their families and/or without proper legal identity are particularly vulnerable.

THE CASE OF XINJIANG

Our research in Xinjiang reveals a distinct profile of trafficked children in the Autonomous Region. They are overwhelmingly male, pre-adolescent, ethnic Uighurs from poor families in southern Xinjiang. Although these children are put to work in conditions of servitude, Article 240 of the Criminal Law does not count them as having been trafficked. Many "brokers" are themselves Uighurs who present themselves as legitimate businessmen recruiting young workers, mainly for service sector jobs in prosperous, eastern areas. They target very poor families with many children.

The broker takes the child away promising to send money to the children's families every year. Sometimes the family receives a significant down-payment to convince them. As far as the family is concerned, their child has voluntarily gone to "Inner China" to work. Parents do not consider their child to be trafficked or engaged in illegal activities. When children arrive in their new environment they find themselves dependent on the perpetrators and in many cases they become enmeshed in an organised criminal network. Many are forced to engage in crime—typically, pick-pocketing, theft or drug dealing.

Unfortunately, many children become accustomed to a lifestyle that they could not afford in their place of origin and go on to become brokers or recruiters themselves. Recidivism is high for children who are arrested and returned to their families. Although less common, some Xinjiang children are directly sold by family members into inden-tured servitude. In even more rare cases, children are abducted and taken against their will and their family's wishes. In Xinjiang and elsewhere, when children are picked up by the authorities, they are kept in Street Children Protection Centres or in temporary detention until a relative or authorised person comes to claim them.

This can be a serious problem if the child is too young to know where she or he comes from. Unidentified children may stay in a Centre for a year or more and if relatives are unlikely to be found the child may be transferred to the local Child Welfare Institute (orphanage). We know from some children that it isn't uncommon for the gangs, finding that the child has been detained, to go to the police and secure the child's release by pretending to be a relative or official come to pick up the child. Besides, children under 16 are deemed below the age of criminal responsibility and so are often released shortly after their arrest, whereupon their adult controllers easily resume control over them.

Governments and communities need to develop multi-sectoral responses to curb the growth of trafficking. National policy and regulatory reform, to bring China's definitions and practice in line with the Palermo protocol, are likely to prove a lengthy process, but local policy to protect children can be developed more rapidly. For example, Save the Children piloted a registration system in a village in Yunnan's Xishuangbanna Prefecture. This requires all recruitment scouts who come to the village to register with the local government office and all persons planning to migrate to inform the office and participate in classes to prepare them for migration. Village-level directives prohibit any young person who has not completed compulsory education from leaving his or her place of origin.

This model was commended by the Regional Women's Federation and preparations are under way to replicate it in a number of counties in Guangxi and Yunnan. Basic education for rural children, especially those from poor, ethnic minority areas, needs to make children aware of risks so they can protect themselves. Migration is inevitable for many poor, rural children in school today. It is therefore logical for the school curriculum to include "safe migration" education.

Such an initiative is now being piloted in middle schools in Pingxiang, Guangxi with support from Save the Children. As well as migration awareness (covering legal and employment rights and preparation for change in the new environment), children are taught about safety at home and in the community (including road and fire safety), parent-child relations, self-confidence and self-esteem, health, hygiene and nutrition, HIV/AIDS and awareness of violence and abuse. We hope to be able to replicate this approach not just to other areas but also to younger children.

A comprehensive and integrated child protection system is desperately needed in a country where the scale of migration is huge and where growing numbers of children are trafficked or living on the streets. Local child protection committees need to be established along with children and youth centres where children, irrespective of their background, can go for support and protection.

This is not unrealistic. The Youth League is currently planning to develop more than 3,000 youth centres across the country. In its work with the Women's Federation, the Youth League and Civil Affairs authorities, Save the Children has been supporting the creation of "children's activity centres" as a starting point for developing local child protection systems. If these centres and the Youth League's youth centres are linked up, they could form the basis for an integrated protection system. Professional social work training will be needed to ensure effective support for the protection system. Work on this has already started.

GOVERNMENT EFFORTS

In the late 1990s, the Government of China (the Ministry of Public Security and the Women's Federation) started to work on anti-trafficking with Save the Children and other agencies such as UNICEF and the International Labour Organisation. ILO and Save the Children efforts are largely funded by the UK Department for International Development.

Since 2001, police at different levels have stepped up their anti-trafficking work. The Ministry of Public Security reports that, from 2001 to 2005, 28,000 human trafficking cases were "cracked down" and 55,000 women and children victims were rescued. By 2001, four provinces had set up centres to help transfer and reintegrate rescued victims. Some community based prevention models have been established in south-west China.

The Public Security authorities have strengthened co-operation with neighbouring countries, especially in Southeast Asia, to combat the rising trend of cross-border trafficking. In 2005, a campaign on the borders of Guangxi and Yunnan led to the arrest of 53 traffickers and the rescue of 38 Vietnamese women who had been forced into sex work. Fifteen trafficking gangs were raided and 115 Vietnamese victims were returned home. Also in 2005, Guangxi Public Security Bureau set up a centre to aid foreign victims. In September 2005, China's Ministry of Public Security had the first high-level official meeting with Myanmar authorities regarding cooperation in fighting cross-border trafficking.

China has also been involved in a Coordinated Mekong Ministerial Initiative Against Trafficking (COMMIT) process that started in 2004 with a memorandum of understanding signed by Laos, Cambodia, Vietnam, Thailand, Myanmar and China. COMMIT's two most important achievements to date are the approval of a sub-regional plan of action (2005-2007) and the development of 11 project proposals covering policy, protection, prevention and prosecution. Signatories have also undertaken to develop their own National Plan of Action (NPA) against trafficking in all its forms.

Yet in China progress on developing an NPA and committing sufficient resources to combat trafficking has so far been quite slow. This may in part because, according to the reporting criteria, the number of cases is relatively low. It is also seen as a regional issue mainly affecting southwest China (even though the number of children being trafficked from Xinjiang is high if the UN definition is applied). Thus, although anti-trafficking offices may exist within the Public

Security system in the southwest, they are not allocated sufficient funds to work effectively.

Meanwhile, however, an important achievement has been the revision of the 1992 Law on Protection of Minors, which comes into effect on June 1, 2007. Save the Children was the only NGO involved in the revision process, which was led by the Rights Department of the Youth League. The Youth League is increasingly visible in the protection of minors and it seems that the lead on child protection is passing from the Women's Federation to the Youth League. In response to this shift, Save the Children is working increasingly closely with the Youth League, both in our child trafficking prevention and our work on children in conflict with the law.

Towards Integrated Protection

Save the Children was the first organisation to start community-based prevention of child trafficking in Yunnan Province and Guangxi Zhuang Autonomous Region. In 1999, we signed an agreement with Yunnan Public Security Bureau to cooperate on trafficking prevention in the prefectures of Honghe and Wenshan. This was the Public Security Bureau's first experience of a community-based prevention approach. Alongside the local registration systems for employers and intending migrants and the school-based education outlined above, collaborative efforts have included pre-migration classes and the use of village broadcasting, blackboard newspapers, brochures, storybooks and folk songs to promote "3-antis" awareness (anti-trafficking, anti-AIDS, anti-drugs) in accessible, local languages or dialects.

We also support the return from overseas of trafficked Chinese girls and women, in cooperation with the International Organisation of Migration, the Thai Bureau Against Trafficking of Children and Women and the Yunnan Women's Federation and Public Security Bureau. Our role is to assist family tracing and assessment and help local partners develop systems to support the reintegration of the returnees. We have supported the reintegration of 40 Chinese women who were trafficked across borders into the sex industry.

In 1999, when we first began to work on trafficking, we developed with the Global Alliance Against Traffic in Women a Chinese version of their "Human Rights in Practice: A Guide to Assist Trafficked Women and Child-ren", and this is still widely used in China. In addition, we routinely support capacity building training for partners, have offered suggestions on the draft NPA and in 2004 co-hosted, with UNDP UNIAP and China's National Working Committee on Women and Children, a conference on trafficking in five provinces.

However, our experience has increasingly convinced us that child trafficking cannot be treated as an isolated phenomenon but needs to be addressed in a more holistic way through the development of integrated protection systems. This conviction has grown out of our work in a number of fields and provinces where the lack of child protection mechanisms is a common denominator. Over the last decade, this work has included:

- Research, training and capacity building work with national and local Civil Affairs authorities responsible for street children and children in the care of government. This has including sponsorship and technical supporting for in-service social work training (at Beijing University) for Civil Affairs officials working with children, as a move towards creating a cadre of child protection social workers in China.
- Support for the National Youth League's Rights Department in its work drafting the recently revision Law on the Protection of Minors.
- Work in Ruili (Yunnan) and Fuyang (Anhui Province) on HIV/AIDS, with particular attention to children affected by the epidemic.
- Work in Hefei (Anhui) and elsewhere on "children in communities" with a focus on vulnerable groups including orphans, disabled children and those at the interface between migrant and settled, urban communities.
- Work with national and local Civil Affairs authorities to develop national guidelines for fostering.

- Work in Kunming (Yunnan) to develop community supervision and support for youngsters in conflict with the law.
- Work in Yunnan to introduce child protection stan-dards in schools, which is particularly important in rural areas where more and more children have to board but is also important in cities where evidence suggests playground violence is on the rise.
- Support for Chinese networks of scholars, lawyers and social activists engaging with issues of child abuse and children in conflict with the law.

Child participation is a key, cross cutting theme in all of these areas, promoted through activities such as child-led research projects and Children's Forums where children voice their concerns, ideas and policy recommendations. Our projects generally also include the establishment of children's activity centres that, as well as creating a useful, community resource—*eg*, a safe and stimulating after-school environment for children whose parents are still working—also serve as a platform for peer education and exchange, including the development of performance and visual art groups.

Our work in these areas clearly interlocks around the common issue of child protection—understood as involving (i) universal access to services (ii) children's and parents' knowledge and understanding of risks and (iii) responsive and coordinated local government agencies. Consequently, Save the Children is now advocating the creation of a National Committee for the Protection of Minors that can be mirrored at provincial level and below and that can support the development of child protection systems in migrant children's places of origin, transit and destination.

Save the Children feels that the National Youth League is capable of playing a lead role in a National Child Protection Committee that would includes the Women's Federation and National Working Committee on Children and Women as well as other government bodies such as the Public Security, Justice, Education, Health and Finance administrations. The numerous children and youth centres that now exist across the country should be networked to provide a strong foundation for such a system.

Child trafficking, migration, street children, and HIV/AIDS are interwoven issues. With government committed to ongoing, large scale migration and urbanisation, the situation for children at risk is very likely to get worse, not better, in the short term. Multi-sectoral responses are urgently needed. Education, health and protection service providers need to work closely together at all levels. Children live in communities and this is where the different strands of provision and protection need to come together in integrated services with a local focus. The community is the site of services to realise children's rights; the government must provide a framework to ensure the quality and effectiveness of services and to monitor standards.

4

Trafficking Phenomenon

Trafficking in persons the recruitment, transport or sale of human beings into all forms of forced labour and servitude is an issue of global concern. It involves grave human right violations, including slavery, forced labour, sexual and physical abuse, torture, arbitrary detention and risks to life and security of person. A minimum of 2.45 million people are victims of trafficking annually and children represent 50 percent of the victims of this highly lucrative (US$ 32 billion each year) human rights abuse. European countries are increasingly aware of the national and regional scope of the problem, but it remains a chal-lenging area to research and assess in terms of figures and trends due to its covert and illegal nature. A myriad of complex factors make children particularly vulnerable to trafficking and these include violent and dysfunctional families, poverty, gender inequality, demand for cheap labour, growth of technology and sex tourism, political and economic instability in countries of origin and the promise of a better future abroad.

INTERNATIONAL LEGISLATION

All source, transit or destination countries, with respect to trafficking, are required under international law to enact specific measures to end this harmful practice. It was first clearly defined by the United Nations Protocol to Prevent, Suppress and Punish Trafficking in Persons, Especially Women and Children supplementing the United Nations Convention against Transnational Organized Crime (2000). Also known as the Palermo Protocol or the Trafficking Protocol, it defines a child as any person under 18 years of age and is the basis for changes in national law.

According to Article 3 (a): "Trafficking in persons' shall mean the recruitment, transportation, transfer, harboring or receipt of persons, by means of the threat or use of force or other forms of coercion, of abduction, of fraud, of deception, of the abuse of power or of a position of vulner-ability, or of the giving or receiving of payments or benefits to achieve the consent of a person having control over another person, for the purpose of exploitation. Exploitation shall include, at a minimum, the exploitation of the prostitution of others or other forms of sexual exploitation, forced labour or services, slavery or practices similar to slavery, servitude or the removal of organs".

Article 3 (c) states: "The recruitment, transportation, transfer, harbouring or receipt of a child for the purpose of exploitation shall be considered 'trafficking in persons' even if this does not involve any of the means set forth in subparagraph (a) of this article." Therefore, it is irrelevant whether force has been used or the child has been misled.

Furthermore, under the United Nations Convention on the Rights of the Child, children's needs are recognised as being distinct from those of adults: Articles 34 and 35 deal with the offences of sexual exploitation and require States to prevent the sale, trafficking and abduction of children. Another legally binding piece of legislation is the Council of Europe Convention on Action against Trafficking in Human Beings. It is currently open to signature, with 15 member States having signed as of July 2005 and will enter into force after ratifications. This convention provides the minimum protection standards for trafficking victims. For example, if a victim's age is uncertain he or she should be presumed to be a child until verified and not returned to a State where he or she would be at risk. The convention also addresses broader issues of prevention, such as discouraging the demand leading to the exploitation of women and children and developing a "protective environment" for children to reduce their vulnerability to trafficking.

UK LEGISLATION

The UK has addressed trafficking offences through legislation. Initially the Nationality, Immigration and Asylum Act 2002 covered the offence of trafficking, but it was only meant to be a temporary piece of legislation and was replaced by the Sexual Offences Act 2003. This Act criminalises trafficking for sexual exploitation and makes it an offence to traffic into, within and out of the UK. The maximum sentence is 14 years and a child is defined as someone below 18 years (not 16 as in the case of the Sexual Offences Act 1956). However, the sentence is higher for those paying for sex with a child below 16 years. In addition, the Asylum and Immigration (Treatment of Claimants etc.) Act 2004 makes it an offence to traffic in all forms of labour exploitation and carries a maximum penalty of 14 years. In January 2005, two Albanian traffickers were prosecuted under the Sexual Offences Act 2003 and received sentences of nine and 18 years in prison. However, in this case the victims were willing to testify, which is rare, given threats to their families and their personal safety and security. The 2005 Council of Europe Convention includes victim and witness protection measures safeguarding trafficking victims and thus securing more prosecutions.

PATTERNS OF TRAFFICKING INTO THE UK

In the UK the issue of trafficking of children first emerged when West Sussex Social Services reported the disappearance of 66 unaccompanied asylum- seeking children from their care in 1995. Since then, UNICEF UK has estimated that some 250 children have been trafficked into the UK over a five-year period, while a Home Office study in 2000 concluded that the scale of trafficking of women (some of whom may include young girls) may range anywhere from a hundred to some thousands annually. However, the true scale of the problem is difficult to assess due to a lack of updated statistics. In addition, there is no clear or constant trend demonstrating a pattern on the routes taken or the nationalities involved. The 2004 research indicates that girls, in particular, are being brought from Africa and Eastern Europe for purposes of domestic servitude and prostitution.

There were 35 cases of child trafficking within 17 boroughs of London, including nine children under 16 years of age; there are many more reported cases that social services did not disclose. Increasingly, an influx of young Vietnamese, Chinese and Thai children, particularly boys, has been noticed by various agencies. In addition, ECPAT UK has received reports indicating the issue is not confined to London. Traffickers appear to utilise a number of ways in which to traffic children into the country through different airports and other ports of entry. The UK has become both a destination and transit country for trafficking. Unaccompanied Minors From 1995 to 2001, West Sussex Social Services came across a number of cases of unaccompanied minors claiming asylum as soon as they arrived at the airport. Most of the children were Nigerian girls and were taken in by West Sussex Social Services.

However, many went missing between one day and six months of being in care. There were indications that they were being further trafficked to other parts of Europe, especially Italy. Those remaining in care were not considered to be safe as some were suspected of having contact with traffickers and being prostituted or dealing drugs. There-fore, care accommodation was considered insecure for such children. The traffickers maintained control over the children by creating a deep distrust of authority, using threats of violence or a fear of voodoo. The fear of voodoo is very real to many of the African children. They are told that the only way of getting rid of the voodoo curse is by paying back a 'debt' to the trafficker. These debts are huge sums of money that are impossible to pay off: some girls owe as much as £25,000. Police assistance was considered ineffective in cases where social workers reported suspicious or abusive characters around children. Some felt that the police viewed the children only as asylum-seekers and not as child protection cases.

Accompanied Minors In 2001, the case of Adam, a young boy thought to have been trafficked for ritual sacrifice, led police to carry out an investigation into the disappearance of young African boys. They discovered that between July and September 2001, 300 African boys disappeared from schools around London. There is no evidence to suggest that these missing children were trafficked or abused, but the case highlights a systemic failure in communication and exchange of information by agencies responsible for the care and protection of children. These ties in with concerns raised about traffickers bringing in children under the guise of the West African practice of sending children abroad to live with a relative or friend for a better education or future. Reportedly, children from Central Africa are brought into the country to be exploited in domestic work and prostitution. Although private fostering regulations require that unrelated guardians of a child inform social services, many fail to do so.

Fostering estimates that there are between 8,000 and 10,000 privately fostered children in the UK. It is often difficult to prove a relationship between a guardian and a child: DNA testing is not the norm. Even when family connection is proven, this is not a sufficient guarantee that a child is safe, as the case of Victoria Climbie severely abused by her great aunt so tragically demonstrated. ECPAT UK found that both the local and immigration services are not entirely clear about their respective roles and responsibilities with regard to carrying out identity checks on children's guardians. Additionally, there are documented cases of Eastern European women (whose exact ages are difficult to establish and may be well below 18 years) being trafficked into the UK, especially from Albania, Kosovo, Russian, Lithuania, Romania and Bulgaria. The case of Albanian children is of particular interest since they have been targeted by a Home Office pilot return's programme for unaccompanied asylum-seeking children, which will be extended to include other countries.

Such a scheme could expose trafficked children to

continuing abuse if suitable child protection structures are not in place in their home countries. The women or girls coming into the UK are often accompanied by their trafficker or meet the trafficker soon after arriving. They invariably have a prior relationship with the trafficker who uses coercive tactics, including deception, threats, the use of physical or sexual violence and debt bondage to control the women and girls. Debt bondage is characterised by the victim having to pay back increasingly high costs to the trafficker. Those assisting these women believe a number of them are younger than the 18 years that they claim to be; age is particularly difficult to measure in older girls and age disputes have been reported in nearly all the boroughs in the ECPAT UK research.

Local authorities expressed concerns that immigration services tended to judge a child to be older than he or she was and this undermined the level of support the child would receive. Concern was also expressed regarding. Nationality, Immigration and Asylum Act 2002, which requires asylum seekers to make their claim immediately; otherwise they would be ineligible for benefits. It was felt that many trafficked children cannot make an immediate claim and if their age is also disputed then they further lose out on any measure of support.

Various authorities are now focusing on the issue of trafficking of children. The strategies need to concentrate on child protection and prevention, not just law enforcement. An important element in developing these initiatives is the cooperation and coordination between governmental and non-governmental agencies at the local and national level. The UK urgently needs to develop a national perspective on child trafficking, including its data collection and documentation. ECPAT UK recommends training for relevant agencies, producing good practice guides, effective support services for trafficking victims and better information collection and management by agencies tasked with the protection and care of children. On a wider regional and international level, greater synergy and cooperation is vital. The implementation of existing legislation is necessary, as is including effective protection measures for victims in national plans of action.

In most countries, human trafficking is acknowledged as a serious crime and crimes are punishable by law in virtually all countries. Yet, owing to dramatic improve-ments in transportation and communication technologies, child trafficking has now developed into a transnational crime, and appears to be on the rise worldwide. The ILO (2001), the UNICEF (2002), and the US State Department (2003) all pulled the alarm warning about the growing scope of this phenomenon as complex transnational crime. As a result, important international standards have already been put in place to coordinate efforts aimed at fighting child trafficking, including the UN Convention on the Rights of the Child and its Optional Protocol on the Sale of Children, Child Prostitution and Child Pornography, and the new ILO Convention. However, very little is known about the mechanics of a successful international cooperation.

For example, while most public discussions of policy responses to child trafficking emphasize actions at the source country level, very little, however, is known about the determinants of the critical level of government effort. The United Nations' 2000 Protocol to Prevent, Suppress and Punish Trafficking in Persons defines child trafficking as "the recruitment, transportation, transfer, harboring or receipt of persons, by means of threat or use of force or other forms of coercion, of abduction, of fraud, of deception, of abuse of power or of a position of vulnerability or of the giving or receiving of payments or benefits to achieve the consent of a person having control over another person, for the purpose of exploitation". A UNICEF report estimated that 1.2 million children are trafficked every year around the world for commercial exploitation.

Notwithstanding, the UNICEF's international flow chart reveals that transnational child trafficking involves the illegal transportation of children from poorer countries to richer countries. In West and Central Africa, for example, children from Burkina Faso, Ghana, Mali and Togo are trafficked to Cameroon, Côte d'Ivoire, Gabon and Nigeria, with the latter group of countries being relatively richer than the first. In South Asia, Nepal acts as a source-country for India—a relatively richer country compared to Nepal. For this region, the Committee on the Rights of the Child reports that in 1995 an estimated 100,000 to 150,000 Nepalese girls and women had been trafficked into India for sexual exploitation. In South-East Asia, Thailand is reported to be the main receiving country, with an estimated 194,180 foreign child labourers reported in 1996, mostly from Cambodia, China (particularly from the Yunnan Province), Lao PDR, Myanmar and Vietnam, all of which are poorer relatively to Thailand.

This pattern of transnational child-trafficking needs to be explained if one is to get a clearer picture of the ingredients of a successful international cooperation in the fight against this phenomenon. This chapter therefore develops a general-equilibrium model in which the supply of trafficked children arises endogenously. In our model, children are kidnapped or abducted from a source-country and illegally shipped into the rest of the world for profit. Children's protection from potential traffickers involves both the family acting as a private protective unit through parental investment in child protection, and a government, which allocates public expenditures to improve enforce-ment of laws against child trafficking. The supply of child trafficking emerges if and only if a positive fraction of the economy's entrepreneurs find it optimal to invest their capital in breaking down protective barriers against child trafficking set up by both families and the country's government, given the state of the international demand for trafficked children.

We use this model to study the determinants of the ability of a source-country government, acting unilaterally, to curb the supply of trafficked children. We argue that when child trafficking is mostly a transnational pheno-menon, setting the critical level of government spending necessary for the complete elimination of the supply of trafficked children presents the source-country's government with an externality problem: if the rest of the world is richer, thus more able to protect their children from traffickers, this may cause the international price of trafficked children to rise. This rise, in turn, coupled with low return to capital in a poorer country, may trigger a higher trafficking effort from return-maximizing capitalists, thus raising the critical level of government's spending necessary to curb the emergence of the supply for trafficked children. In other words, rich countries' ability to protect their children from traffickers, makes it harder for poorer countries to unilaterally follow suit, without the help of the former.

This then explains the pattern of transnational child trafficking flow observed in the data. The starting point of our analysis is the observation that since by nature, children are most vulnerable when left unprotected, building a protective environment for these children requires both parental and public investments. Parents are usually call upon to provide for their children's basic needs, including nutrition, adequate clothing, health, and education, which may reduce the risk of these children being lured by the false promise of better lives outside their home environment. However, for many reasons, including poverty, families often fail to be effective protective units for their children, thus making them the perfect victims for lurking traffickers. To help protect children from traffickers, government officials may launch public awareness campaign, in addition to recruiting, training, and equipping of customs officials, police officers and other law-enforcers.

Notwithstanding, even well-intentioned government officials may fail to prevent children from being trafficked out if, when acting unilaterally, they are unable to affect the international price for trafficked children. The higher this price, the higher the return to creating a supply of trafficked children, which, in turn, may induce well-organized criminal groups to step up the effort to break down barriers against child trafficking. In other words, a high international price acts as a "ladder", helping well-organized criminal groups to "climb up" the protective walls set up by families and government officials. The critical law-enforcement effort is therefore one that raises the wall higher than the "ladder" used by potential traffickers. The higher the ladder, the higher the wall should be and thus the more public funds will be needed, which is a negative externality.

The ILO classifies child trafficking as one of the worst forms of child labour, under Convention 182. Due to the outrageous nature of this phenomenon, an international consensus has developed on its elimination, often prompting policy actions, which, unfortunately, preceded research by many years. Dessy and Pallage (2002) and Rogers and Swinnerton (2002) are the first papers to attempt a theore-tical exploration of the economics of this phenomenon. Using a model of parental investment in child's education, Dessy and Pallage (2002), show that when a country is very poor, in order for a ban on the worst forms of child labour to bring a Pareto-improvement, appropriate mechanisms must be designed to mitigate the decline in child labour wages caused by a ban-induced reduction in employment options for children.

Rogers and Swinnerton (2002) offer a counter-argu-ment in a model exploring the welfare effects of banning exploitative forms of child labour. They argue that because the ban push both the exploited children and the exploiters towards the non-exploitative side of the market, this has beneficial effects on child labour wages. Both models, however, do not discuss the determinants of government's ability to enforce the ban on the worst forms of child labour. Yet this is a very important question and here is why. First, in Rogers and Swinnerton (2002), while a ban has the potential to raise child labour wages, it also has the adverse effect of depressing the return to capital, due to reduced market options.

Capitalists therefore may have a vested interest in opposing such a ban, or in bringing down barriers to child exploitation set up by law-enforcement. Second, in Rogers and Swinnerton, parents are passive and do not invest in child protection. Although parent in their model know that their children can fall victim to traffickers, they do not allocate household resources to reducing the probability that their child may be trafficked away. Parents in our model may do that. By focusing on the microeconomics of both children vulnerability to trafficking and capitalists' decision to supply trafficked children, our research seeks to explain the determinants of the critical level of public expenditures a source-country government must allocate in order to stop child trafficking at the source. It also seeks to explain why poorer countries are more likely to be source-countries for child trafficking: since building a protective environment for children involves household investment, poverty may make households too dependent upon government officials for the protection of their children.

In other words, poorer families may substitute public for private barriers against child out-trafficking. As a result, higher public funds are required in poorer than in richer countries in order to curb the supply of trafficked children. With economic development, in contrast, households become richer; this enables them to become more effective as protective units for their respective children, thus lessening their dependence upon the government to build barriers against child out-trafficking. In that case, the critical level of government effort is lower, which therefore reduces the level of public funds necessary to curb the supply? If child exploitation or the worst forms of child labour have not been studied much, there exists, however, a large literature on child labour, both theoretical and empirical. The theoretical literature was initiated by the seminal work of Basu & Van (1998).

Already burdened by brutal civil wars, internal con-flicts, socio-political unrest and economic difficulties all of which have retarded development West and Central African countries have woken up to another challenge: child trafficking and exploitation. The phenomenon is an emerging problem that the countries have realised they will have to address. UNICEF, for instance, estimates that 200,000 children are trafficked each year in the region. On 8-10 January, regional experts met over the issue in a seminar held in Yamoussoukro, Cote d'Ivoire. Organised by the international police organisation, Interpol and the Ivorian government, the "First Specialised Meeting on Child Trafficking and Exploitation in West and Central Africa" proved an opportunity to share experiences, exchange information and review national strategies.

Participants at Yamoussoukro agreed on the need to combat child trafficking through increased cooperation. The conference's final declaration-The Yamoussoukro Declaration-states as a first point that the participants, including government ministries, NGOs and UN agencies, pledge to conduct synchronised information campaigns to fight against a phenomenon whose existence governments acknowledged only recently. Child trafficking, the conference heard, was first acknowledged as a new scourge in West and Central Africa during a regional workshop organised by UNICEF in Cotonou, Benin in 1998. Yet the problem can be traced to earlier years.

Susanne Aho, director general of Togo's child protection department, told IRIN that the first significant news reports of child trafficking in her country were in 1992. But it was in 2001 that child trafficking gained unprecedented international attention. In April, a boat "The Etinero" grabbed the region's attention when it was re-ported that it had left the port city of Cotonou carrying over 200 "child slaves" destined to work in central African countries. After two weeks at sea, during which period the Etinero was refused docking in Gabon and Cameroon, the boat returned to Cotonou. Authorities then found that it carried about 140 people, including 40 children and youths aged between five and 24 years old, who after interviews, confirmed they were heading to work in the central African region.

Following the event, the media started paying closer attention to the phenomenon. Consequently, it labelled several countries in the region "slave states" including the Atlantic coast-countries, from Cote d'Ivoire to Gabon and others like Burkina Faso, Mali, Niger. All these countries were represented at the Yamoussoukro seminar. But while defining child trafficking, it is important to note that not all population movement is illegal, the regional experts said. Child trafficking, they said, was "a phenomenon where an individual (called an intermediary), who for a fee and through violence or ruse, displaces within or outside a national territory an individual less than 18 years old for sexual or commercial exploitation, generally with the complicity of the parents".

Child trafficking and exploitation are banned by the International Labour Organisation (ILO), the UN agency that regulates labour practices around the globe. Partici-pants also clarified the difference between this practice and the "socialisation" of the African child. "Socialisation" is a process in which skills are taught by family members during a child's years of growth, they said, such as skills learned during school holidays when children are sent to relatives in neighbouring countries. Performing household chores, farming, selling at the market, working in a relative's mechanical shop, falls in this category. Equally, trafficking is different from the traditional population movement or seasonal displacement that has linked West and Central African countries for centuries. Two types of trafficking were identified - internal and external. Internal trafficking occurs within the boundaries of a national territory, while external trafficking occurs across national borders. The states involved were also classified.

A supplier state is the victim's state of origin while the final destination is a receiver state. Victims can transit through states to reach a final destination. In West Africa, Cote d'Ivoire is a receiver state for Malian and Burkinabe children. In Central Africa, Cameroon is a transit state for Togolese, Nigerian and Benin's e children heading to Gabon which is considered an "Eldorado" because of its relative prosperity due to the oil industry. According to the seminar, child trafficking is encouraged by several causes including poverty, constant demand for manual labour, traditional migratory flows, some of which have turned into illicit flows of persons, youth seeking independence, high birth rates and polygamy, porous borders, lack of legislation and deficient school systems. It was agreed that in the fight against the practice, the first obstacle was the lack of reliable statistics. At the moment, no scientific study exists that would provide accurate data on the problem. Even where some statistics exist, they are believed to be often underestimated. Still participants had some statistical indicators of the magnitude.

In 2001, there were 297 trafficking victims in Togo, according to Suzanne Aho, while in Senegal, 400,000 children are "at risk" of prostitution, underage labour and other unlawful practices, Senegalese representative Amadou Yoro N'Diaye told IRIN. Mali's minister for women, child and family affairs, Afoussatou Thiero Diarra, told IRIN about 500 youth fell victim between September 2000 and August 2001, to trafficking between Cote d'Ivoire and Mali. Countries at the seminar pledged to conduct a study that will accurately reflect the state of affairs of child trafficking in the region. Emphasis was also placed on the need for governments to create national crime databases. But they are also hindered by insufficient technical equipment, human capacity, financial resources, and adequate legis-lation, it was heard. For example, Gabon which has an 800-km coastline does not have enough a large enough coast guard to prevent illegal entries, partly due to a lack of funds, Gabonese ambassador in Cote d'Ivoire, Henri Bekalle-Akwe, told IRIN. Togo, which has been under economic sanctions for years from the EU, does not have enough money to devote to child trafficking, Aho said.

And across the region, existing legislation does not specifically address child trafficking, but rather children's well being and in general terms. To counter some of these constraints, the final declaration called for specific anti-trafficking legislation and for harmonisation of these laws across national borders. Participants said a more concerted effort against the scourge would complement some of the already existing initiatives. For Michel Gregoire of the ILO office in Abidjan, the convening of the conference was in itself a positive step because it proved that the region acknowledges that the phenomenon exists. The 1996 agreement between Ghana, Togo, Benin and Nigeria, and the September 2000 protocol between Mali and Cote d'Ivoire are some of the other earlier efforts that the region could build on in the coming years.

Three aspects were identified as priorities for the region in tackling child trafficking: establishment of legislation that is specific to child trafficking and ensuring uniformity across the region, injecting the necessary amount of money, and providing the necessary equipment for security opera-tions and more accurate and efficient administrative activities. Interpol Crime Intelligence Officer, Jan Austad added another element - that police and prosecution work in tandem to ensure that when police arrest a suspected trafficker, prosecution moves quickly on the case. This has not always been the case for many reasons including corruption, Austad explained. But N'diaye, a lawyer and presently chief of staff of Senegal's Ministry of Family and early Childhood, took the problem back to what he thinks is its root cause: poverty. Asked what the region should do, he said: "To eradicate this scourge, we have to fight against poverty and in favour of development". Burkina Faso agreed to host the next meeting in 2004, at which the region will review progress made since this year.

Child Trafficking is an inhumane offence against defence-less and innocent children. Millions of children are forcibly trafficked or coerced across borders only to be sold in the sex trade, for illegal adoption, for criminal activities, for work as domestic servants, beggars, soldiers or for other purposes.

The urgency to combat trafficking in children is under-standable considering the heinous nature of the pheno-menon – it is an affront to principles of human dignity and morality and a severe violation of basic human rights. Principle 9 of the Geneva Declaration of Rights of the Child of 1924 states explicitly that the "The child shall be protected against all forms of neglect, cruelty and exploitation. He shall not be the subject of traffic, in any form". Despite being in existence for centuries, Child Trafficking has only in recent years emerged as an issue of global concern due to the worldwide consensus and co-operation to join hands in fighting this heinous crime; With the amplification of international and national legal apparatus, the trafficking of human beings is perceived to be more than a crime it is a serious violation of human rights, children's rights, labour rights and basic fundamental freedoms.

Child Trafficking has become highly lucrative and increasingly worthwhile as women and children are considered commodities which can be "sold" several times over. With the permeable borders and the advancement of technology child trafficking has expanded around the Globe where the routes for trafficking children alter according to local conditions or supply and demand factors. It is no longer adequate to say that victims are trafficked from poor to the wealthier ones. Violence is not the necessary mode for child trafficking, as has been often misconceived, as the victims are tricked, deceived, forced, sold by their parents or otherwise coerced into situations, which they later cannot escape from.

Predominantly, women and children are trafficked in for the "sexual trade". The lack of employment in their native countries, force women and children into illegal migration, through migrant traffickers who offer "package deals". Deceptive means such as false promises of careers in business, factories and households, are used to lure the women and children to being trafficked. They are inevitably then found imprisoned in brothels. In many cases, the women are lured to foreign countries in the hope of obtaining legitimate work, where they are then paid meagre salaries and the poverty eventually forces them to resort to prostitution or to prostitute themselves under duress. The trafficking of children is usually by way of kidnapping or abduction, once abducted, threats and acts of violence are used to hold on to the victims. In Thailand for instance, brothel managers employ agents to collect photos of young girls as they go to school. The girls are then selected by the managers and upon selection the girls are ordered by them for the agents to kidnap.

Aside from the kidnapping or abduction, Asian Countries have also faced the poverty driven selling of "daughters" by the impoverished families to "agents" for sometimes as low as US$200 a child, which children are then re-sold to traffickers. The sale of the girl child by her family, due to poverty, in turn places the financial burden of supporting her family on the girl child. Such trafficking is an example of non-violent trafficking of children. Also of large incidence is where the agents pose as "potential husbands" used to deceive the family of the girl child into believing the girl child and her "rich" husband will take over their financial burden, inevitably however, the girl child is then either sold to traffickers or forced into prostitution. However, one must remember that it benefits the traffickers to keep their victims in a foreign environment where not only are they vulnerable for having entered a country illegally, but are also disadvantaged because of their ignorance of the law, culture and language of that country.

As Reported by Francis T. Miko, Specialist in International Relations trafficking affects virtually every, country in the world. The largest numbers of victims come from Asia, with over 225,000 victims each year from Southeast Asia and over 150,000 from South Asia. The former Soviet Union is now believed to be the largest new source of trafficking for prostitution and the sex industry, with over 100,000 trafficked each year from that region. An additional 75,000 or more are trafficked from Eastern Europe. Over 100,000 come from Latin America and the Caribbean, and over 50,000 victims are from Africa. Most of the victims are sent to Asia, the Middle East, Western Europe and North America.

The increasing spread of the AIDS epidemic and the rise in the risk of being infected with sexually transmitted diseases, has contributed to the popular demand for "virgin" girls and boys who are sourced out from remote villages around the globe. The trafficking of children is rampant in South East Asia namely, countries such as Malaysia, India, Nepal, Indonesia and Sri Lanka and an analysis of the statistics of child trafficking and the laws that purportedly guard against the offence in these countries to some extent exemplifies the magnitude of the issue and highlights the shortcomings of the penal law in combating it.

In 1997,4,200 Malaysian girls were reported missing and a

significant fraction of these girls were estimated to have been victims of trafficking. In 1998, 2, 250 prostitutes trafficked in from foreign countries were arrested by the Malaysian Police. Also estimated were 4000 boy children trafficked into from Thailand to beg and engage in the sexual trade. The Malaysian Penal Code which was drafted in accordance with the Indian Penal Code, like India has prohibited the inducement of girls under the age of 18 years to go some place or to be removed from her guardian or to perform any act with intent or knowing that it is likely that the girl will be seduced or forced to sexual intercourse. Such provisions are provided for under the provisions relating to the kidnapping of minors and statutory rape.

Malaysia faces the problem of being a prime location both for the trafficking in and trafficking out of women and children, as well being used in transit for the trafficking of women and children from Countries such as Indonesia, Thailand, Singapore, Taiwan, Sri Lanka, India, Pakistan, Bangladesh, Philippines, Cambodia, China and Russia. In 2002, newspapers reported the arrest of 3, 607 foreign prostitutes, mainly from Russia and its neighbouring countries. Those arrested are sent to detention centres and are eventually deported after being subjected to imprisonment or detention for 6 months or more. The sad truth is that the punishment is faced by the victims and not the traffickers, pimps and procurers who profit from the trade, as to the victims, they are nameless and their whereabouts are unknown.

Legislation relating to trafficking is found in the Indian Penal Code and in the Immoral Trafficking Act. The Penal Code prohibits the buying, selling, letting to hire or otherwise disposal of or to obtain possession of a minor (a person under 18 years of age) with intent or knowing that it is likely that the minor will be used for the purpose of prostitution or any other immoral and unlawful purpose. The provisions apply to both male and female children. It is also an offence to induce a girl under the age of 18 years to go some place or perform any act with intent or knowing that it is likely that the girl will be seduced or forced to sexual intercourse. If the girl is "imported" to India from abroad the age limit is raised to 21 years. Offences of such nature carry a penalty of up to 10 years imprisonment and a fine. A Conspiracy to commit such an offence under the Penal Code is generally also punishable.

For women and girls additional protection is provided in the Immoral Traffic Prevention Act. This act was amended in 1986 to provide for more severe penalties for offences involving children and minors. Under this act anyone who detains a woman or girl in a brothel or on any other premise with the intent that the female person shall have sexual intercourse with other persons is liable to punishment. To facilitate prosecution, certain circumstances are presumed to constitute illegal detainment. Thus if someone is found with a child in a brothel or a child that has been sexually assaulted is found in a brothel it is presumed that the child is illegally detained. Offenders are liable to a prison term from 7 years to life. These strict liability provisions allow for a higher possibility of curbing the offence, which would otherwise not be possible without the reversal of the burden of proof as has often happened in drug-related offences.

Nepal faces the catastrophic issue of child prostitution with 5,000 to 7,000 children being trafficked out of Nepal every year. Current statistics reveal up to 200,000 Nepalese have been trafficked out into neighbouring countries, 60,000 of whom are children ranging from the age of 8 years to 15 years old. The children are subjected to violence, beaten up and starved to ensure compliance with the orders of brothel operators. The children are mistreated to the extent of being given opium to ease the pain endured in the first weeks of intercourse.

In Indonesia, Article 297 of the Indonesian Penal Code prohibits trafficking. It is applicable to females regardless of age and to males under 18 years of age. It is also illegal to take a minor from the legal custody of another person or to hide a minor that has been taken away. The use of violence, threat of violence or deceit or if the victim is under 12 years of age are listed as aggravating circumstances. The maximum penalty is then 9 years imprisonment instead of 7 years.

Additional protection is awarded by making it a criminal offence for legal guardians to hand over or submit their child to other persons knowing that the child will be subject to work that is harmful or affects the child's health. This provision applies to children under 12 years of age. Under the Indonesian Code, victims who are under 12, only then is the crime it prohibits sufficiently aggravating. The code does not provide a definition of trafficking in the legal text and no examples are given.

This is a glaring inadequacy of the code to afford protection to children who are victims of trafficking and even prostitution (which the provisions are mainly concerned with). In contrast the legislation in India has the age limit at 18 years and in situations where girls are trafficked or "imported" (as stated in the provision) into India from another country, the age limit is raised to 21 years. A provision of this nature seemingly takes into account the seriousness of the offence of trafficking in children. The Indonesian Code in this regard provides negligible pro-tection against the violation against children. The provision is inconsistent with the definition of a "child" stated in Article 1 Convention on the Rights of the Child (hereinafter referred to as "CRC") as "every human being below the age of 18 years unless, under the law applicable to the child, majority is attained earlier".

While the second part of the Article may be interpreted as a proviso to the age of majority being 18 years, the spirit of the convention *vis a vis* the protection of children against abuse of basic human rights must be appreciated. The Convention sets out the yardstick against which governments, as custodians of fundamental freedoms and human rights, ought to measure to attain and realize the rights for children set out therein globally. It is a universally recognized and most internationally ratified international instrument pertaining to the rights of children. It has placed the child at the nucleus of the universal call and pledge for human rights.

In Sri Lanka, Penal Code 5 was amended in 1995 which introduced two new offences of sexual exploitation (Section

360B of the Amendment to the Penal Code) of children and trafficking (Article 360C of the Amendment to the Penal Code) of children. Under Article 360C (2) and 360B (2) a "child" is defined as "a person under eighteen (18) years of age. Where the offence of "trafficking" is committed in respect of children the offender, if found guilty, will be punished with imprisonment for a term not less than five years and not exceeding 20 years and may also be punished with a fine.

Essential to combating trafficking of children is the co-operation between the legal systems, the government bodies and the non-government bodies around the globe. The passing of deterrent laws for the trafficker, as opposed to the victim is a step towards reducing the occurrence of trafficking in children, however one must bear in mind that the criminal mind will always find its ways to circumvent the laws passed.

Most societies are plagued by the malady of child trafficking, making it today a "global phenomenon" yet it remains somewhat "unknown". The exact magnitude of the offence is not represented in terms of data and statistics and the exact modes of perpetration are still oblivion. There is lack of awareness amongst citizens - possibly due to the chauvinism of state authorities to disclose ills that affect national dignity and recklessness. Co-operation amongst countries need to be fostered to counter this phenomenon, for instance by uniformity in penal provisions between countries which would be a welcome consideration to reciprocal enforcement of protection and prevention in trafficking which is mainly a "cross-border" crime. This uniformity can be achieved through ratification of international instruments and national implementation of these international humanitarian instruments relating to trafficking of children.

Since 1991, June 16 has been marked annually as the Day of the African Child. The date is a commemoration of the 1976 Soweto uprising when school children in Soweto, South Africa took to the streets protesting against the imposition of Afrikaans as the language of teaching, and against the inferior quality of their education. On that day hundreds of children and adults were killed and thousands more injured. In 1991 the Organization of African Unity, as the regional body was then called, earmarked the day to honour those who died as well as to draw attention to the lives of African children.

In year(2007), the theme of the Day of the African Child was child trafficking, a phenomenon that has scourged the continent in different forms. It is estimated that 17,500 children and young women are trafficked out of Kenya annually, while 1000 are trafficked each year from Mozambique to South Africa alone. Global trafficking is a USD 10 billion per annum industry, putting it at par with illegal trade in small arms and drugs.

CHILD TRAFFICKING IN AFRICA

Children are trafficked mainly for forced labour and sexual slavery. A number of children are kidnapped for these purposes. In conflict situations, such as in northern Uganda, girls are captured and forced to be soldiers, wives, domestic workers and porters. Where force is not used, traffickers lure children and young women with promises of marriage, education or jobs. Cases of kidnapping and other means of direct force however, form just a small percentage of the child trafficking cases in Africa; poverty is a major factor. If there was less poverty, there would likely be less trafficking. In many cases, the conduits of trafficking are parents themselves, whether or not they know that they are getting their children into exploitative conditions. The lure of money or jobs is just too great for many parents to resist or permit them to make the effort to investigate.

Children who are trafficked live and work in extremely exploitative conditions. They typically receive meagre or no pay, work long hours and are deprived of childhood rights to education and play. Many children who are trafficked at a young age know nothing else other than the situation they are in and would prefer to stay in their exploitative situations as they remember nothing of their home or family situation and have nothing else to fall back on. Legislative and policy measures to combat trafficking in Africa are weak, though improving. Celebrated child rights campaigner, Former First Lady of Mozambique Graca Machel has lent her voice to the clamour against the practice, urging for heavy penalties to be inflicted against traffickers.

The Economic Community for West African States (ECOWAS) has launched an awareness raising campaign aimed at combating trafficking. ECOWAS has 15 members, 11 of which have ratified international conventions against trafficking in persons, all of which have task forces to combat the practice and most of which have legislated against it. There has been an increase in the number of prosecutions and convictions for child trafficking and child sex tourism and in inter-governmental cooperation to address trafficking. However this is not enough and trafficking is on the increase. Poverty has been cited as one of the underlying factors in trafficking and without combating poverty it will be difficult to make inroads into eliminating the trade.

Children's Voice

Most African countries have ratified the Convention on the Rights of the Child, which articulates children's rights and expands democratic space for children. In most initiatives to address child rights issues, children are regar-ded as silent victims. During the Soweto uprising children demonstrated that they understand their rights, can articulate their own issues and are prepared to take a stand on them, sometimes even to the death. In the spirit of the Soweto uprising, the African Day of the Child should give a platform to children themselves to raise their voices and give an opportunity for older people to appreciate their perspective. A study on Ethiopian children's perspectives on violence against them revealed that children appreciated the inter-relation of violence and poverty and the need to have adequate legislative and policy measures entrenched. It also revealed that children have an appreciation not only of their rights, but also of their own responsibilities and roles in addressing violence against them. As the Day of the African Child is commemorated, it is important that the children of Africa are not only seen, but heard as well.

IN THE AFRICAN UNION

The use of religion, language, and political power, are a fundamental part in the perpetuation of slavery in the African Union. The process of enslvement is extremely abusive and the psychological violence especially is designed to produce docile captives. Neocolonialism and the international economic system play a vital role in African slavery, through the disruptions produced by lawless multinational corporations, through unfair terms of international trade, and through the general maginalization and exploitation of African society. In April 1996, UN Special Representative for the Sudan, Gaspar Biro, reported "an alarming increase...in cases of slavery, servitude, slave trade, and forced labor".

Allegations that a Nigerian-registered ship had left a Benin port carrying 200 child slaves bound for Gabon made international headlines and shocked the world in 2001, renewing calls for efforts to end child slavery. A joint statement released by the Benin government and United Nations Children's Fund (UNICEF) confirmed that indeed at least a dozen of the 43 children eventually found on the ship, the Etireno, were slaves (the whereabouts of the other 150 children alleged to have been on board remains a mystery), hinting at the existence of a modern-day slave trade between Benin (once known as the infamous "Slave Coast") and other West African nations. Thousands of children are bought and held captive to labour in Cocoa, or in palm nut plantations.

THE SUDAN

Estimates put the number of people who have been enslaved in Sudan at 200,000. In the Sudan, northern militias, armed and organised by the Government in Khartoum, come down from the north on horseback to loot, burn and abduct women and children to sell as slaves. In 1996 the SPLA charged that the Government of Sudan and its paramilitary auxiliary militias use slavery to destroy the Southerner dimension of Sudanese identity. The Sudanese government permits international monitors to travel into Sudan to observe the slavery activity. The Sudan government is at war with the SPLA and the SSMA. Regular Sudanese Army troops fight alongside auxilliary militias including the PDF. The Popular Defense Force is one of the institutions set up by Omar Beshir after his junta ousted an elected civilian government in June 1989, scrapped political parties and trade unions and established a radical Islamic regime. PDF recruits are sent to an advanced course in fighting techniques before being dispatched to zones in south Sudan to fight against the Sudan People's Liberation Army (SPLA). With regard to auxilliary militias, in 1996 Omar Beshir said the government was bent on military training in line with Islamic commands to ready and mobilize forces to "intimidate the foes of Allah".

A language of hyperbole characterises all belligerant forces in Africa, and leaders on all sides in Sudan are given to making extravagant claims. The government has previously boasted of divine support; armies of angels were said to fight side by side with the government forces. The flora and fauna of the south were declared government-friendly; trees shouting Allahu Akbar in unison; monkeys self-sacrificially treading on land mines and detonating them. It is unlikely that these things are true, however, many desparate villagers and soldiers appear to talk as if they believe these and other fantastic occurances (confirmed instances of soldiers abandoning posts because of ghosts and supernatural phenomenon are not uncommon).

Selective interpretation of this kind of language by religious activists and by the international media, as well as interpretation of the statements and accusations made by either side have reduced the war to appear as matter of religion and ethnic rivalry and have obscured critical ele-ments such as dire poverty, dictatorship, cultural isolation, multinational corporate interests, and neocolonial pressures from the West and from Asia as key factors in the per-petuation of the violence, human rights abuses, and community dislocation. These conditions have excerbated social failure and it is in this context that slavery must be understood.

Many observers are puzzled about US activists' sharp focus on Sudan when experts estimate that 17 million children worldwide are being "held in conditions amounting to slavery", and on the African continent, child-trafficking plagues not only the war-ravaged societies of Angola, Congo and Sudan, but also impoverished nations of West and Central Africa. Christian groups led by the Zurich-based Christian Solidarity International, have purchased the freedom of thousands of Sudanese slaves since 1995, paying an average of $50 per person. The CSI has bought and redemeed over 11,000 slaves. But critics ask whether buying slaves (even for the purpose of freeing them) perpetuates the slavetrading economy and wonder why Christian groups haven't brought the same efforts to bear in Angola, Congo and parts of West Africa, where many of the children bought and sold are also predominantly Christian.

On 8 July 1999, a UN agency accused a Christian human rights group of encouraging the slave trade in southern Sudan by handing over $100,000 (£64,000) to Arab traders to buy the freedom of more than 2,000 slaves. Julianna Lindsey, a spokeswoman for the United Nations Children's Fund Operation Lifeline Sudan, said that, while she appreciated the benefits to the individuals concerned, there were fears that paying money to redeem slaves would serve only to support the market. "The issue is the same whether it is 500 or 2,000 slaves", she said. "Money in southern Sudan is very attractive and the people involved in the trade will use that." Slave-Redemption trade has encouraged more trafficking." There are also reports that the well-meaning redeemers are frequently exploited by people posing as slaves, who have never been abducted - as well as by families willing to sell their children or other relatives to slave traders several times over, if necessary, for financial gain.

Life in slavery is one of appalling hardship and cruelty, where unpaid hard labour is often combined with physical and sexual abuse. The victims, mostly women and children are sold off far from their communities for as little as $15 each. Boys have been forcibly circumcised and girls subjected to ritual genital mutilation. The boys work as cattle herders or field hands in the plantations, the girls as domestic servants. Young African women reported stories of violence, rape and murder at the hands of their captors. "When one woman tried to escape, we were all beaten with axes and sticks", Ayak, an exslave, said. She was pregnant when she was abducted fromher village of Rianwei in The Sudan, and remained in slavery for 4 years. "I fell uncon-scious. When I woke my leg was paralysed and I was bleeding. Then I lost my baby". She still walks with a limp but is lucky in one way - she has heard that her husband is still alive and hopes that he will accept the young baby she has brought home with her, the product of rape by her captor. Amel has spent five years in captivity. She saw her husband die when they were captured, and had two of her three children taken from her when she arrived in the north. "I don't know what happened to them or if they are alive", she said. "When I asked my master about them, he would beat me". She too has a baby whose father was her captor.

and sexual abuse. The victims, mostly women and children are sold off far from their communities for as little as $15 each. Boys have been forcibly circumcised and girls subjected to ritual genital mutilation. The boys work as cattle herders or field hands in the plantations; the girls as domestic servants. Young African women reported stories of violence, rape and murder at the hands of their captors. "When one woman tried to escape, we were all beaten with axes and sticks," Ayak, an ex-slave, said. She was pregnant when she was captured from her village in Kiarwel in The Sudan and remained in slavery for 4 years. "I fell unconscious. When I woke my leg was paralysed and I was bleeding. Then I lost my baby." She still walks with a limp but is lucky in one way—she has heard that her husband is still alive and hopes that he will accept the young baby she has brought home with her, the product of rape by her captor. Amel has spent five years in captivity. She saw her husband die when they were captured, and had two of her three children taken from her when she arrived in the north. "I don't know what happened to them or if they are alive," she said. "When I asked my master about them, he would beat me." She too has a baby whose father was her captor.

5

Theological Reflection on Trafficking

Migration as a phenomenon occurs in nature where though individual and group boundaries exist do not however prevent crossing wide territories. In the animal world, seasonal or periodic movements take place in response to changes in climate, availability of food or to ensure reproduction. These range from microorganisms in freshwater lakes which migrate seasonally from deep to shallow water due to changes in temperature to whales, which move in autumn from the sub-polar to subtropical seas to have their young, then return in later spring to wider food-rich waters. For some animals and birds, it may take a lifetime to complete a round-trip or return migration. Species of pacific salmon born in freshwater streams, migrate to ocean waters, and then return to the stream where they were born to breed before dying. The Tanzania-Kenya animal migration is no different from the experiences of migrants across the world – the "river crossing", the "do and die points" and the predators that feed on them! The migration of large number of animals in Tanzania and Kenya have become big tourist attractions so much that it is described as a wonder of the world. How ironic? Human migration has also become a global wonder especially as one thinks of what humans do to fellows for labour, trade, profit and self-satisfaction and reenactment of the slavery stories.

The most dramatic moment is the migrating wildebeest

crossing Mara River. Wildebeests will amass in their thousands at banks of river Mara which is rife with the dreaded Nile crocodiles and raging currents. When the pressure from behind becomes unbearable the animals take the plunge into the river. Over a quarter of a million wilde-beest die from drowning, stampede, crocodiles and the predators every year. But even this annual carnage is not enough to reduce their numbers. The wildebeest deaths during migration are replenished with almost a double number of births in a year. The deaths during migration are now considered as a natural population check, natural selection at its best.

Migration in its various forms has been part of life from time immemorial. This will continue to be the case both within national boundaries and cross-continentally. There is hardly any ethnic group and race, which does not have a form of migration entailed in its origins and historical experience. We are either offspring of migrants, are involved in a kind of migration or are seeking one. We may even discover that we are beneficiaries of migration events or have become victims of it. Consciously, unconsciously or both, one can be on the promoting side of migration or be opposing it for varied reasons. In effect migration and issues surrounding it have become part of our lives, part and parcel of daily living locally and globally from which we cannot truly dissociate ourselves, be neutral, or become uncon-cerned on-lookers. Many of the causes and consequences of migration in times past can still be seen today, some of which have taken greater scope while new trends have also emerged. The pull and push factors of migration, its lights and shadows, the life it has enhanced and the death following it, its sinful manifestations and the grace that also becomes present in the midst of it, are all shared by both communities of crigin and destination.

The International Political Camp on Ecology and Politics: "Globalization and Local Experiences How to Avoid Sawing Through the Branch We Are Sitting On" which was immediately followed by the International Theological Camp on "On Word, Different Voices! Let's read the Bible Together (Genesis 1-11)". Delegates temporarily migrated from all continents of the world cutting across many nationalities to encounter each other as strangers, live together for a while, share experiences and search for possible alternatives and solutions to issues affecting the world in which they dwell. The world they all share in common. It ended with calls that having come together as strangers we should not return to our homes remaining strangers to one another. In other words we should be in solidarity with each other, as a newly discovered, created family. The point to note here is that the creation of forums, platforms and exposures which makes it possible for people of different nationalities to meet and interact in some meaningful way is a relevant panacea for making them more receptive to others. Crossing the numerous borders to encounter each other was by no means easy for some of us.

Meeting the requirements and processes for crossing the borders did not only take a lot of time–months–but was quite a struggle to organize and manage from both ends of the inviting center and the invitee. Howbeit I found the Italians I met to be very welcoming, right from the Visa Officer and his jokes, to the Prali community. A lady minister from Italy, however, pointed out that the reality on the ground was still a big challenge for the church and Italy in receiving and integrating migrants, even when they are "legal" migrants. Indicators to the struggle include separate church services for migrants and Italians within same church building or separate worship centers. While on one hand there seems to be some reservations in opening up to migrants from less developed nations, it has been in the interactions of Italy with the wider European Union Community that the standard of living of Italy on the one part has improved! This clearly shows that there are discriminatory migration preferences.

HUMANS OR THEIR RESOURCES

On another front, Nigerian crude petroleum for example, is explored, drilled and exported across borders easily into Europe and North America to service the insatiable developmental quest and affluent lifestyle. This is courtesy of multinational oil companies from Europe and America such as Royal Dutch Shell (British Dutch), Chevron (American), Exxan-Mobil (American), Agip (Italian) and Total (French) oil companies. 40% Nigerian crude exports go to United States of America accounting for 10% of its oil imports and ranks as the fifth largest source of its imported oil. Crude oil production by these multinational companies is carried out at a very high cost of environmental degradation and pollution resulting from oil spillage and bunkering in the Niger-Delta region of Nigeria. Meanwhile, thousands of Nigerians queue up daily for visas at the American, British and Italian Embassies in Lagos Nigeria, where most are turned away after gruesome, tedious, long, complicated, costly and very detailed procedures. The shadow of these failed migration attempts are the human trafficking of Nigerian women and girls to European (particularly Italy), American and some Asian destinations. The same can be said for many other nationalities.

WALLS AND TOWERS

Human migration, the movement of individuals and groups of people from one place to another, is inherent in the creation narrative. God blessed the male and female, He created to be fruitful, multiply and replenish the whole earth. God intended people to migrate in order to fill the earth. Following the flood, the families of the sons of Noah after their generations became nations. The major event, which led up to the tower of Babel project, was a mass movement of people of one language in search of a suitable dwelling place. They found a plain and decided to dwell there. The insecurities, unsettledness, vulnerabilities and uncertainties of a migrant life informed the idea to build a city, have a tower and make a name for themselves. The city would be walled which not only defined it's boundaries but also immediately secured those within it while at the same time kept away those outside of it. The tower would stand as a symbol of their power, enterprise and ingenuity.

The city would be named, well known, intimidating and domineering, a pointer to its sovereignty. The driving motive for all this was that "lest we be scattered abroad upon the face of the whole earth". The Babel enterprise was contrary to the purpose of God. It was anti-migration and also an anti-migrants solution, a self-protection and exclusion wall. It seems, therefore, that we have situations where the forces, motives, and reasons which cause people to migrate or give in to migration are same factors which make others to seek to prevent, limit or exploit migration. Since "lest we be scattered abroad upon the face of the whole earth" was at variance with "Be fruitful, and multiply, and replenish the earth..." God "babelled" them to keep them open to migration its consequences not withstanding. It is possible then that migration could both be desirous and at the same time feared, acceptable and rejected depending on what situation is prevailing or purpose it serves.

This, therefore, could form a point for our reflection to look at where we are on the issues surrounding mig-ration, our own understanding. What will we consider desirous and what fears do we have about migration.... the stranger in us which we seek to protect and the stranger we see in others we try to prevent? What stranger are we ready to become? What stranger do we fear to be? What makes us welcome or reject someone from another race? The basic question then will be how are our own basic desires and fears about migration different from that of the other? What common grounds do both of us share? Our Christian understanding leads us to know that "All people are born in the image of God" whether they have a skin that is pigmented white, black, brown or without any pigmentation. We all are fellow-creatures of God as Malachi 2:10 reminds us. "Have we not all one father? (Luke 13:34 pictures God as a mother also) hath not one God created us? Why do we deal treacherously every man against his brother...?" Leviticus 25:35 gives an even wider scope of who a brother or sister is, "And if thy brother be waxen poor, and fallen in decay with thee; then thou shalt relieve him yea though he be a stranger or a sojourner, that he may live with thee".

The creation itself is one whole collective. The responsibility for sustenance of the earth rests on every part of it and therefore everyone. What happens in one area of the globe affects the other. In a sense therefore we all have a common ownership of the earth. We all should then have common right to not only have access to it but also dwell in any part of it. This common individual or group right does not necessarily work against the right of sovereignty of nations .The Psalmist declares that the whole world and all in it, the beasts, forest and mountains belong to God, who bequeathed it to all. Every human being shares the same basic needs for existence food, shelter, clothing, safety and human dignity. Every person will take every necessary possible step to meet these necessities, which at times entails having to migrate to other lands. Though generally a person will not ordinarily want to leave his or her country for another if most of the essential needs are met, but other reasons do arise which could make one to migrate.

The Bible describes all human beings as pilgrims on earth. We are strangers on transit in the world. We are all temporary dwellers. No one had a choice in being born an African, American, European or Asian. We see how divine acts can be manifested in migration. The call of God required that Abraham and his household be migrants for most of his later life. In other words this instance of migration was an action initiated by God, an act of God Himself. As Christian students today, are there acts of God, which we can see in migration today? How can the divine and divine presence in migration affect the destinies of a people and of a world? "Even in the harsh stories of migration, God is present, revealing himself. Abraham stepped out in faith to respond to God's call. He and Sarah extended bounteous hospitality to three strangers who were actually a manifestation of the Lord, and this became a paradigm for response to strangers of Abraham's descendants.The grace of God even broke through situations of sin in the forced migration of the children of Jacob, Joseph, sold into slavery, eventually became the savior of his family- a type of Jesus, who, betrayed by a friend for thirty pieces of silver, saves the human family".

The salvation from famine, which came through Joseph,

went beyond his immediate family to save the Egyptian nation and those around it. The presence of the stranger impacted the whole nation. We can think of how the migrants have challenged and changed the way people think, act and live. The history of the chosen people in experiencing enslavement and subsequent liberation by God gave rise to laws regarding strangers. The people of Israel were not only to imitate God in the conduct to a stranger but were to draw from their experience in loving the neighbor as ones self. "For the Lord, your God, is the ...Lord of lords, the greater God, mighty and awesome, who has no favorite, accepts no bribes, who executes justice for the orphan and widow, and befriends the aliens, feeding and clothing him. So you, too, must befriend the alien, for you were once aliens yourselves in the land of Egypt".

These command-ments went beyond personal exhortations to being instituted within the laws for gleaning and tithing. In reaping the harvest of the land, which is a type of the wealth of the nation provision was to be made for the poor and the stranger. They were not to use up everything for themselves but actually allow the stronger to dine with them to satisfaction. The Lord Jesus Christ said the judgment of his followers would be based on the manner they responded and treated those in need, including, strangers. The Lord Jesus said, "...whatever you did for one of these least brothers of mine, you did for me". In the incarnation the Saviour came to his own but they knew him not. He was a stranger to them. Just like an alien Jesus left all that made him God to come to the world, to be sacrificed. The church today and as Christians we need to relive the experience of the disciples on the road to Emmaus. The risen Lord presented Himself as a stranger to his disciples. It was after they received Him as a stranger that their eyes were opened to His resurrection, which became their own resurrection, a newness of life and hope.

The Roman Catholic Church in the United States and Mexico recognized the following rights:

1. Persons have the right to find economic, political and social opportunities in their homeland to live in dignity

and achieve full life through the use of their God-given gifts with a just and living wage.

2. Persons have the right to migrate to support themselves and their families. All the goods of the earth belong to all people. It becomes necessary for sovereign nations to provide ways to accommodate this right.
3. Sovereign nations have the right to control their borders. This however should not merely be for the purpose of accumulation of more wealth. More power-ful economies have stronger obligation to accommodate migration flows, those who flee wars and persecution.
4. Refugees and asylum seekers should be afforded protection by the global community without incarceration.
5. Regardless of their legal status, migrants, like all persons, possess inherent human dignity that should be respected without punitive laws and hard treatment by enforcement agents..

TRAFFICKING

Trafficking in human beings is a modern-day form of slavery. The United States "Victims of Trafficking and Violence Protection Act of 2000" describes severe forms of human trafficking as "Sex Trafficking in which a com-mercial sex act is induced by force, fraud or coercion or in which the person induced to perform such act has not attained 18 years of age or the recruitment, harbouring, transportation, provision or obtaining of a person for labour or services through the use of force, fraud or coercion for the purpose of subjection to involuntary servitude, peonage, debt bondage, or slavery". David Ford (2007) in his comments on "The Theological Legacy of the Slave Trade" touched on the root cause of this modern-day slave trade when he wrote: "It is a harrowing realization to appreciate that the fundamental building blocks of the transatlantic slave trade remain virtually untouched by modern notions of equality and social justice. The drive for growth, cultural imperialism and control of the world's resources and wealth continue to be the primary motives in the economic and political policies of the world's leading, and (in terms of where power resides) white, industrialized nations.

Slavery, such as bonded labour and human trafficking, continues to exist today... not simply (as) evidence of humanity's continuing capacity for sin... (rather) the dominant political and economic ideas that underpin 21st century society in the west are precisely those albeit in a more benign form - that create the conditions in which these practices and structures can exist. Not only is equality not a reality, but also the value of some people and people is deliberately emphasized (and exploited) over that of other. The continuing distance between the reality of exclusion and invitation to equality in the sight of God is self-evident". Trafficking in human persons is a global phenomenon, which affects men, but especially women and children. Every year 700,000 to 2 million women and children are trafficked across national and international boundaries. A significant factor in human trafficking is the economic gain. It is observed that trafficking of adult and young women reaps greater economic gain than drugs! It is the third largest source of profit for international organized crime, after drugs and arms, mounting to billions of dollars annually.

Cultural influences also play a role in the trade of human beings. Cultural perceptions of women and discriminatory views of prostitution involving men as against women might affect ones disposition or concern for women who are involved in prostitution who became victims of trafficking. Another contributory factor to human trafficking is the manner in which the media, commercialism and marketing projects manipulate the image and role of women. "We live in a culture, which thrives on a high level of con-sumption and convenience, often without awareness of or concern for how that level is achieved or maintained. We don't often stop to consider the migrant field labor or sweatshop factory labor at huge department stores or shopping centers".

The questions then to consider will be how our participation in a consumer culture relates to the exploitation of workers and the use of people as commodities for our enjoyment or convenience. In addition to the economic status and states of poverty, low status of women, which underline human trafficking, other factors are the strong international criminal networks. The trafficking of both girls and boys, almost always involves to some extent deception, or agreement between adults, including at times parents and relations! Girls between the age of 13 and 18 constitute the largest group (with estimates of 500,000 girls below 18) within the sex industry. Virtually every country in the world is affected, whether economically developing or developed from the north or south. The majority of those trafficked are women under the age of 25. The fear of contacting HIV/AIDS by sex clients and the erroneous thought that young girls are not infected have led traffickers to recruit younger victims, even as young as under 10. It is estimated that about 1 million women and girls of various nationalities are trafficked into Thailand, with 20,000 to 30,000 women and girls from Myanmar (Burma) trafficked into brothels in Thailand while 5000-7000 Nepal girls get trafficked into India every year.

We yet recall how the dreams of Joseph became a source jealousy, fear and hatred by his brothers. They sold him in a foreign land to "see what would become of his dreams". His dreams made him vulnerable. Portiphar's wife harassed him sexually and falsely accused him. He did not get a fair trial and was thrown into prison. In prison Pharaoh's chief butler forgot him after making use of his gift. We can see a parallel in the actions of Joseph's brothers, the Ishmaelite traders and Portiphar's wife in what happens in human trafficking today. One also notes the abuse of power in handling the case of a domestic servant. However, Joseph's faith and knowledge of God, his moral values and sense of self-dignity in labor together with the gift of interpreting dreams became a tool with which God intervened to effect liberation. We also note how most people in the story used Joseph for their own ends his brothers, the merchants, Portiphar and his wife, the prison guard and Pharaoh's officers, including Pharaoh himself.

No one was thinking of protecting Joseph's dreams and

interests. Joseph however knew that God had not forsaken him. He felt the presence of God. The recognition of Joseph's industry and gift only brought him more work but which also brought elevations to higher positions of responsibility. We also read about the Pharaoh and his generations, which did not know Joseph and how they began to put the people of Israel into forced labour. This is similar to many who benefit from the sweats, deprivation, exploitation and sufferings of forced migrants and forced labour, and turn against them still. The experience of Tamar, king David's daughter, is an example of the way young girls are forced unto sex, through deception, collusion, force and indifference. Amnon, David's first son lusted after his cousin a virgin Tamar. With the collaboration of subtle Jonadab, Tamar was lured and deceived into believing that she was going to care for a sick brother.

The unexpected was the case. Amnon being stronger than her forced her and raped her, in spite of her pleas. Amnon throws Tamar out who goes on the street wailing. The father of Tamar, the king gets angry but does nothing to punish Amnon, or about Tamar's situation. "So Tamar remained desolate in her brother Absolom's house". After two years of concealing his hatred, Absolom, kills Amnon in revenge yet Tamar is left ostracized and her condition unchanged. Those whom Tamar felt safe with and trusted the most gave in to her forced defilement. Jonadab exploited the innocence of Tamar to satisfy the selfish desire of Amnon. When Tamar is defiled nobody cared about giving her justice or rehabilitation. The societal stigma left her desolate for life. We see the providential acts of God to prevent the destruction of forced migrants, as with Queen Esther and her people in Shusan and also Daniel, his colleagues and the worship of the god of the land.

Migration is in a sense a demand for equity. Migrants represent a physical presence asking for a piece of the cake belonging to all. The presence of migrants often reveals the level of human selfishness and self-centeredness. God would allow migration to reorder and reposition the world. It becomes the correct interpretation of the dreams of kings of the nations, just like that of Pharaoh, which differs from the advice of the astrologers representing today's experts on safeguarding the national well-being. What challenges does migration and human trafficking hold for a Christian student group? The challenge of building a community of young people and students from all nations:

- When conferences and assemblies occur-creating actual interaction and building relationships and friendships which would reduce the bias toward strangers.
- Creating other platforms of interaction and communication like internet discussion groups which cuts across human and territorial boundaries.
- Group exchange programmes beyond continental spheres.

The challenge of discovering and examining where we are in relating to strangers and people looked down upon then take deliberate actions to get closer to a "stranger". We are actually brought up not to talk to the stranger! The challenge of creating awareness and education among students and family circles on issues of trafficking, forced prostitution, and sexual exploitation. The challenge of seeking out trafficked persons and becoming "dog sniffers" within our neighbourhood.

Personal and Group Reflection Points

(a.) Jesus makes a whip of cords and drives out those who exhibited lack of respect for the temple.

(b.) Though the situation was overwhelming, Jesus found a way to respond (John 2:13-22). What are our feelings towards the lack of respect shown to women trafficked around the world, together with young men under servitude? What responses will be appropriate?

(c.) On the Sabbath, Jesus calls over a woman crippled by a spirit for eighteen years; touching her, He said "women, you are set free from your ailment" (Luke 13:10-13) What "spirits" or forces contribute to crip-pling women and men who are trafficked today? What "spirits" cripple us? What would help free those trafficked? What would help free us to respond? How can we suffer with them, bear their shame, exploitation and fear? How can we touch them?

(d.) Can SCM offices become distress call centers? How can we support groups and networks focusing specially on migration and human trafficking? How can we even symbolically, support, stand by or accompany a victim of human-trafficking or stranded "legal"/"illegal" migrant? How can we engage in a programme of recovery, repatriation and integration at the student level?

PROSTITUTION ISSUES AND TRENDS

Prostitution is one of the oldest professions of the world practiced since the birth of the organized society. Prostitution is practiced in almost all the countries and every type of society. In India, the Vedas, the earliest of the known Indian literature, abound in references to prostitution as an organized and established institution. In Indian mytho-logy there are many references of high-class prostitution in the form of celestial demigods acting as prostitutes. They are referred to as *Menaka, Rambha, Urvashi, and Thilo-thamma.* They are described as perfect embodiments and unsurpassed beauty and feminine charms. They are highly accomplished in music and dance. They entertained divinities and their guests in the court of Lord *Indira,* the Lord of Hindu Gods. They were also sent to test the real depth of 'tapasya' (penance) and devotion of great saints.

An apsara named Menaka caused the downfall of the great sage *Vishwamithra* and became the mother of *Shakuntala,* the immortal heroine of the greatest drama of the world, *Abhigyan Shakuntalam* written by the great poet *Kalidas* of India. Aryan rulers of India followed the system of celestial court and developed the system of guest prostitution. They presented well-accomplished maidens in token of friendship of kings. They were also offered as ransom to the victor to part with his most beloved prostitute. Empires fell and came up for her sake. Another class of girls from infancy were carefully selected and fed on poisonous herbs and venomous foods. They were called Vishkanyas (Poisonous virgins). The kings to destroy their enemies utilized these prostitutes.

Prostitutes were common during the reign of the Pandavas and Kauravas (Historical Indian rulers). They were an important part of the court and both dynasties possessed harems of aristocracy in Brahmanic India. Having concubines is common among the aristocracy. Kautilya's famous 'Arthasasthra' contains rules for prostitutes and their activities and gives an account of how prostitutes should behave and how their lives are ordered. A code of conduct was prescribed, for people seeking their favor and for them. They had certain definite prerogatives, rights and duties. Vatsyayan, the noted Indian sage of the Third century B.C. devoted a number of pages on prostitutes and their amorous ways of life in his monumental treatise Kamasutra. Rules of conduct for popular and successful practice of their trade have been prescribed. His classification of the prostitutes indicates that the common, private and the clandestine prostitutes of today had their prototypes in those olden days.

The sanctified prostitution in the third century A.D. in the Sanskrit works of Mahakavi Kalidas. Religious prostitutes were attached to the famous temples of Mahakala of Ujjain and the system of holy prostitutes became common. This class consisted of girls who had been offered by the parents to the service of the God and their religion. In the south India, they are known as Devadasi and in North India as Mukhies. These dancing girls were considered essential at the time of offering of prayers and were given a place of honor. Gradually due to the laxity of morals among the priests, they misused the systems for immoral purposes. Under the garb of religious dedication of girls to temples, clandestine prostitution developed. The medieval period gave great importance to women and wine.

The Muslim rulers with the exception of Aurangazeb recognized prostitution and the profession flourished under royal patronage. After the downfall of the Mughal Empire, hoards of concubines, dancing and singing girls women came out of the royal palaces. They were not trained for any profession and society had no jobs to offer them. When faced with economic problem they had no choice but to take recourse to the laziest of all the trades, the trade of sex. The place of women in India did not improve during the British regime. Conditions continued to deteriorate and in the absence of state control and regulation, prostitution thrived on a large commercial scale. Social disabilities and economic hardships of women made them an easy victim to the gangsters of this profession.

This shows that prostitution existed in India in some form or the other from time period to period but the evil has continued to persist. Today prostitution exists in almost every big city of the country. Women from third world countries are given allurement to work in India, as waitresses, models, artists and cabaret performers which subsequently lead to their exploitation by the flesh traders. Besides there are "high class call girls" who are engaged on lucrative jobs and yet return to these vice activities during nights in every discrete manner. If the traditional brothels or red light areas are on the wane, the evil of prostitution has manifested itself in posh localities of Metropolitan cities in the guise of singing and dancing schools. Prostitution in India can therefore be called as an "Ancient Vice in Modern Garb". The current laws in India that legislate sex workers are fairly ambiguous. It is a system where prostitution is legally allowed to thrive, but which attempts to hide it from the public.

THE IMMORAL TRAFFIC (SUPPRESSION) ACT (SITA)

According to this law, sex work in India is neither legal nor illegal; it is tolerated since prostitutes can practice their trade privately but cannot legally solicit customers in public. In particular, the law forbids a sex worker to carry on her profession within 200 yards of a public place. Unlike as is the case with other professions, however, sex workers are not protected under normal workers laws and are not entitled to minimum wage benefits, compensation for in-jury or other benefits that are common in other types of work. They do, however, possess the right to rescue and rehabilitation if they desire and possess all the rights of other citizens. In practice this is not common. Recently the old law has been amended as The Immoral Traffic (Prevention) Act or PITA. The Indian Penal Code (IPC) which predates the SITA is often used to charge sex workers with vague crimes such as "public indecency" or being a "public nui-sance" without explicitly defining what these consist of.

Sections 366A and 366B of Indian Penal Code, are intended to punish the export and import of girls for prostitution. Section 366A deals with procuring minor girls from one part of India to another. Section 366B makes it an offence to import into India from any country outside India girls below the age of twenty-one (21) years for the purpose of prostitution. Section 5, of the Immoral Traffic Prevention Act, 1986 defines procuring, inducing or taking persons for the purpose of prostitution. Section 6 of the Immoral Traffic Prevention Act, 1986 provides punishment not less than seven years for detaining a person in premises where prostitution is carried out. A survey of prostituted women in India reveals their reasoning for staying in prostitution (in descending order of significance): poverty/ unemployment; lack of proper reintegration services, lack of options; stigma and adverse social attitudes; family expectations and pressure; resignation and acclimation to the lifestyle. Most of the research done by Sanlaap (an NGO) indicates that the majority of sex workers in India work as prostitutes due to lacking resources to support themselves or their children. Most do not choose this profession out of preference, but out of necessity, often after the breakup of a marriage or after being disowned and thrown out of their homes by their families. The children of sex workers are much more likely to get involved in this kind of work as well.

One of India's most striking characteristics is its material poverty. An estimated 40% of India's population lives in poverty. This means that almost 400 million people cannot meet basic survival needs like food, clothing and shelter. This is an overwhelming, almost unimaginable statistic. Poverty does not create imbalances in gender and sex. It only aggravates already existing imbalances in power and therefore increases the vulnerability of those who are at the receiving end of gender prejudice. In a patriarchal set up, the section in families in societies that is affected is women and girl children. Caste wars, political strife, domestic conflicts through their manifestations and repercussions reflect strong gender prejudice against women.

Violence against women, assault and rape on women are not individual sexual or physical crimes. It has become a tool of a political statement for aggression and gender persecution, which amply reflects on the degree of human degradation and commoditization of women in the eyes of the state, community and society. Indeed, such poverty belongs to an almost surreal world in which only the "wealthy" are certain to meet basic needs. Desperation seems to characterize the lives of India's poor. This desperate poverty is often cited as the root of India's growing prostitution problem. In some cases, a woman may prostitute herself in order to obtain material possessions she could not otherwise afford. While fundamental needs like food, clothing and shelter may be provided, some girls pursue dreams of greater prosperity and economic opportunity through prostitution.

A review of Prostitution in India would be incomplete if it not refers to the special class of women known as devadasis. For centuries the devadasis or dancing girls serving in temples were taught music and dancing with all wealth of detailed technique. As they were hereditary employees of the temples, they enjoyed economic security. Further, they had an advantage of receiving training under technically competent traditional teachers. Unfortunately the system deteriorated and devadasis came to be increasingly identified with prostitution. The Devadasi system has a significant place in the history of prostitution in India. The term Devadasi literally means servants (slaves) of God and perhaps originally denoted a class of women who gave themselves to a life of religious service and austerities. These devadasis who were not supposed enter the bond of matrimony often functioned as temple singers, dancers, concubines and prostitutes. The term Devadasi became a euphemistic way of referring to women prostituting in the name of religion.

The Devadasi system was set up, according to a Times of India report (10-11-1987) as a result of a conspiracy between the feudal class and the priests. The latter, with their ideological and religious hold over the peasants and craftsmen, devised a means that gave prostitution their religious sanction. Poor, low-caste girls, initially sold at private auctions, were later dedicated to the temples. They were then initiated into prostitution. A Times of India report (10-11-1987) confirms that the practice of dedicating young dalit girls at childhood to a goddess, and their initiation into prostitution when they attain puberty continues to thrives in Karnataka, Andhra Pradesh and other parts of South India. This is largely due to social backwardness, poverty and illiteracy, according to a study by two doctors of the India Health Organization.They noted in their study on -"Devadasis - the link between religious culture and child prostitution".

The study revealed that girls from poor families are married to God Krishna and are sold after puberty at private auctions to a high caste master who initially pays a sum of money to the families ranging from Indian Rupees 500/- to 5,000/-.The study, made during health camps organized by the World Health Organization (WHO) in the Devadasi populated areas, revealed that the dedicated girls formed 15 percent of the total women involved in prostitution in the country, and as much as 70 percent to 80 percent of the prostitutes in the border districts of Karnataka and Maharashtra. The devadasi tradition, still prevalent in many parts of India, continues to legitimize child prostitution.

A devadasi is a woman married to a god and thus sadasuhagan or married, and hence at all times blessed. As such, she becomes the wife of the powerful in the community. Devadasi is known by different names in different states. In the Bijapur district of Karnataka, girls are given to the Monkey God (Hanuman, Maruti), and known as Basvi. In Goa, a devadasi is called Bhavin (the one with devotion). In the Shimoga District of Karnataka, the girls are handed over to the goddess Renuka Devi, and in Hospet, to the goddess Hulganga Devi. The tradition lives on in other states in South

India. Girls end up as prostitutes in Bombay and Pune. The Banchara and Bedia peoples of Madhya Pradesh also practice "traditional" prostitution.

The view of women as a commodity is pervasive in popular manifestations of Hindustan culture in India. Women who have had sexual experiences are considered to be 'used goods' and are unlikely to ever marry. Without a husband, a woman has no source of income; she also cannot wear the marriage bindi. She is an impoverished cultural outcast. The prevailing line of reasoning is that she at least has a useful place as a prostitute. Women who have been widowed or divorced are also confronted with this social stigma. If a woman's husband dies, she has essentially outlived her purpose. Since she is not a virgin, she obviously cannot marry again. In rural areas, "bride burnings", in which a woman burns herself to death on her husband's funeral pyre, still occur. The social stigma, which leads a woman to believe that her life is worthless after her hus-band's death, is also attached to a woman whose husband chooses a different woman as his wife.

When strong cultural notions are combined with the potency of religion or poverty, even more people are pressured into prostitution. For example, a girl may become a street child because her mother died and her father's new spouse will not accept her. As a street child, she may be periodically arrested along with her fellow vagabonds for crimes, which they may or may not have committed. While in police custody, instead of simply being beaten as her male cohorts are, she may be sexually abused by the police officers. She may decide to become a prostitute to support herself and to find her place in the broken world in which she is fated to reside. Her children will likely be prostitutes as well.

India is a receiving, sending, and transit country for prostitution. Due to its geographical proximity to Nepal and Bangladesh as well as Pakistan, all of which are economically less developed than India, the constant illegal movement of people is a perpetual phenomenon. Every day, about 200 girls and women in India enter prostitution, 80% of them against their will. Prostitution is widely rampant in India and its main markets are in the big cities. The statistics available on the number of prostitutes operating in the country is not exact because there is so much of clandestine prostitution, in spite of such undetected prostitution the situation is horrifying. A very accurate, comprehensive picture of prostitution in India is not available since sexual exploitation and sale of women and children are mostly unreported crimes; since many cruel episodes are caused by middlemen and procurers who act secretly and in a very organized, criminal manner. However, some intensive project studies and research work reveal following facts: According to a recent publication on trafficking, there are about 2.3 million prostitutes in India. This data may seem to be on the higher side but authentic data of a survey of Bombay (Mumbai) city alone indicates an alarming figure of more than 0.1 million prostitutes in its 12000 brothels. Approximately 20% women in prostitution are under 18. A sample survey of 12 states and 2 union territories reveals that women who are sexually exploited and sold are usually children (under 18 years) at the time of their initial exploitation or abduction.

A survey by the Ministry of Human Resource and Development reveal that only 4.9 % of the prostitutes in Calcutta are born within the city. More than 70 districts supply prostitutes to Delhi. The survey also revealed that two third of the original families of prostitutes lived below the poverty line and 60 % of the prostitutes covered in the survey belonged to Scheduled Castes or Scheduled Tribes or Backward Classes. A study of 12 states and 2 union territories reveals that the majority of rural girls are forced to take up prostitution. One can conceptually see that these prostitutes are mainly from two groups. They have no education and belong to the lower income group or they belong to castes, which are lowly placed - they come from a backward community with little education.

Prostitution is increasing in India where there have been fears over the spread of AIDS and reports of young girls being abducted and forced into prostitution. It takes up to fifteen years for girls held in prostitution via debt-bondage to purchase their freedom. Children of prostituted women are victims of sexual abuse as well. Children are forced to perform dances and songs for male buyers, and some are forced to sexually service the males. There are three routes into prostitution for most women in India. (1) Deception; (2) Devadasi dedication and (3) Bad marriages or families. For some women their marriages were so violent they preferred prostitution. Husbands or families introduced some women to prostitution. Many families knew what the women had to do, but ignored it as long as they got the benefits from it.

Karnataka, Andhra Pradesh, Maharashtra, Tamil, Nadu and Uttar Pradesh are the high-supply zones for women in prostitution. Belgaum, Bijapur and Kolhapur are some common districts from which women migrate to cities either through an organized trafficking network or due to socioeconomic forces. Bangalore is one of the five major cities in India which together account for 80 percent of child prostitutes in the country. 90% of the 100,000 women in prostitution in Bombay are indentured slaves. In West India, Mumbai leads in prostitution. There are more than 100,000 women in prostitution in Bombay, Asia's largest sex industry center. The red light district in Bombay generates at least $400 million a year in revenue, with 100,000 prosti-tutes servicing men 365 days a year, averaging 6 customers a day, at $2 each. In Bombay, on average the girls are bought by six men a day, who pay US$1.10 - 2 per sex act, the madam gets the money up front. To pay for movies, clothes, make-up and extra food to supplement a diet of rice and dal, the girls have to borrow from moneylenders at an interest rate of up to 500%. They are perpetually in debt.

The largest red light district in India, perhaps in the world, is the Falkland Road Kamatipura area of Bombay (film, "The Selling of Innocents" 1997). In Kamatipura, brothel district in Bombay three men a day buy more than 70,000 prostituted women and girls. Condoms are seldom used. Escape is rare. 60% of commercial sex workers in Bombay's red-light district areas are infected with STDs and AIDS (CATW - Asia Pacific,

Trafficking in Women and Prostitution in the Asia Pacific). More than half of Bombay's 100,000 prostitutes are infected with HIV. A magazine publisher in Bombay said AIDS would benefit the country because it will depopulate the vast underclass. In 1991, Bombay's 100,000 prostituted women averaged 600,000 sexual contacts a day. At the time 30% were HIV positive, the chance of transmission was 0.1%. On that basis, 200 clients were being infected with HIV everyday, 6,000 each month. After Mumbai police raided Kamatipura, 160 women were sent to the St Catherines Rescue Home. Many women were HIV positive and a large number were pregnant or already had children.

Eunuch Lane in Bombay has more than 2,000 eunuchs in prostitution. The eunuchs, or hijras, have deep religious roots in Hinduism. As young boys they are abandoned or sold by their families to a sex ring and taken into the jungle, where a priest cuts off their genitals in a ceremony called nirvana. The priest then folds back a strip of flesh to create an artificial vagina. Eunuchs are generally more available to perform high-risk sex than female prostitutes, and some Indian men believe they can't contact HIV from them. In West India after Mumbai, Goa leads in prostitution, especially child prostitution. At least 2,000 women are in prostitution along the Baina beachfront in Goa. The main frequenters of prostitutes in Goa are tourists, local men and college boys. United States "seamen" ask locals in Goa which bars to find prostitutes in. Taxi drivers take tourists from Delhi, Gujarat, Bangalore, Bombay and Punjab to brothels in Baina. Some men have taxi drivers bring prostituted girls from Baina back to their hotels in Panjim. The next morning, the taxi drivers rape the girls before taking them home. In Goa, there are at least 400 children in prostitution. After Ms. Mohini Giri, chair of the National Commission for women, visited and declared there to be rampant child prostitution in the area, police have conducted some raids in order to find prostituted children. Although police conduct raids, brothels receive tip-offs and hide the minors before raids are conducted.

In South India, Andhra Pradesh, leads in prostitution. There are many dhabhas, or small-scale brothels, along the

Solapur-Hyderabad highway, which provide women as an "additional service" to truck drivers and motorists. The women and girls in the dhabhas, or brothels, along the Solapur-Hyderabad highway, are threatened, harassed, forced to service, freely and beaten by men and police. Local farmers abuse them also. Police do not register any complaints of assault. In one cases, a woman who was running over unfamiliar fields to escape the police in pitch darkness; she stumbled into a well and was killed. Sometimes, bodies of women are found on the fields, half eaten by animals. Another woman had her ears cut off, was robbed and left unconscious on the road. In Chennai, Tamil Nadu, an ethnographic study to map the areas of prostitution was done to streamline strategies for HIV prevention among commercial sex workers (CSWs) in the city. Mobile brothels manned by cell-phone toting operators are proving to be a hit in Chennai, according to the study.

For those in the trade, running a mobile unit makes sound business sense as it cuts down on operational costs of renting a building and bribing the cops. As for the client, it promises 'pick and drop' facility of sex workers at a place of his choice. More than 17 mobile units operate from cars in the city, according to Chennai-based NGO Indian Community Welfare Organization (ICWO), which works with Commercial Sex Workers (CSWs). The ICWO estimates the volume of sex business in the city at Rs. 3.33 crore per month in its study. According to the study, there are 6,300 women sex workers operating from all over the city, around the year. The sex workers have been broadly classified as family girl, street worker, brothel based, and mobile. Family girls form the majority of the lot, numbering 4500. There are 350 street workers and 90 mobile workers, according to the study.

It was found that 55 percent of the sex workers came from Andhra Pradesh, 24 percent from Tamil Nadu and 11 percent from Kerala. The study identified 150 full time brokers and an estimated 4500 part time brokers. It has been found that clients are serviced at 'normal houses', besides brothels, hotels and lodges. These houses are used for short-term stay and rent is paid for the hours used. At least 91 such houses exist in the city. According to the study, an estimated 11,111 paid sexual encounters take place in the city. It was found that 93 percent of the CSWs were into the trade out of compulsions and not out of choice. 78 percent of the respondents said they would not allow their children to enter the profession. It was found that 68 percent of the respondents used condoms regularly during sex. The 32 percent who did not use condoms on a regular basis gave different reasons for not using them. Thirty percent said they couldn't use condoms with regular clients. Another 30 percent said they would forget to wear it at times and 10 percent felt that condom usage would prolong sexual activity. Another 10 percent said some clients would object to it. About 20 percent said they knew better techniques to avoid infection.

As for reasons why they chose to be sex workers, 31 percent respondents said they entered the profession due to family debts and 29 percent said their husbands deserted them. About 29 percent said their lovers had ditched them. Clients were asked why they visited sex workers. 21 percent said their wives had health problems. At least 17 percent said they came for oral sex and 10 percent said their wives were not interested in sex. Seven percent said they had grown up children at home and six percent said their wives refused to have sex with them. Eleven percent came for a change, for 22 percent it had become a regular practice and for six percent, sex was a passion. The objective of the study was to map areas in the city where commercial sex workers operated and to "understand the sex industry" in Chennai.

The Tamil Nadu State AIDS Control Society supported the study with the intention of using the information to frame suitable strategy for HIV/AIDS intervention programs. About 43 percent of the sex workers who were interviewed for the survey were in the 26-35 age group. 26 percent was in the 19-25 age group. About 20 percent was in the 36-40 age group and 10 percent was in the above-40 age group. The team interviewed 300 women sex workers. Among the 300, 180 belonged to the family category, 80 street workers, 30 brothel based, and 10 from the mobile units. Twenty pimps, 20 lodge/house owners, and 20 hotel room boys were also interviewed.

In India, despite the many laws against the sex industry and traditional caste-bound prostitution, prostitution and trafficking is still common. However, Indian laws are little ambiguous when it comes to the issue of defining prostitution. The sale of one's own bodily sex to a male customer by an adult woman on her own free will in her private premises in not illegal and hence not punishable as per the Indian laws. At the same time, Indian law does not give a special recognition by way of registration, documentation or license for the sale of one's own bodily sex to a male customer in her private premises or in public premises on her own free will. Organized prostitution is illegal in India. The text and spirit of the existing law does not allow anyone (*e.g.* the anti social elements) to take disadvantage of the helplessness and vulnerability of a woman and therefore it makes brothel keeping, procuration of person for prostitution, living on earning of other person's prostitution, giving ones premises for the business of prostitution, detaining anyone in brothel etc illegal and punishable. There are two views in India regarding of prostitution. One view is to further criminalize it and other to totally decriminalize it.

We are of the view, that a total eradication of prostitution is impossible. It is time to repeal laws used to punish prostitutes in seeking to protect public decency and order. Legalizing prostitution is one solution, though not a panacea. "Legalized" prostitution refers to a wide range of situations. It can simply mean that prostitution is not against the law. More often the case, though, legalization is synonymous for regulation, with laws enforced by police. Licenses can be issued, for example, with mandatory health-checks. Zoning laws may set up "prostitution centres" should be removed from residential areas. Total prostitution elimi-nation would require restructuring social setup, which would give greater sexual freedom to men and women in which women's identity is respected as a human being. Education and economic independence of women will counter their vulnerability and lead to the recognition and respect of women's dignity as that of a human being.

6

Issues and Framework of Laws in Trafficking

Trafficking of human beings is the recruitment, transportation, transfer, harboring or receipt of people for the purpose of exploitation. Trafficking involves a process of using illicit means such as threat or use of force or other forms of coercion, of abduction, of fraud, of deception, of the abuse of power or of a position of vulnerability. Exploitation includes forcing people into prostitution or other forms of sexual exploitation, forced labour or services, slavery or practices similar to slavery, servitude or the removal of organs. For children exploitation may include also, illicit international adoption, trafficking for early marriage, and recruitment as child soldiers, for begging or for sports (such as child camel jockeys or football players). Trafficking in human beings is a global issue, but a lack of systematic research means that reliable data on the trafficking of human beings that would allow comparative analyses and the design of countermeasures is scarce. There is a need to strengthen the criminal justice response to trafficking through legislative reform, awareness raising and training, as well as through national and international cooperation.

The support and protection of victims who give evi-dence is key to prosecuting the ringleaders behind the phenomenon. The trafficking of Human beings is a matter of global concern as it involves the violation of fundamental rights. Although numerous separate abuses that contravene both national and international law are committed during the course of trafficking, it is the combination of the victim's displacement from their community and their commer-cialised exploitation that makes trafficking distinct. There is a large body of international and national instruments like declarations, conventions and prohibiting trafficking. An overview of selected International conventions that regulate trafficking is presented below.

The United Nations obligates States to refrain from committing human rights violations and also to take positive steps to ensure that individuals are able to enjoy their human rights. A State's legal obligations are articulated in human rights instruments, such as treaties and conventions. The UN also drafts politically binding documents that do not have the force of law, such as declarations and resolutions, but which nevertheless represent important guidelines on States' obligations. More information about the United Nations system, human rights documents and enforcement mechanisms can be accessed from the International Law section of this site. The United Nations addresses trafficking in women from various directions. First, the UN human rights instruments apply to women and men equally and are relevant to the kinds of abuses that women suffer in cases of trafficking. In addition, the UN international standards on the treatment of crime victims also obligate States to protect victims of trafficking. Second, of the types of violence against women addressed by this site, trafficking in women was perhaps the first to receive the attention of the UN as a transnational crime. This section, therefore, includes a historical overview of the UN conceptualization of trafficking, prior to the emergence of an international women's human rights movement.

Third, the UN treaties and resolutions that articulate the rights of women are applicable to the situation of trafficking and define trafficking as a form of gender-based violence. Since the early 1990's, all major UN instruments on States' commitment to ensure women the full enjoyment of their human rights and their protection from violence have included specific obligations to combat trafficking in women. Fourth, the UN Convention Against Transnational Organized Crime entered into force in September 2003. The accompanying Protocol to Prevent, Suppress and Punish Trafficking in Persons, Especially Women and Children received its 40th ratification in September 2003 and entered into force on December 25, 2003. The Trafficking Protocol contains the international consensus definition of trafficking and sets forth State obligations to prevent trafficking, to protect victims and to prosecute perpetrators of trafficking.

Finally, at its 60th session in April of 2004 the United Nations Commission on Human Rights appointed a Special Rapporteur on Trafficking in Persons, specially Women and Children for the explicit purpose of focusing on the human rights of victims of trafficking. To do so, the rapporteur's job is to gather and exchange information from governments, non-governmental organizations and victims of trafficking in order to propose appropriate measures to prevent and remedy trafficking violations. Working within the major international instruments and definitions of trafficking, the Special Rapporteur will conduct country visits, publish reports and take up cases where individual or widespread rights abuses have occurred. States are obligated to protect the rights of trafficking victims under general human rights instruments. The International Covenant on Civil and Political Rights guarantees women the right to life, the right to be free from torture and cruel, inhuman or degrading treatment, and the right to security of person. This Covenant also grants trafficked persons the right to an effective remedy for acts violating their fundamental human rights.

The International Covenant on Economic, Social and Cultural Rights provides such basic guarantees as the right to an adequate standard of living (including food, clothing and housing), the right to the highest attainable standard of physical and mental health, the right to education and the right to favorable work conditions, which includes fair wages, equal pay for equal work and reasonable limitation of working hours.

- International Agreement for the suppression of the white slave traffic - 1904. The agreement was formu-lated with the intension of securing for women of full age who have suffered abuse or compulsion against criminal traffic know as the white slave trade.
- International convention does the suppression of the white slave Traffic 1910. This convention criminalised the procurement enticement or leading away of women or girl under the age of 21, even with her consent for immoral purpose irrespective of whether may have been committed in different countries.
- Slavery convention 1926. States parties are enjoyed to discourage all forms of forced labour slavery means the owner's control over another person, without the salve's full informed consent for exploitation.
- Forced Labour Convention (ILO) 1930. Article-1 of this convention calls for the suppression of the use of forced or compulsory labour in all its forms as soon as possible.
- Universal Declaration of Human Rights (1948). Article 4 of the Declaration prohibits slavery and the slave trade. Article - 13 recognise the right of persons

  Unconventional for the suppression of the traffic in persons and of the exploitation of the prostitution of others (1949).

This convention is a compilation of four previous international conventions 1904, 1910, 1921 and 1933. It made procurement, enticement, etc for prostitution punish-able, irrespective of the age of the person involved and his/her consent to the same (Article -1). Brothel keeping was also denounced as illegal and punishable Article 20. However, it is limited to trafficking for prostitution and related activities.

- Abolition of forced Labour convention (ILO) 1957. Under this convention, states parties under took to abolish any form of forced or compulsory labour that is used as a means to establish political coercion, economic development, labour discipline or racial, social, National or religious discrimination.

- United Nations convention against Torture and other cruel; inhuman or degrading treatment or punishment (1984). The convention provides against the expulsion or return of a person another state if there are substantial grounds for deeming him/her to be in danger of torture. Victim compensation measures are also stipulate in it.
- Tourism Bill of rights and the Tourist code (1985). Adopted by the WTO, the code enjoins that state parties should preclude any possibility of the use of tourism to exploit others for the purpose of prostitution.

IN SOUTH ASIAN COUNTRIES

BANGLADESH

The Bangladesh constitution guarantees equal rights and equal protection to every one regardless of gender. The fundamental principles of state policy require the state to prevent prostitution. Article 34(1) prohibits all forms of forced labour. The suppression of Immoral Traffic Act 1933 protects all children up to the age of 18 from sexual exploitation. The women and children repression; prevention Act 2000 provides stringent penalties against trafficking, Kidnapping, collection random, rape, the sexual exploitation etc., These provisions also apply to both internal and cross border trafficking. These were the some of the legal framework in Bangladesh Against Human Trafficking.

BHUTAN

There is very little information available on the laws of. Bhutan on trafficking. In 2001, the UN committee on the Rights of the child considered Bhutan's initial report and noted the absence of legislation on the minimum age for employment. There is insufficient data and awareness regarding the Human Trafficking. It also suggested that new laws need to be promulgated and existing law need to be suitably amended to address these issues.

MALDIVES

There is no specific law to prohibit or prevent the trafficking in persons. There are no reports of persons being trafficked to from or within the country following Nationwide consultations, the Government has drawn up a National plan of action on the basis of the Beijing platform for action and the common wealth plan of Action on Gender and Development.

NEPAL

The constitution of Nepal enshrines the principles of equality and Justice for every citizen without any dis-crimination on the basis of race, caste, sex, creed, etc., and safe guards the human rights of all citizens. Code of law 1963. Lays down provisions against Inter-state and other of slavery and domestic trafficking-section decrees prison sentences of 20 years for International trafficking and 10 years for attempted sale, plus fines equaling to the amount of transaction.

PAKISTAN

One of Pakistan's major problems is the smuggling of children to countries in Gulf for camel Jockey and racing. The high profits and the lessening fear of harsh punishment have bolstered syndicates of Human traffickers across "Asia, the middle east and Europe". The prevention and control of Human Trafficking Ordinance 2002 has been promulgated to deal with all types of human trafficking. However the legislation suffers from certain limitations. Also legislation is focused on trans border trafficking and not on domestic trafficking. And the Human trafficking ordinance 2002 defines human trafficking to include trafficking for any purpose, via, prostitution Forced labour and services. It also takes into considerations the Organised nature of the crime and presumes the vicarious liability of each member of the trafficker's group by providing for stringent punishments; the ordinance also includes provisions for the compensations for the victims.

SHRI LANKA

In country trafficking is one of Sri Lanka's major problems s.360 of the Sri Lankan penal code deals with the offence of trafficking defined as the act of buying or sealing or bartering of any person for money or for any other consideration. Those assisting, arranging the travel, recruiting, etc., said to be trafficking and be prostituted. The National Child Protection Authority act is a landmark initiative that can help in preventing child abuse and in protecting the rights of children.

INDIA

The Constitution of India, under Article 23(1), prohibits trafficking in human beings and forced labour; this right enforceable against the state and private citizens. However, trafficking was never defined in Indian laws except in the Goa Children Act, which is specified to the state of Goa. In India the law has no express provision for confiscating the assets amassed by the traffickers, nor does it have provisions for the victim protection. The concerned authorities should consider these points so that the laws and provisions are made victim friendly. Let us prevent commercial dealings in human beings.

7

Developmental Partnership in Asia

The trafficking of human beings is nothing new. Indeed, it is as old as civilization itself, as the trafficking of women and children (particularly girls) can be traced back as part of early slavery systems where girls and women were auctioned off as domestic labour or into brothel bondage. What is new, however, is that today women and children are ever more vulnerable to trafficking and the phenomenon is increasing and acquiring new dimensions borne through rapid globalization. Today, irrespective of cultural differences and geographic location, women and children are bought and sold on a daily basis for purposes of prostitution, forced labor, begging, drug smuggling, sexual exploitation, adoption and forced marriage, just to name a few. And though they can be sold for trifling sums of money, the trafficking industry is recognized as one of the world's largest transnational organized crimes after drugs and arms and is worth many billions of dollars.

The Asian continent is extremely diverse in terms of cultures, traditions, peoples, political ideologies and religions. Nevertheless, there are commonalities shared by people that create and enable environments where human trafficking can flourish. Poverty, gender discrimination, consumerism, lack of education, lack of economic opportunities, unsafe migration, marginalization and the patriarchal nature of Asian society are all factors which contribute to the exploitation and trafficking of women and children. As an active member in the Asian community for over three decades, APHD has long committed itself to pursue integral human development, stop social injustices, and to work toward a peaceful society from the perspective of the Gospel and the social teaching of the Catholic Church.

APHD fundamentally believes in the intrinsic rights of human beings and views with alarm the increase in both scope and pace of human trafficking. Therefore, APHD seeks answers to the questions: "Why do women and children get trafficked?" and, "What can we do, as an Asian Catholic development network, to stop women and children from being trafficked?" Our Pan-Asia Program Against the Trafficking of Women and Children embodies APHD's effort to put an end to this gross violation of human rights against women and children. The Asia Partnership for Human Development holds firm that through its concerted and collaborative actions at the local, national and regional levels, trafficking can eventually be stopped on the Asian continent. As an Asian Catholic development network committed to this cause our refrain is now and always will be: "Stop human trafficking, you and I can."

In a letter to Archbishop Jean-Louis Tauran on the occasion of the International Conference: Twenty-First Century Slavery-the Human Rights Dimension to Trafficking in Human Beings, Pope John Paul II said the following:

"The trade in human beings constitutes a shocking offense against human dignity and a grave violation of fundamental human rights. Already the Second Vatican Council had pointed to, 'slavery, prostitution, the selling of women and children, and disgraceful working conditions where people are treated as instruments of gain rather than free responsible persons', as 'infamies' which 'poison human society, debase their perpetrators' and constitute a 'supreme dishonour to the Creator'. Such situations are an affront to fundamental values that are shared by all cultures and peoples, values rooted in the very nature of the human person."

A modern day form of slavery, human trafficking is an abomination that violates human dignity. APHD adopts the definition for human trafficking in human beings as stated in the United Nations Protocol to Prevent, Suppress and Punish Trafficking in Persons, Especially Women and Children, Supplementing the UN Convention Against Transnational Organized Crime (2000).

UNITED NATIONS PROTOCOL (VIENNA CONFERENCE 2000)

According to this UN Protocol:

(a.) "Trafficking in persons shall mean the recruitment, transportation, transfer, harbouring or receipt of persons by means of the threat or use of force or other forms of coercion, of abduction, of fraud, of deception, of the abuse of power, or of a position of vulnerability or of the giving or receiving of payments or benefits to achieve the consent of a person having control over another person for the purpose of exploitation. Exploitation shall include, at a minimum, the exploitation of the prostitution of others or other forms of sexual exploitation, forced labor or services, slavery or practices similar to slavery, servitude or the removal of organs.

(b.) The consent of the victim of trafficking in persons to be the intended exploitation set forth in paragraph (a) of this article shall be irrelevant where any of the means set forth in subparagraph (a) have been used;

(c.) The recruitment, transportation, transfer, harbouring of receipt of a child for the purpose of exploitation shall be considered "trafficking in persons" even if this does not involve any of the means set forth in paragraph (a) of this article;

(d.) "Child" shall mean any person less than eighteen years of age".

United Nations Human Trafficking Protocol (Article 3)

There are some key features of the Protocol, which:

- Defines trafficking as a crime against humanity, marked

by intent to deceive and exploit;

- Expands the range of actions considered as part of the trafficking process–recruitment, transportation, trans-fer, harboring, and receipt of persons in end-institutions;
- Addresses a wide range of means used, from blatant force to subtle inducements that capitalize on vulnerability, to achieve 'consent';
- Makes consent to the intended exploitation irrelevant, where any of the means outlined in the definition are used;
- Recognizes a range of purposes of trafficking, in addi-tion to sexual exploitation;
- Contains rights-based and protective social, economic, and political and legal measures to prevent trafficking, protect, assist, return and reintegrate trafficked persons, and to penalize trafficking and related conduct;
- Calls for international cooperation to prevent and combat trafficking.

Some of the main points that emerge from the Protocol are as follows:

- There is an international consensus on the definition of trafficking together with an agreed upon set of prosecution, protection, and prevention mechanisms on which to base national legislation against trafficking, and which can serve as a basis for harmonizing the laws in various countries.
- The trafficked persons, especially women in pros-titution, are not viewed as criminals but as victims of a crime.
- All victims of trafficking in persons are protected and not just those who can prove force (Article 3a and b).
- The definition ensures that the victim will not bear the burden of proof (Article 3b).
- The consent of the victim is irrelevant (Article 3b).
- The definition provides a comprehensive coverage of criminal means by which trafficking takes place, including not only force, coercion, abduction, deception of abuse of power, but also less explicit means, such as abuse of a victim's vulnerability (Article 3a).

- The exploitation of prostitution and trafficking cannot be separated. The Protocol acknowledges that much trafficking is for the purpose of prostitution and for other forms of sexual exploitation (Article 3a).
- It is not necessary for the victim to cross a border. Women and children who are domestically trafficked for prostitution and forced labour within their own countries are also protected.
- The key element in the trafficking process is the exploitative purpose, rather than the movement across a border (Article 3a).
- The Protocol is the first UN instrument to address the demand which results is women and children being trafficked, calling upon countries to take or strengthen legislative or other measures to discourage this demand that fosters all forms of exploitation of women and children (Article 9.5).

HUMAN RIGHTS VIOLATION

APHD takes the view that the violation of one person's human rights should be viewed as an affront to the dignity of all humanity. Trafficked victims are subject to the worst mental, emotional, physical and sexual abuses. They are denied their basic rights to health, education, nutrition and their full earnings, amongst other abuses.

GLOBAL SCOPE OF HUMAN TRAFFICKING

"This scourge is often responsible for taking away the hope for a decent future of the most vulnerable, especially women and children. In order to face this growing phenomenon, it is of the utmost importance that national and international systems of criminal justice identify not only criminals, but also those who suffer as victims from trafficking".

In the modern age of globalization, human trafficking has truly become an issue without borders that has reached enormous proportions and requires urgent action both on the part of the nation-state and civil society. Women and children are not only trafficked within and across national borders, but also across continents. Current global trends, underscored by free markets and movements of labor, facilitated by the diffusion of information and transportations technologies, have added an international dimension to the issue of trafficking in Asia.

Today's trafficking involves the recruitment and transportation of persons, using deception, coercion and threats in order to place and keep them in a situation of forced labour, slavery or servitude. Persons are trafficked into a variety of sectors of the informal economy, including prostitution, domestic work, agriculture, the garment industry or street begging. While exact data are hard to come by, estimates of the number of trafficked persons range from 500,000 to two million per year, and a few organizations have estimated that up to four million persons are trafficked every year. Although women, men, girls and boys can become victims of trafficking, the majority of victims are female. Various forms of gender-based discrimination increase the risks of women and girls to become affected by poverty, which in turns puts them at higher risk of becoming targeted by traffickers, who use false promises of jobs and educational opportunities to recruit their victims. Trafficking is often connected to organized crime and is developed into a highly profitable business that generates an estimated US$7-12 billion per year.

Trafficking is in most cases a trans-border crime that affects all regions of the world. According to a 2006 UN Global Report on Trafficking, 127 countries have been documented as countries of origin and 137 as countries of destination. The main countries of origin are reported to be in Central and South-Eastern Europe, the Common-wealth of Independent States and Asia, followed by West Africa, Latin America and the Caribbean. The most commonly reported countries of destination are in Western Europe, Asia and Northern America.

ASIAN DIMENSION

It has been estimated that over 225,000 people are trafficked from Southeast Asia and over 150,000 from South Asia.

SENDING, RECEIVING AND TRANSIT IN ASIA

Within Asia there are two geographical forms of trafficking: domestic and cross-border or regional trafficking. Domestic or internal trafficking happens within a specific country. In this scenario, women and children from rural areas are trafficked into the cities to work as domestic servants, sex workers, beggars, drug sellers, and/or factory workers, often under inhumane conditions. Regional trafficking or cross-border trafficking occurs in the case where women and children leave their respective country and are brought into another country. Nearly all countries in Asia are affected by the trafficking of women and children, either as sending country (such as Indonesia) or as receiving country (such as Japan), or as transit or passage country (such as Thailand) before final destination.

Countries prone to natural disasters, political instability and underdevelopment are typically sending countries (such as Bangladesh and Nepal), because women and children from vulnerable domestic situations and from poor areas are desperate to improve their conditions. Owing to eco-nomic necessity, coupled with complete absence of social safety nets, many are lured into promises of better living conditions and jobs in urban centres. Transit countries, such as Thailand and India, offer an entrepôt for traffickers sending their victims on their way to a receiving country. Consequently, receiving countries in East Asia like Japan, South Korea, Hong Kong and Taiwan, can be the final destination for women and children trafficked around the region. Upon their arrival in the country of destination, these women and children are then coerced and forced into the activities that contravene their basic human rights.

TERRAIN OF TRAFFICKING IN SOUTH AND SOUTHEAST ASIA

South Asia and Southeast Asia are Asia regions in which

human trafficking flourishes and thousands of women and children are trafficked for various exploitative ends every year. Although a great deal of the human trafficking remains within countries, cross-border trafficking is on the rise. Examples are incidents of trafficking from Myanmar to Bangladesh and then onward from Bangladesh to India and Pakistan. Many countries in the Middle East are the final destination of those who are trafficked for sex work and domestic servitude. Within the region, Nepali women are trafficked to India, primarily for commercial exploitation in the sex industry. According to some estimates, 2.5 million women work in the flesh trade in India. The vast majority of trafficked women consist of Indians while the rest are from Bangladesh and Nepal. Certain social, cultural and religious beliefs and practices contribute to an environment in which trafficking can flourish. Social and religious marginalization of certain castes in Nepal and India, for instance, leads to these groups being vulnerable to prostitution, which in some cases is even widely culturally accepted. Emphasis on the tourist industry in Asia has also contributed significantly to the trafficking of women and children for sexual exploitation. For example, since the 1980s Sri Lanka has been internationally known as the child sex paradise. Furthermore, it is known that in Thailand a child sex worker can cost US$ 3-4, while in Sri Lanka a child sex worker can be bought only one dolla.."

In Southeast Asia, one of the main hubs for trafficking is the Greater Mekong Sub-region (GMS). This region sees trafficked victims coming into Thailand from Burma, China, Laos and Cambodia. Also, trafficking occurs from Vietnam to Cambodia and to China and Taiwan. Finally people are being trafficked to Malaysia, Singapore and Japan from Indonesia, the Philippines, Cambodia and Thailand. There have also been incidents of trafficking into South Korea. In the context of Asia, cross-border trafficking is fostered by uneven economic development, porous borders, need for cheap labor, demand for commercial sex, poverty, natural disasters and migration between countries.

GENDER DIMENSION

It is very crucial to ask ourselves the question, "Why women and children are more vulnerable to trafficking?" There are many reasons for such gender distinctiveness. First and foremost, women and children are too often voiceless in the family and community; and the patriarchal nature of the Asian society also contributes to their vulnerability. This is why APHD focuses on vulnerable women and children. A useful social barometer for this imbalance is seen when how trafficked women have different experiences than men and their degrees of vulnerability are different. Once repatriated the recovered and healed woman is treated differently than a man. In many societies in Asia, when a man is repatriated into his society he is viewed as a hero. But a woman is always referred to as a 'spoiled good'.

WOMEN TRAFFICKING

The dehumanizing aspect of women trafficking and sexual exploitation in Asia is fuelled by demand for commercial sex in the region. It is unfortunate that today some religious and socio-cultural practices have justified the sexual exploitation of women for male entertainment, in South and Southeast Asian particularly. Certain tradi-tional beliefs exacerbate the vulnerability and marginali-zation of Asian women; notably the caste system existing in many countries of South Asia. Additionally, some cul-tural practices justify the sexual exploitation of women in these communities. In many Asian societies women are viewed as comparatively inferior to men, which increases their vulnerability. Nowadays, young women from remote villages, minority groups and indigenous communities, broken homes, and those who are economically disadvant-aged, are the prime target for traffickers. Many of them are lured into promises of better living conditions in the city, job offers and/or marriage proposals, which they believe as a means to improve their conditions and support their families. However, they are often sold to brothels, drug lords, factories, gangs or sent abroad to be exploited.

CHILD TRAFFICKING

Culturally in Asia, children, particularly girls, are raised to accept their responsibility as an income contributor. Many children are forced to work in dangerous conditions as a mean to show their gratitude to their parents. Filial piety is a value that is widespread in the region. Frequently, girls are sold by their family members or traffickers as domestic workers or trafficked for marriage, and later forced into prostitution. Although girls are favored, boys are.also trafficked to work as camel jockeys in the Middle East. How-ever, it is important to note that in many instance chil-dren sold by their parents who believe that they own their children, thus they can do as they please. In many cases, children are kidnapped by traffickers and taken into the city.

A child in the legal sense, means any person under the age of eighteen. Sexual exploitation is the fate of many victims of child victims of trafficking. However child trafficking is different from the trafficking of women in some important respects. A child, in the legal sense, means any person under the age of eighteen. Simply put, it is the recruitment, transportation, transfer, harbouring or receipt of a child for the purpose of sexual exploitation, regardless of the means. Children are less able to navigate the risks and threats; have less negotiation power with traffickers and societies; and have special rights and needs that are all-too-often not respected. Like the trafficking of women, child trafficking is a modern-day abomination that traces its roots to the past or to some deep cultural value within a given society. All minor under eighteen years old are considered 'trafficked' regardless of consent.

FACTORS CONTRIBUTING TO HUMAN TRAFFICKING IN ASIAS

In recent decades, the Asian continent has experienced rapid political and economic change. However, the level of development has not been even within and amongst countries, and socio-economic gaps have ultimately widened between 'have' and 'have-nots', contributing to the vulnerability of the poor. Trafficking thrives where poverty has forced the population to seek different methods of sur-vival for themselves and their families. Amongst the myriad factors contributing to the vulnerability of women and children to trafficking are globalization, materialism or consumerism, cultural and religious beliefs, gender insen-sitivity and inequality, human migration, demand for cheap labor, demand for commercial sex, lack of education, discrimination against minority groups, lack of economic opportunities, porous borders, weak law enforcement, breakdown of families and family values, male migration into urban areas, growth of the tourist industry in Asia and the patriarchal nature of the Asian society.

DRIVERS AND ROOT CAUSES

Human trafficking is a highly complex, multi-dimensional problem, with many contributing factors that can be differentiated as supply or 'push factors', demand or 'pull factors', and pervasive 'catalytic' factors. Studies increasingly reveal that the major factors that increase the risk of trafficking for women are poverty, lack of economic opportunities, low level of education, domestic violence, inadequate law enforcement to uphold the status of women and children and a general lack of political, social and economic stability. In countries or regions fuelling the supply of trafficked persons, strong contributing factors (which disproportionately impact women) include: poverty, particularly the feminization of poverty; lack of economic opportunities or possibilities for human development; lack of access to education; domestic violence and the disintegration of the family structure; vulnerability of women and children; the low status of women in some cultures; and armed conflict and oppression.

In countries and areas of the world fueling the "pull" for trafficked persons, strong contributing factors include: the rise in demand for commercial sex workers as part of a globalizing sex industry; demand for cheap, exploitable and disposable labourers; and a pervasive erosion of moral norms and values in consumerist societies in which such wanton abuse of people is not openly challenged. Catalytic factors that contribute to human trafficking around the world include: a lack of public awareness of the dangers of trafficking, particularly amongst the vulnerable groups themselves; the financially lucrative nature of trafficking to organized crime; the sophisticated nature and capacity of today's traffickers, who make use of mass communication and transportation tools; lack of counter-trafficking legislation and effective enforcement; global policies that contribute to inequality and marginalization of vulnerable groups; and the non-existence and elimination of social protection and societal safety nets for people in vulnerable situations.

SUPPLY AND DEMAND FOR HUMAN BEINGS

The buying and selling of a human being is but an extension of the runaway capitalist philosophy and unbridled free market economics. Human trafficking is thus governed by the law of supply and demand and the open movement of labor, such as the growing movement from rural to urban areas. By looking at some of the supply and demand factors that foster the growth of trafficking, one can identify some of the specific causes of trafficking, which can then be sub-categorized into different aspects of life such as socio-economic, economic and political.

SUPPLY

Socio-cultural

- Illiteracy and inadequate educational and employment opportunities as well as lack of gender perspective in education.
- Patriarchy, which is the main cause for discrimination of women and girl-children.
- Erosion of traditional family values, and the pursuit of consumerism, encourages the sale of women and children.
- Racial discrimination, racism and related intolerance, which makes the women from such communities more vulnerable to trafficking.
- The media and new technologies, which through advertising and the commercialization of sex, present women's bodies as objects for sexual pleasure.

Economic

- Economic disparities within the countries, and between countries and regions, which is the primary cause for the growth in trafficking in women.
- Feminisation of poverty because women constitute 70% of the world's poor and they support their families through precarious employment in the growing informal sector.
- Globalization and its differential impact on women through economic restructuring and transition with cuts on social spending which affect women.
- A lucrative business with high monetary returns be-cause women are sold and resold a number of times. The relative danger of being apprehended is low and this attracts crime syndicates.
- Economic difficulties in relation to economies in difficulty or in transition.

DEMAND

Socio-cultural

- Male attitudes and perceptions of women in society and women's unequal socio-economic status.
- Pornography and its role in demand for sex. This is coupled with and ever increasing use of the internet as its vehicle and as a means for traffickers to market women and children.
- Patriarchy resulting in the unequal power relations bet-ween men and women and the discrimination of women.
- Consumerist behaviour with the commodification and the commercialization of sex leading to the consideration of women's bodies as commodities and objects for sexual pleasure.

Economic

- Demand by employers for unskilled and cheap labour markets. Women's labour is usually in low status work in the domestic and entertainment spheres and in the informal sector.
- An expanding commercial sex industry and increase

demand for sex. The variety of ways it merchandises women and children are: prostitution, sex trafficking, sex tourism, mail-order brides, to name but a few. The growth in child sexual exploitation is due to male client preferences for younger women and girls because of a fear of HIV infection.

- Development policies promoting tourism, and patterns of development that depend on temporary migrant workers.

SUPPLY

Political

- Feminisation of International Migration as women enters the labour market-together with a lack of regulation for labour migration-which provides in-creased opportunities and channels for trafficking.
- Civil and military conflicts push people to flee their homes and their countries. Of the 25 million refugees in the world, 80% are women and children. They be-come easy prey in the hands of the traffickers.
- The growth of transnational crime and the expansion of drug trafficking networks act as mechanisms for other forms of exploitation.
- Weak law enforcement mechanisms and measures to penalize offenders.
- Corruption by police, law enforcers, officials and peace-makers.

DEMAND

Political

- Unequal and exploitative political and economic re-lations dictated by the North, which results in the deterioration of conditions of life in the South.
- Military bases both past and present have created enor-mous prostitution infrastructure.
- Restrictive migration policies, which have decreased the possibilities for regular migration.
- Sales of arms and the increase of armed conflict within

and between with the consequent increase of displaced people and refugees who fall victim to traffickers.

- Weak law enforcement mechanisms and measures to penalize offenders.

The profile of trafficked victims:

- Women and children are the key target group because of their marginalization, limited economic resources and predominance in the 'invisible' informal sector.
- People from impoverished and low income households in rural areas and urban slums, especially women engaged in small farming, petty trading, vending, as labourers, scavengers and other low status work or services.
- Ethnic minorities, indigenous peoples, hill-tribes, refugees and illegal immigrants.
- People with low levels of education, a few years of formal schooling, some primary school education or illiterate.
- Young girls running away from home or girls from families that expect their daughters to financially contribute to their support are easy targets for traffickers.
- People who lack awareness of their legal rights, their exploited situation, and have no channel for seeking redress.

PURPOSES OF TRAFFICKING

Actual profiles from the Asian Countries Where We Work

Trafficking of women and children is often considered interchangeable with sexual exploitation. In many ways, the purpose of traffic of women and children leads to sexual exploitation, prostitution, forced marriage, adoption, slavery like labour, organ removal, domestic servants, and/or camel jockeys. There are a wide range of purposes associated with trafficking. A large percentage is for prostitution, but others include the entertainment industry, sweatshops, illegal adoption of children, organ transplants, forced marriages, mail-order brides, domestic work, forced labour, drug trafficking, begging, other exploitative forms of work.

BANGLADESH

Women and children from poor rural areas are highly prone to trafficking in Bangladesh. They are trafficked for the purposes of sexual exploitation, mainly prostitution, and are sent into cheap bonded labour in cities of Pakistan India and the Middle East.

Kamy's Story

Kamy was only thirteen years old when she was trafficked from her home in Bangladesh to the neighboring country of India. She hailed from a very poor family of a remote village straddling the Indo-Bangladesh border. One day a distant relative brought a man to their house who proposed to marry Kamy. But Kamy's mother did not accept the proposal, since the man was an Indian and rather elderly. However, after much persuasion and a cash donation to the family of 3000 Bangladeshi taka (US$44) Kamy's mother gave her consent to the proposal.

It was agreed that after the marriage Kamy's new husband would stay in the village to run a small shop to earn a living. But soon after the marriage, Kamy's husband decided to take Kami away from the village, saying he sought better employment opportunities at an unknown destination in India. After crossing the border with India illegally, they reached a place which was obviously new and unknown to Kamy. On arrival she was confined to a house where many other young girls of her age were residing and many people visited them. On that very night she was introduced to four men who were so-called friends of her husband.

They raped her one after another. Kamy now realized how she had been deceived by her husband. For nearly a month, she had to entertain a number of clients every night on regular basis. As a result she became ill. Luckily, one day she somehow managed to escape from their clutches and coincidentally met her maternal uncle. With the help of her uncle, Kamy was able to return back home to her house in Bangladesh. At the tender age of thirteen, Kamy spent her days in confinement and forced prostitution.

PHILIPPINES

Trafficking for sexual exploitation comprises the majority of instances. Other purposes are for begging, child labour for bonded labour in factories and fishing operations. There are also cases for domestic work, for mail order brides and for child adoption to Europe.

Girls from ethnic minorities of Mindanao

Eleven-year-old Mandaya, a domestic helper, confides that seven of her sisters and a number of others from their village came to Davao City to seek employment. She said they were willing to do anything, even to become 'commercial sex workers' just to earn money. "Life is so hard on our communities. We only eat twice a day because of the price of copra, our main source of living, is so low. It's so hopeless but life can be better here in Mati because we can get employed. We need money to send to our parents in the mountains". But they have learned that earning money in the city is not as easy as they thought. Commercial sex workers earn 50 pesos a day while those working as household help earn 300 pesos a month.

INDIA

In India, women and children are trafficked mainly for prostitution in brothels. However, evidence has also proved that alarming numbers of women and children are trafficked for cheap labour or slavery-like practices and domestic work. There is a growing pattern of trafficking in child prostitutes from Nepal.

Can we trust our Chacha? Sisters Julia and Promila were brought to Delhi by their uncle (chacha) when they were sixteen and fourteen years old. They are members of a lower caste from a village in Gumla District of Jharkhand. Seeing the glamour of girls who worked as domestic workers in the cities, they were tempted to go to the city. Their family was poor and the parents were finding it difficult to fulfill the minimum basic needs of the children. Hence to help the family financially, they were brought from the village by their uncle (chacha) to Delhi. On rea-ching Delhi, they met with another man who promised them to find a good job for both of them. Their chacha left them with the man and never came back to see the girls to check on their safety. Although their chacha used to stay at Delhi, the sisters knew nothing about his whereabouts and address. The man who had falsely said he would get them both jobs raped the elder sister. One lucky day, the sisters happened to meet a very senior and married domestic worker, whom they told their stories.

She kept the two girls in the safety of her home for few days. Julia and Promila were them taken to one a domestic workers'welfare center located in West Delhi in order to find a means to help them out. The center was also informed about the situation of the girls. But its resources were limited and the girls were referred to the Society for Development of Tribates. The society tried to help the girls by trying to find the man who had sexually exploited them. They also tried to trace their location of the girls' chacha. However, as they did not have any information about the uncle or the man who sexually abused Julia, they were finding it very difficult to do anything for Julia and Promila. The mental trauma that Julia went through was difficult to heal. As the situation got worse the society thought it best to send the pair back to their own village and made the nece-ssary arrangements for them to reach home safely. The dream of a glamorous life they once saw in becoming a domestic worker had become a nightmare as they asked themselves, "Is our chacha trustworthy?"

COMBODIA

Begging and soliciting are significant purposes along-side trafficking into prostitution. Children are trafficked for their labour into domestic work, food processing, sea-food factories, fisheries, manufacturing plantations, logging and others.

NEPAL

Sexual exploitation or prostitution is the main purpose of the trafficking of Nepalese women and girls. The majority of these trafficked victims are sent mainly in India to work as sex workers in brothels. Though trafficking for the purpose of commercial prostitution is very common, it is only one side of the coin, religious traditional forms of prostitution are also practiced in Nepal.

Ganga

My name is Ganga. I am twenty years old and my home is in Makwanpur. I come from a family of eight members. I lost my mother when I was very young and my father found it difficult to look after all of us. I order to manage our difficulties he remarried. His second marriage freed him only of his problem of taking care of the children as most of the problems and responsibilities were passed to me, but I was only a girl myself. I had to do a lot of the household chores, from cleaning the house to washing and cooking. Because I had to look after the house, I never had a chance to go to school, which I longed to attend. I've never entered a school building in my life and I can not read or write.

My neighbors were quite friendly to me; they always spoke to me and listened to my stories. There was one girl in the neighborhood who was like a sister to me. She promised to free me from my struggling life by providing me with a job outside the village. I was really happy as I would be away from my stepmother and could stand on my own feet. I was pleased with the whole idea of going out to work. So I accompanied this so-called big sister away from my village to a big city. When we reached the city she left me in a house with many other girls like and that was the last time I saw my neighbor. When I started to mingle with the other girls in the house I realized that I was in a brothel in Mumbai, India and that I had been sold to be-come a prostitute. I had no other choice but to accept this situation. I received hope of freeing myself from captivity from one of my clients who visited me regularly. He took pity on me and promised to take me away from this place. With the help of the client I did manage to get out of the brothel in Mumbai. In the end I was able to return to Nepal, where I received some support and care from an NGO working to help women and girls like me.

THAILAND

Trafficking exists for large-scale commercial sexual exploitation. Also evident is trafficking for drug trafficking, begging and soliciting, domestic labour. There is significant child trafficking for child labour in jewelry making, cloth weaving, construction, fisheries and other agricultural businesses.

A Daughter Sold For the Price of a TV

When Ngun Chai sold his 13-year-old daughter into prostitution for the price of a television set, he had a single regret that he did not get enough money for her. Later the mother La Chai cried when she discovered that her eldest daughter was not working in a nearby city as the agent, who had bought her daughter, had promised. Instead the young girl was forced to sell her immature body in a Bangkok brothel to as many as eight men a day. But her tears were not for her daughter. "I should have asked for 10,000 baht," (US$ 250) she said, "not 5,000". "He (that agent) has robbed us." The family live in a thatched hut in Pa Tek village on the outskirts of Mae Sai, a bustling township sit-uated on Thailand's northernmost border with the military state of Myanmar, formerly known as Burma. The United Nations Children's Fund estimates that one third of the sex workers in South-East Asia are aged between 12 and 17. Many are bought and sold in places such as Mae Sai.

PAKISTAN

Female sexual exploitation, drug smuggling, organ sell-kidney transplant, begging, camel jockeys, forced labor, forced marriages and domestic servitude, pick pocketing, stone crushing are some of the many purposes women and children are trafficked within and from Pakistan. It was known that sexual exploitation of male children is a growing phenomenon.

Bishti

Unlike most trafficking victims, Bisthi was an educated young women belonging to a well-off family. The daughter of the Police Commissioner of district Bagrat, she was a student of fifth standard in her hometown. At school one day, she felt drowsy. She had her own car and driver; she left the school premises to return home. Feeling faint, she asked her driver to take her home. In the car she lost consciousness and when she awoke to her horror she found herself across the border in India. In a drugged state, she was then trafficked into Pakistan, where she is sold into prostitution at a brothel. She was made to stay in a room with fourteen women and twelve men, and a pimp seemed to be in charge.Themadam'sson, LalMian who worked as a police employee, legalized a marriage contract with her and used this to prevent her from escaping. A fight between pimps led to this case being reported and Bishti was arrested as a result. The officials of Badin Police Station arrested her on 28th August 2001. Lal Mian gave her intoxi-cating drugs, which kept her unconscious for much of the journey between India and Pakistan. In Lahore, Lal Mian sold her for a fee of 100.000 Pakistani rupees. The Naika (female brothel owner) forced Bishti into prostitution with the help of her son. During the fourteen months that she stayed in the house, Bisthi was raped countless time, some-times by her father-in-law. Her husband, Ghulam Shabir, was a police employee and whenever she tried to escape or report the matter to the police, he would promptly produce the Nikah Nama and bring her back home.

SRI LANKA

Commercial sex and cheap labor force are the two main significant purposes of trafficking in Sri Lanka. Female migrant workers often resort to prostitution to meet their subsistence needs. Moreover, Sri Lanka has been known internationally for the past two decades as a so-called 'child sex paradise'.

Shemen

Shemen remembers herself and her siblings starving for days on end, after their father abandoned them and her mother had to take up a petty, low income job. She fell in love with an army deserter and eloped with him after her mother objected to the affair. But the man proceeded to prostitute her to his friends, until she was arrested by the police and placed in a shelter home. There, she received counseling and support services, instilling in her some hope. Shemen's mother became a labourer at the Municipality Council after her father, a fish seller, abandoned the family. Recalling her childhood, nineteen-year-old Shemen says that there was a time when she and her brothers had no food to eat for several days at a stretch. She left school in the second grade and went to work as an assistant in a garment factory at the age of fourteen. There, she fell in love with an army deserter. When her mother opposed the affair, Shemen eloped with the man and started living with him in Katunayake.

After a few days, her lover started to quarrel with her and began avoiding her. He then proceeded to sell Shemen off to his friends for sexual purposes at the rate of 500 rupee. The police arrested her on suspicion of prostitution while she was at a musical show in another town. During interrogation, the police informed her that her lover was a trafficking agent and had trapped and sold many other girls for sexual purposes. She was directed to Nisala Diya Sevana Institution where her life changed for the better. The care and counseling she received finally gave her some comfort. Today, she is interested in finding employment under the guidance and security of the nuns there and hopes to rebuild her life.

APHD PAN-ASIA APPROACH

The sad reality is that as long as there are poor, vulnerable and disadvantaged individuals, specifically women and children, there will always be people to be trafficked. So APHD sees its mission to make it difficult for traffickers to exploit vulnerable women and children by empowering them and providing them with means to have a sustainable livelihood. In the context of Asia, our anti-trafficking stra-tegies can be linked with economic development and social inclusion, so that holistic, long-term approaches to anti-trafficking are developed that address the root drivers and contributing factors. A turning point for APHD along its path to combat human trafficking in Asia was a 1996 police raid in Mumbai, India, where numerous Nepali girls were found to be working as sexual workers in brothels. Surprisingly, these trafficked young women were jailed in India before being sent to Nepal.

During efforts to repatriate these girls, the Nepali government sought support from different NGOs to facilitate their recovery and healing. However, some of these organizations were not experienced in handling this task. In this regard, APHD offered its support and expertise on human development to organizations who offered to assist these Nepali girls. Suddenly aware that only collective efforts can combat trafficking, due to the magnitude and complexity as a regional issue, APHD and its partner agencies committed themselves to protect women and children in Asia. In 1997, APHD began its counter-human trafficking work, starting with its South Asian Programme against the Trafficking of Women and Children. APHD received tremendous support from its Partner Agencies in the region, most notably Caritas India, Caritas Pakistan, Caritas Bangladesh, Caritas Nepal and Caritas Sri Lanka; all of whom organized advocacy trainings, educational workshops and campaigns in their respective countries. From 1999 to 2005 APHD's programme focused on the South Asia region.

An external evaluation of the South Asia Programme Against the Trafficking of Women and Children concluded that human trafficking was prevalent not only in South Asian countries but also Southeast Asia and East Asia. Importantly, the study noted that East Asia is home to destination countries for trafficking victims, most notably from Southeast Asia. Since trafficking of women and children touches Asia as a whole, APHD decided to expand its programming towards a continental or Pan-Asian approach. Given the current trend of trafficking across Asia's many borders, in 2005 APHD expanded its work to the current Pan-Asia Programme Against the Trafficking of omen and Children. In true spirit of cooperation, APHD pledged to link and network better with NGOs and intergovernmental bodies involved in working against human trafficking in order to avoid duplication and to boost the programme's efficiency. Trafficking can be viewed as a matter for international security since it is a form of organized crime that transcends national borders. But most of all trafficking is a threat to the human security of women and children.

From this perspective, APHD has undertaken a programme using a Pan-Asian approach, along with its different Caritas partners and with like-minded organizations, to create a network to raise awareness on and prevention of human trafficking. Since many of APHD's development projects focus on addressing situations of poverty and lack of education, our programme focuses on these two areas in the context. As a human development organization, APHD directs its work and efforts to focus on the supply aspect of trafficking. APHD works to empower young women and children, by providing them with an education and means to achieve their sustainable livelihood. APHD's fundamental purpose is to make it difficult for traffickers and those demanding such services, who ultimately take advantage of women and children by their actions. To achieve this goal, the APHD Pan-Asia Programme has added other members of the civil society community, besides women and children, in its awareness building campaign and education efforts.

APHD'S POSITION

In order to set goals to end or reduce trafficking, it is necessary to understand the entire aspect of human trafficking-from the time the person is trafficked, then transported, and brought from one place to another. To combat this situation, we are obliged to examine the root issues that contribute to the existence of trafficking. APHD chooses to examine this social plague's spread through the microscope of poverty (particularly the feminization of poverty) and gender inequity. Today, the sheer magnitude of the issue demands redress of governments and international bodies. Therefore to tackle trafficking in Asia, all stakeholders must adopt a common definition reflecting the transnational nature of women and children's trafficking in the region. APHD believes that with the collaboration of governments and non-governmental entities, new and important channels can be opened-up to protect women and children from trafficking.

Our vision is to ensure the rights of Asian women and

children to be protected from the horrors of trafficking. Pan-Asia Programme Against the Trafficking of Women and Children. The APHD Pan-Asia Programme aspires to enable women and children to protect themselves from trafficking, by building on the efforts undertaken by APHD's partners in grassroots animation, organization and mobilization. It strengthens the collaboration of the APHD partners with other national and Pan-Asian networks. The program focuses on mobilizing Asia religious and civic leaders to become partners of the anti-trafficking campaign. This will culminate in Asia-wide events to be celebrated in many Asian countries.

APHD's primary goal is to contribute to the significant decline in numbers of Asian women and children being trafficked. Our program:

- Ensures the empowerment of women and children and young people in order to protect them from exploitative conditions;
- Sensitizes religious and civic leaders and mobilizes them to work towards eliminate trafficking;
- Advocates and lobbies for the enactment and implementation of policies, legislation and declarations against trafficking.

Objectives:

- To develop and strengthen programs of APHD partners which sustain efforts for empowerment of women, children and young people against trafficking.
- To convince religious and civic leaders of the gravity of trafficking so that they become partners in address-ing the trafficking issue.
- To include the trafficking issue into the training curricula of religious and professional training institutions so that participants will become actively involved in preventing trafficking.
- To ensure enhanced networking among APHD partners for legislative advocacy and maximize the sharing of resources and expertise in combating trafficking.

APHD Program Implementing Partners' Profile:

There are ten partner agencies, spread over 12 countries in South Asia, Southeast Asia and East Asia as indicated below:

- Caritas Bangladesh
- Caritas Nepal
- Caritas India
- Caritas Pakistan
- Caritas Sri Lanka-SEDEC
- NASSA-Caritas Philippines
- Caritas Cambodia
- Fountain of Life Center, Thailand and Caritas Thailand (CCHD)
- Caritas Mongolia
- Asia ACTs Against Child Trafficking, representing Lao PDR
- Karuna Myanmar Social Services (KMSS)
- China (Linked to APHD) via our partner agency Caritas Australia
- Caritas Bangladesh has taken anti-trafficking as a cross-cutting issue. It has been integrated to the animation program and savings and credit schemes. Weekly meetings and other training courses, especially in gender, disaster management, human rights, HIV/AIDS, etc are maximized to disseminate information on the issue. It sensitized its and partner NGO's staffs, self-help group members, indigenous leaders through training courses, workshops at national and local level.
- Caritas Nepal works for people's empowerment and social justice. It's main programmes center on the women's economic empowerment, agriculture and micro-credit. It is also focused on awareness raising, literacy and building up the people's organizations, plus emergency relief and providing education for Bhutanese refugees. The anti-trafficking programme is integrated into the animation and cooperatives development program.
- Caritas India emerged as a leading capacity building organization in India. Its interventions cover various

areas ranging from disaster management and natural resource management to programme support at the grassroots. Mainstreaming gender is an ongoing effort that the organization is working towards. The main focus of the anti-trafficking programme has been on trafficking of domestic workers.

- Caritas Mongolia is the socio-developmental arm of the Catholic Church in Mongolia. It has undertaken projects like: providing water wells in the desert areas; repairing school dormitories for very poor school villages; food and medical relief to victims of disasters; non-formal education; support for street children and charity to the poor.
- *Caritas Pakistan*: During 2004 and 2005 Caritas Pakistan took the lead to coordinate and produce APHD's 2005 South Asia Regionial Anti-Trafficking Directory. The organization is moving forward with its anti-trafficking programmes.
- The Fountain of Life Center based in Pattaya, Thailand, has been working directly to support trafficked and prostituted women. It also has another project to assist street-children and the children of migrant workers.
- Catholic Commission for Human Development (Caritas Thailand) supports mutual education processes by promoting the formation of personnel for development work in order to build networks and foster the genuine growth of people's organizations. It conducts its development work through programmes in Education, Sustainable Agriculture, Capacity Building, Publi-cations, and Religion and culture.
- *Caritas Sri Lanka*: SEDEC is the social arm of the Roman Catholic Church in Sri Lanka. SEDEC has many units that work on various issues with the grass-roots. The Women's Development Unit has been invol-ved in the issue of trafficking since 1999. Caritas Sri Lanka also launched a major research on the issue focused in two districts in Sri Lanka. Based on the study's findings, a documentary video titled "The Sigh of a Woman" was produced to assist awareness raising campaigns.

- NASSA-CARITAS PHILIPPINES is the social action and development arm of the Catholic Bishops' Conference of the Philippines, which aims to respond to the calls of the Philippine Church for greater and deeper social involvement and people empowerment through an alternative social development agenda.
- Caritas Cambodia works through its Village Development Associations (VDA). It supports the VDAs with education, health and other social services. It is now in the process of developing its relationships with other networks to gather the necessary information and guidelines for working to combat human trafficking.
- Asia ACTs Against Child Trafficking is a network in Southeast Asia working in seven countries: Philippines, Thailand, Indonesia, Burma, Cambodia, Laos and Vietnam. It launches advocacy and public information, conducts community education, advocates for the strengthening and reactivation of child protection network, conducts lobbying for laws to fight child trafficking, conducts research, assists in capacity building of partner groups and extends direct services to prevent child trafficking and assists victims of trafficking through its campaign partners. Many of its publications and network activities have been supported by APHD.

STRATEGIES FOR CONGREGATIONS AND THEIR COLLABORATORS

Trafficking in women and children is an issue of such proportion that is requires urgent and concerted response to halt its spread. A comprehensive approach is required to address the many dimensions of the issue, and colla-borative networking among the various actors and at different levels is crucial to finding success in combating trafficking. Religious congregations can also collaborate to become agents for stopping trafficking by making use of some of the following approaches.

Research, data collection, and the dissemination of information:

- Collect data on trafficking as a basis for sound policy

and programme formulation.

- Prepare a directory on national and sub-regional organizations working on trafficking.
- Disseminate data and information in various local languages.
- Link tertiary institutions with persons working on the ground and at the grassroots.
- Use a human rights framework to document human rights abuses in the trafficking of women and children

Awareness raising and advocacy:

- Conduct awareness campaigns about trafficking at local, national, and sub-regional level to mobilize diverse groups; from women and children at the grassroots to policy makers, government, non-govern-mental organizations, religious congregations and ecclesial bodies.
- Make strategic use of the media to provide national and international coverage of the issue, generate public opinion and pressure to stop trafficking.
- Strengthen advocacy efforts to reduce demand, and include a strong component of gender sensitization on issues pertaining to women and girls.
- Encourage theological reflection and discussion, within churches and parishes, on the undoubted existence of buyers of sexual services and the implications of this for the community of women and men in the Church.
- Integrate programmes about the economic and gender justice into school curricula.
- Find out which organizations in your area are working on the issue and join them.
- Ask your school, parish, social service to explore the issue and become more aware about how to help.

Prevention:

- Address the underlying causes of poverty, improve access to education and employment opportunities, in particular women's access to productive resources.
- Promote education, particularly for men and boys on trafficking of women and girls and its dehumanizing effects.

- Offer ways of doing theological reflection on the dignity of women and womanhood and God's plan that men and women should live a mutual relationship.

Protection, return and reintegration:

- Physical, economic, legal, psychological and spiritual assistance for women and children who are victims.
- Job training facilities and support for alternative means of livelihood.
- Programmes for recovery, healing and reintegration into the society.
- Assistance to the family of the victims.
- Engage local churches and community groups in assisting families at risk, especially those with a histories of domestic violence.

Advocacy and lobby:

- Ratify and implement the United Nations Protocol to Prevent, Suppress and Punish Trafficking in Persons, Especially Women and Children, Supplementing the UN Convention Against Transnational Organized Crime (2000).
- Review, improve and implement comprehensive legislation at national level.
- Accelerate training of law enforcement agencies and personnel, including gender sensitization.
- Promote legal literacy and improve access to affordable legal assistance.
- Improve treatment of trafficked victims.
- Develop guidelines and strengthen multidisciplinary reintegration programmes such as health care, counseling, education and training, social integration.

Networking:

- Create effective networking between Church congregations on the issue of trafficking.
- Build up networks with NGOs and other actors at local, national and international levels.

- Work in collaboration with other churches and religions.

INTERNATIONAL INSTRUMENTS

(i.) UN Protocol 2000 to Prevent, Suppress and Punish Trafficking in Persons, especially women and children, is the first universal treaty that covers almost all aspects of trafficking in persons. "Trafficking in persons shall mean the recruitment, transportation, transfer, harboring or receipt of persons by means of the threat or use of force or other forms of coercion, of abduction, of fraud, of deception, of the abuse of power, or of a position of vulnerability or of the giving or receiving of payments or benefits to achieve the consent of a person having control over another person for the purpose of exploitation. Exploitation shall include, at a minimum, the exploitation of the prostitution of others or other forms of sexual exploitation, forced labor or services, slavery or practices similar to slavery, servitude or the removal of organs".

(ii.) UN Convention for the Suppression of the Trafficking in Persons and of the Exploitation of the Prostitution of Others States that "...prostitution (is) incompatible with the dignity and worth of the human person".

(iii.) Convention on the Elimination of All forms of Discrimination Against Women (CEDAW), 1979 - Article 6 of CEDAW obliges State parties to take all measures including legislation to suppress all forms of traffic in women.

(iv.) UN Convention on the Rights of the Child (CRC), 1989– Article 34 and 35 enjoin State parties to take all appropriate national, bilateral and multilateral measures to prevent the abduction, sale or traffic in children for any purpose or in any form. Article 39 ensures that State take all appropriate measures to promote the physical and psychological recovery and social inte-gration of a child victim from any form of neglect.

(v.) Vienna Declaration of 1993 at the World Conference on Human Rights stresses the importance of working towards the elimination of violence against women in public and private life, the elimination of all forms of sexual harassment, exploitation and trafficking in women.

(vi.) Beijing Declaration and Platform for Action 1995 of the Fourth World Conference on Women held in Beijing, in its strategic objective D 3 aims to "eliminate trafficking in women and assist victims of violence due to prostitution and trafficking."

(vii.) ILO Convention on the Worst Forms of Child Labour of 1999 (Convention 182) has identified commercial sexual exploitation as a worst form of child labour and its obligate members to eliminate as a priority such worst forms of child labour.

(viii.) Outcome Document of the Beijing Plus Five UN General Assembly Special Session, 2000 in its Recommendations for Actions to be taken at the National level: 104 a) take appropriate measures to address the root factors, including external factors, that encourage trafficking in women and girls for prostitution and other forms of commercial sex, forced marriages and forced labour in order to eliminate trafficking in women including by strengthening existing legislation with a view to providing better protection of the rights of women and girls and to punishing the perpetrators, through both criminal and civil measures.

8

Child Trafficking in the International Community

Trafficking in general and child trafficking in particular has received increased attention over the last decade. International agencies, governments and non-governmental organizations (NGOs) are clearly eager to take actions to stop trafficking. However, the statistical data available is, at best, illustrative because of the illegal nature of trafficking. A number of indepth studies have been produced in the last decade though these have been uneven in their geographical coverage as well as in the issues they have addressed. For example, there are many more studies covering trafficking for sexual exploitation, with fewer dealing with trafficking for labour exploitation. This imbalance is brought to light in the studies that define trafficking and traffickers only in relation to the sex industry. Geographically speaking, most studies focus on trafficking in Asia and Europe. Africa has also received some attention, especially more recently. The most neglected region is South America. Here, trafficking has yet to start gaining some attention. Although there is a general perception that trafficking is not as significant in South America as it is in the other regions, until more research on this issue starts emerging, this cannot be confirmed with certainty. More-over, available information indicates that trafficking is, as in some African countries, linked with traditional forms of patronage and, therefore, it is often not perceived as trafficking.

The aim of this study is twofold: (1) to present the problem of child trafficking for labour exploitation in the migration of Bolivians to Argentina, and (2) to assess the usefulness of the trafficking framework within the context of the international movement of people taken into consideration in this paper. Four case studies will be used to illustrate the main mechanisms involved in child trafficking for labour exploitation, such as the reasons for wanting to migrate, recruitment practices, working conditions, and consequences. The last part discusses the way these issues relate to policy initiatives. Specifically, it questions the usefulness of the trafficking framework in contexts where teenagers are considered old enough to work locally as well as abroad. The general assumption of the negative consequences children and teenagers face as a result of having been trafficked are also questioned by the case studies presented in this paper given that the "trafficking event" eventually developed into adult economic migration.

The case studies presented in this sectionform part of a larger study on gender, race and ethnicity issues in the migration of Bolivians to Argentina, undertaken as part of a doctoral degree. Fieldwork was conducted in Cocha-bamba, Bolivia (May-June 2002) and in Buenos Aires, Argentina (January-March 2003). The study focuses on a particular neighbourhood on the outskirts of Cochabamba, mainly inhabited by ex-miners who migrated from a mining community situated on the border between the departments of Cochabamba, La Paz and Oruro.

The collection of life stories was the main data collection method used. These were collected from Bolivian migrants living in Buenos Aires as well as returnees. A total of 38 life stories were collected from both women and men migrants and returnees. The life stories were complemented by a survey conducted in a neighbourhood consisting mainly of ex-mining families on the outskirts of Cochabamba in Bolivia to establish general migration trends. About one-quarter of the community was surveyed, which included 157 households and 605 cases being recorded. The aim of using such an approach in the study of international migration is to look closely at the experience of a small number of people in order to gain a better understanding of their subjective experience of migration. This approach follows calls for increased attention to be paid to the social actors who under take migration, including their personal narratives and generally, the arguments made for a biographical approach to the study of migration. By allowing the researcher to analyse a person's subjective experience and understanding of a particular issue, the biographical approach can enable researchers to arrive at new understandings of human trafficking. It also gives space for gaining a longer time-dimension on particular issues and specifically, understanding the way an issue develops through time in a person's life.

The four people whose cases are presented in this paper are those of migrants living in Buenos Aires at the time of the interview (one) and returnees (three). Two (a man and a woman) are originally from rural areas while the other two (two women) were born and raised in a mining town. All are bilingual Quechua and Spanish speakers and all migrated during the 1990s when they were between the ages of 13 and 16. Human trafficking, including child trafficking, is generally treated within the international framework for combating human trafficking. The United Nations' adoption of the Protocol to Prevent, Suppress and Punish Trafficking in Persons, Especially Women and Children (A/55/383) on 2 November 2000 was a welcome development aimed at setting a common international ground for fighting trafficking-related crime. It provides a common definition of trafficking and makes a useful distinction between adult and child trafficking. Children are given a special status within this Protocol. Article 3, subparagraph (c) of the Protocol specifies that "the recruitment, transportation, transfer, harbouring or receipt of a child for the purpose of exploitation shall be considered 'trafficking in persons' even if this does not involve any of the means set forth in subparagraph (a) of this article".

Difficulties arise in relation to the lack of clear definitions about the circumstances that can be classified as "child trafficking", especially in view of the fact that key concepts such as "exploitation", "coercion"and "vulnerability" have been left undefined. Many have also pointed out the additional constraints inherent in the Protocol which are related to the fact that it is essentially a crime prevention instrument, rather than a human rights instrument. As it will be shown in this paper, the nature of child trafficking is based on complex patterns of human movement and, therefore, its boundaries are not always clear-cut. In particular, it is important to recognize that use of the Protocol imposes the need to define people according to their status as "victims of trafficking" to make them eligible for receiving protection and support from the government of the country they find themselves in. Eligibility for protection and support for victims of trafficking are in themselves not guaranteed since they are an optional rather than compulsory part of the Trafficking Protocol. Rather, they have to avail themselves of other international human rights instruments.

CHILD TRAFFICKING IN LATIN AMERICA

There is, relatively speaking, very little information about human trafficking in Latin America and where such information exists, it is often not distinguished from human smuggling. This lack of information stems from the fact that most of the literature on trafficking is in English and also that the issue itself is just starting to filter in through the international organizations working there (ILO, 2002). However, this does not mean that trafficking is not a serious problem in Latin American countries.

The International Labour Organization (ILO) has identified adult and child human trafficking for the pur-poses of sexual exploitation in relation to the tourist industry in countries such as Brazil, Costa Rica, Guatemala, El Sal-vador and Mexico. A study conducted by Mike Dottridge (2004) as well as that published by Social Alert (2000) concluded that the most widespread form of child trafficking in Latin America is that of illegal international adoptions. For the specific case of Bolivia, a review by the international NGO Terre des hommes has identified a number of sectors in Bolivia where child trafficking takes place: commercial sexual abuse; work, including hard labour (in agriculture, housework, craft and industries); international adoptions; and organ transplantation.

Moreover, many different forms of trafficking are widely practiced but are apparently unrecognized as such because they are embedded in traditional forms of patronage. For example, in Andean countries it is common for poorer families to entrust some of their daughters to better-off families to "help" with domestic work in exchange for education. This alleviates the economic burden posed by daughters who are often considered unproductive workers in rural households, while at the same time giving them in theory the opportunity to further their education. This form of exchange is common between households who have formed a fictitious-relative bond called compadrazgo, for example, by a better-off person sponsoring the celebration of a major event in another person's life.

One of the few studies available on child trafficking in Bolivia argues that the parents who give their children away often do so in good faith, thinking that they are providing the child with better opportunities and suggests that they do not seem to be aware of the situations of vulnerability they are placing their child in or the extremely exploitative working conditions these children often have to endure. The same NGO, Defensa de los Niños y Niñas Internacional (DNI), argues that in-country trafficking is very common while at the same time the legal framework for combating it is non-existent. Bolivia has as yet signed but not ratified the Trafficking Protocol, which is in any case weak in terms of dealing with adult and child trafficking that takes place within national borders. When cases of child trafficking come to light, they are generally dealt with within the provisions of the Children's and Adolescents' Code and the National Labour Law.

The regional as well as Bolivian national situation in relation to trafficking- related initiatives is still lagging behind that of other countries but is slowly improving. Argentina was last year placed in the Tier 2 Placement while Bolivia on the Tier 2 "Watch List" according to the United States Trafficking in Persons Report. The still low but never-theless increasing number of studies dealing with adult and child human trafficking indicates a growing awareness and interest in the issue regionally as well as nationally. Notable examples include a study of internal as well as international child trafficking in Bolivia conducted by DNI, which also deals with cases of child trafficking under their child protection objective. The International Organization for Migration (IOM) has a project for Combating Irregular Migration and the Trafficking of Persons in the Countries of the Andean Community (CIMAC project). Child trafficking is covered at the regional level by the Inter-American Convention on International Traffic in Minors, which was ratified by both Bolivia (in 2003) and Argentina (in 1999). It has also been addressed as a specific issue under the provisions of the UN Convention on the Rights of the Child by both Bolivia and Argentina. However, both countries still lack specific laws and an anti-trafficking enforcement strategy while corruption of law enforcement agents is likely to pose persistent barriers to effective anti-trafficking action.

International child trafficking in Bolivia is often undertaken as a result of national as well as personal crisis and is, at the time it takes place, the best available option open to the persons who are being trafficked. International child trafficking for the purposes of labour exploitation takes place for work in the agricultural sector, textile workshops and services, for example, domestic work and sex work. The causes for child trafficking are closely related to those that sustain international migration the prolonged political and economic crisis, collapse of traditional industries such as mining, inadequate land distribution for sustaining the rural population engaged in subsistence agriculture, structural adjustments implemented since the 1980s, gender-based discrimination, and income differences as compared to the countries of destination. In addition, existing inequalities based on ethnic, racial, class, and gender differences place specific groups of adults as well as children at a greater risk of being trafficked. This is also the case in other geographical regions such as Asia, where girls and those belonging to ethnic minorities are much more likely to be trafficked than others.

Internal and international trafficking can have very different consequences for the people being trafficked, especially in terms of their legal situation and the levels of support to which they are entitled. However, from the point of view of the person being trafficked, it is the exploitation to which they are subjected that matters, rather than which side of the border they are in. In cases where international migration patterns are merely an extension of internal migration patterns, the causes of international trafficking can be considered the same as those of internal trafficking. This is particularly the case in Bolivia, where international movements of people have been described by some as an extension of internal migration. Adult as well as child trafficking, therefore, needs to be understood and analysed in conjunction with other, non-trafficking modes of population movements. It is encouraging to note the grow-ing recognition of the close connections between human trafficking and economic migration.

Most victims of trafficking are first and foremost economic migrant workers who have fallen into the hands of traffickers. As far as child trafficking is concerned, the issues become more complicated as a result of the relevance these arguments have with regards to national and international child labour discourses. Trafficking in human beings is, therefore, closely related to established patterns of human movement and generally responds to similar push-pull factors as employment-related migration. However, the policy implications are less likely to be taken up by governments which are at the receiving end of the migration flows given their reticence in recognizing real demands for migrant workers and the general trend toward the closing of the borders.

BOLIVIAN MIGRATION TO ARGENTINA

Given the fact that adult as well as child trafficking takes place within existing movements of people, it is useful to review migration trends between these two countries in order to better situate the life stories presented below. The migration of Bolivians to Argentina is a long-standing phenomenon since the presence of Bolivians was recorded in the first Argentine census in 1869. Since the 1950s, however, this migration flow has been increasing in signi-ficance, both numerically as well as in terms of the way it is perceived by the Argentine population and its government. There are three recent trends in Bolivian migration worth highlighting. In the first place, these are related to the changing destinations. While Bolivians used to migrate to the northern regions of Argentina, they changed their preferences in the 1970s in favour of the capital, Buenos Aires. The shift of the economy toward the tertiary sector and the mechanization of agricultural work, which decreased the demand for seasonal agricultural workers, have contributed to this change.

Secondly, there has been a feminization of migration in general and of Bolivians in particular. In the past, it was mainly men who migrated. In fact, the migration of Boli-vians was one where men pre- dominated to a greater extent than in the migration of people from other neighbouring countries. Since the 1980s, however, women have started playing a much more active role in this migration flow. The increased labour market participation of Argentine women, their higher educational attainments, as well as the aging population are all factors that lead to an increased demand for domestic services, which are mainly met by migrant women. Bolivian women are generally employed in informal street trading in both clothes and vegetables, textile manufacturing and to a lesser extent in domestic work. In contrast, Bolivian men who migrate to rural areas or the outskirts of Buenos Aires usually work in agricultural production while those in urban areas usually work in construction and textile manufacturing.

Thirdly, this international migration has become increasingly irregular. Until the mid-1980s it was relatively easy to regularize one's stay in Argentina. Also, a number of amnesties have been implemented since 1949 with the aim of facilitating the regularization of foreign workers. However, in the last decade it has become increasingly more difficult for migrants to become regular residents due to increased costs, and the requirement of a working contract or close relatives who are already residents in Argentina. In particular, some observers have argued that during the 1990s the Dirección Nacional de Migraciones (DNM), the governmental agency responsible for managing migration as well as implementing migration policies, started imposing additional obstacles for migrants originating from neighbouring countries. Without implementing a specific policy, such practices increased the likelihood of migrants remaining in an undocumented situation.

These wider patterns are clearly visible in the migration of people from the communities taken into account. Survey data suggest that Buenos Aires is the main destination. This is explained by the fact that they started migrating relatively late (late 1980s and early 1990s), when the Argentine capital had already taken precedence as the migrants' favoured destination. Survey data also show that both men and women migrate for work. However, while men's migration began to intensify in the early 1990s, especially since 1993, women's migration started increasing in 1997. This confirms the wider patterns of Bolivian migration to Argentina in relation to the feminization of migration. Finally, the migrants' stories also confirm the trend toward illegality and the increasing difficulties migrants face in their attempts to regularize their stay in Argentina.

The Case Studies

Child trafficking is undertaken within the wider process of labour migration in the long-standing migration flows from Bolivia to Argentina. Bolivian teenagers often migrate to Argentina for the purpose of working as part of their family's livelihood strategies. Children are in this case treated as an economic asset by their families but migrating to a neighbouring country often puts them in a vulnerable situation and exposes them to exploitative working conditions. While it is often assumed that this "vulner-ability" is generally a characteristic of child trafficking itself, it is important to acknowledge that the exploitative working conditions are for Bolivians in Argentina not limited to children. They are a result of the particular labour relations migrants engage in and are heavily influenced by the current migration policies. It is also often argued that being trafficked can prejudice children's long-term interests, for example by restricting their educational potential, but the cases considered here contradict the general assumption that being a victim of trafficking necessarily entails negative long term consequences.

The following case studies illustrate some modes of trafficking. The first two cases belong to what could be classified as "typical" child trafficking cases for the purpose of labour exploitation. The two girls were 16 years old when they were contracted by a "lady" looking for young girls to employ in her textile workshop in Buenos Aires. Debt bondage was involved and the girls were kept in what could be classified as "slavery-like conditions": working 12 hours a day or more, insufficient time off, bad food, and restricted freedom. The other two cases are somewhat ambiguous because the youngsters, a teenage boy and a teenage girl, migrated to Argentina with members of their respective families. Their cases do not fall within the scope of the Trafficking Protocol. However, as will be shown later, they can be classified as victims of trafficking under the Inter-American Convention on International Trafficking in Minors. The fact that they were employed in exploitative working conditions and in contravention of Bolivian child protection legislation makes their situation very similar to that of other teenagers who were trafficked. These four cases raise a number of issues related to child trafficking and teenage migration more broadly.

Maria

Maria worked in a textile workshop while in Buenos Aires and is currently finishing high school. She is single with no children. She was born in 1975 in a mining town in Cochabamba, Bolivia. In its heyday, this mining town used to be an important centre, not only providing employment for miners but also provisioning the neighbouring rural communities with education and health services. It used to attract people from the neighbouring communities and beyond.

Apart from a small number of families that worked in the

service sector, most families relied on the mining industry for their livelihood. The dominant gender ideology assigned reproductive roles to women, who were brought up to be homeworkers while men, the "miners", were assigned the breadwinning role. However, families were numerous and mining a dangerous occupation, which led to many miners' death due to accidents or illness. Many women, therefore, had to take jobs in the mining industry as well. The dominant ideology forbids women entry into the underground mining tunnels. Despite this, some women did work underground, albeit within a strict sexual division of labour. But these women were few. Most women worked in other occupations, such as nightwatching or "palliri", an occupation usually undertaken by women, especially widows, involving sorting out rocks containing ore from those that do not. In the past it was not uncommon for children to start working at an early age. However, education was given priority, wherever possible, to those born since the 1970s.

The mining town was severely hit by the crisis in mining during the 1980s which forced many to look for employ-ment in larger Bolivian urban centres, in the lowland rural colonization areas such as the Chapare region or abroad. Maria moved to a neighbourhood on the outskirts of Cochabamba when she was 16 but stayed only for a week. She went to Buenos Aires as part of a group of 12 girls who were trafficked to work in a textile workshop. She stayed in Buenos Aires until 2001, making regular annual visits home.

The woman who took the group to Buenos Aires promised them a good wage and a return home if they so wished. Maria felt tricked because when she got to Buenos Aires she was made to work from 8 a.m. to 8 p.m. with a 30-minute break. They were not allowed to go out, not even on Sunday, their day off, in case they escaped and left the debt unpaid. As part of the agreement, Maria owed US$360 for documents and travel. Her monthly wage was US$200 but she was forced to work unpaid for three months before her boss let her go. After this period, she left her employers and found a job in another textile workshop with the help of a friend. She eventually recovered the money her employer owed her, though this was returned to her in small amounts.

Isabel

Isabel was born in the same mining centre in Cochabamba, Bolivia. Her father had an accident in the mine when she was young and as a result her family moved to a neighbourhood on the outskirts of Cochabamba. Because her mother did not earn enough to enable her to study, when the opportunity arose at age 15, she went to Buenos Aires with an unknown person who was looking for girls to work in a workshop. In contrast to the promises of training and light work made before migrating, upon arrival in Buenos Aires Isabel was not treated well. She was unhappy with the food she was receiving and that she could not leave the workshop. Her parents signed a contract with this person a guarantee in case she did not come back but Isabel escaped with a couple of other girls who were part of the same group. They found work elsewhere and worked for one month until they were discovered by the person who brought them to Buenos Aires.

Isabel returned to the workshop where she was treated better, was taught how to use the machines and was paid. She remained at the same workshop for five years. During one of her visits home, she met her partner and returned to Buenos Aires with him but did not go back to work. When she became pregnant her partner wanted her to return to Bolivia to give birth, promising her that he would con- tinue to support her, but she refused. Her daughter was born in Buenos Aires in 1999. Following the crisis that hit Argentina in 2001 she returned to Bolivia. She was expecting her second child at the time of the interview.

Juan

Juan was born in Nor Chichas, Potosí in 1982 and has been going to Argentina with his father since he was 13 years old. He is single with no children and has only recently moved to Cochabamba. His migration patterns followed a seasonal logic: during his school holidays he used to accompany his father to the north of Argentina to Salta, Santa Fe, and Mendoza to work on farms. They would earn US$300 to US$400 per month as a family unit, including a rent-free room which enabled them to keep expenses to a minimum. He had some longer stays in Argentina, for example, he stayed in Salta for one year and during his last trip he stayed in Mendoza for three years. Working conditions were rough but comparable to those in Bolivia for similar types of work. He would work up to 13 hours a day. He now plans to finish high school and enter university to study languages.

Miriam

Miriam was born in 1982 and brought up in Nor Chichas, Potosí, in a rural community. Her father died when she was two years old. She is the youngest of six brothers and sisters, two of whom have died. Her brothers and sisters left home as they were growing up, usually around age 15. Miriam stayed the longest and left home at age 18, as it is customary for the youngest child to take care of the parents. Her life was marked by poverty. She started migrating to Argentina when she was 15 years old. She undertook sea-sonal trips on a yearly basis, spending January to April in Argentina and returning to Bolivia for the harvest at the end of April. Her income was crucial for the household's survival and complemented the subsistence agriculture practiced by her mother. The fact that she had never considered migrating to a Bolivian city illustrates the institutionalization of migration as a fundamental element in the management of rural households' livelihoods in the southern regions of Bolivia.

During her first trip to Argentina she travelled with her cousin, but later she also travelled with her brother. She took various jobs in the agricultural sectors in different locations in the same vein as other seasonal agricultural labourers. For some jobs she was paid piece-rate, for example, picking tomatoes she would earn 30 to 40 cents per box, managing 50 to 60 boxes per day averaging a daily wage of US$15 to US$24. However, she considered agricultural work hard, especially for her age. A crucial turning point in her life occurred in her late teens, when she was coming under increasing pressure to get married because it was customary for girls in her community to marry around age 15. The situation became unbearable when she was 18 years old so she ran away and remained in Argentina to escape marriage. This time she looked for work in the domestic sector and found an apprenticeship in Mendoza. She moved to Buenos Aires with her employers.

In Buenos Aires she found life hard as she was very lonely. Additionally, her employers refused to increase her salary, despite the fact that now she was fully trained and was also working in the kitchen. Lacking a residency and work permit decreased her bargaining power in relation to her employers as they used her irregular status as an excuse for not increasing her salary. When the crisis hit Argentina in December 2001, Miriam's employers decreased her salary by more than 10 per cent. She left her job and moved in with Mario, whom she had met in Mendoza and who had by then arrived to Buenos Aires. She had a daughter in January 2003.

The Mechanisms

There is little doubt that trafficking is very closely related to internal and international migration in various ways. Trafficking often "picks up" on regular migration flows, generating a trend parallel to that of "ordinary" labour migration. The routes, as well as parts of the trafficking process, are often similar, whether this is the recruitment, transportation, or stay abroad. In fact, an "ordinary" migration can turn into a case of trafficking if any of the issues associated with trafficking take place along the migration "chain". The remainder of the "chain" or process can, therefore, be exactly the same for ordinary migrants as for victims of trafficking. Thus, wherever cases of trafficking occur, it is very likely that there already exists an established migration flow. In most of these cases, there needs to be a motivation for wanting to migrate in order for trafficking to take place unless it is an outright case of abduction (which constitutes a small minority of all cases of adult as well as child trafficking). What follows is a detail-ed analysis of the four cases, which highlights the main issues involved in child trafficking for labour exploitation, including the reasons for wanting to migrate, recruitment procedures, the working conditions, and the consequences of child trafficking.

Reasons for wanting to migrate

The main reasons for wanting to migrate are economic and related to poverty and limited working opportunities. All four cases presented above migrated for work. They were all similar in that they felt compelled to migrate in order to help their parents support their families due to financial difficulties. Juan explains that working abroad was the only option available to his family at the time, "We really didn't have a choice, it was the only way we could keep going, you see. [...] Because we were really struggling economically".

Seasonal migration is customary for those coming from rural areas. Households maximize their income and subsistence options by alternating subsistence work on their own plots of land in Bolivia with income-generating opportunities, often in the form of taking employment in urban areas of Bolivia and/or in Argentina. Miriam used to return home every year to help her widowed mother work on her plots, "So, I always used to go and help my mum, always. Every year when I returned, I would arrive by the 25 [or] 20 of April". The mining communities where most of the interviewees originated from suffered severely during the 1980s from the imposition of structural adjustment programmes and the mining crisis in general. The lack of working opportunities in the mining centres compelled many to look for work in larger Bolivian cities, from where many decided to migrate abroad.

Poverty often forces families to send their children to work. The fact that movement or migration is involved in the process does not necessarily matter, especially where migration to the neighbouring country is an established source of employment to the point that, in some cases, it sidelines completely any consideration of employment within the country. A study on child trafficking in Bolivia has identified poverty as the main problem behind internal as well as international trafficking. The parents' inability to feed, dress and educate their children often forces them to "entrust" them to relatives or other people. This is echoed by examples in other countries.

The case studies also confirm this. Miriam's description of her life before going to Argentina speaks for itself:

> My life was quite poor. When I was in Bolivia, how can I tell you, in Bolivia I lived with my mum and it was fine. Bah, it was OK but we always needed something, since my father wasn't there. Always, many things ... [...] My father died a long time ago. He left me when I was two years old. [...] I left when I was 18. But until then, I was with my mother and all was well but we always needed something. Do you understand? I used to come here, and used to go back, four, three months. The money that I used to take back, it was all for food, the necessary, nothing more. When it was finished, I had to come again.

However, child trafficking is the result of complex dynamics; therefore, locating its causes solely in poverty is simplistic. It should always be kept in mind that complex processes related to gender, ethnic and class differences put some people into a more vulnerable position than others and work in such a way as to determine who does the least desirable jobs at the national, regional, as well as household level. Gender-based discrimination and oppressive patriarchal structures sometimes also play a part in women's decisions to seek employment abroad (Chant, 1998; Chant and Radcliffe, 1992). This was clearly the case in Miriam's life. She was increasingly under pressure to get married at an early age and despite the fact that this was customary for girls in her hometown, she did not find this appealing and chose migration instead.

I had problems, problems, problems. And I had to get married. Because of that, and also I run away. They wanted to get me married. My mother didn't particularly want that but [the boy] was running after me too much. [...] They were running after me because they wanted to marry me, that's why I ran away [and came] here, that's why I didn't return to Bolivia. [...] I didn't want to get married yet but he insisted. Getting to know me and getting married, quickly, he wanted. But I didn't want to get married quickly. And I didn't want him for living with, like this. So, because of that I run away.

While it is fairly straightforward to establish why these teenagers migrated, the decision-making process related to seeking work abroad is somewhat more elusive. Isabel's story illustrates the fine line between a personal voluntary decision to seek work abroad and wider family pressures to do so. While she initially states that she decided to migrate "for work", in a later statement she explains that she was sent to Argentina because her father had an accident in the mine. Given their age and the situation their families were in, it is fair to assume that all four teenagers came under great pressure to seek work to contribute to their households. At the time this situation arose, working abroad was perceived as the most favourable of the options available to them.

Recruitment

Issues related to recruitment are clearly more relevant for those who were trafficked than for those who migrated with family members. Maria and Isabel travelled as part of a group to Buenos Aires. They were recruited by a woman neither they nor their families knew, who came to the neighbourhood looking for young girls to work in a textile workshop in Buenos Aires. She recruited a group of 12 girls, most of whom were teenagers, to take to Buenos Aires to work in her textile workshop.

Both Maria and Isabel felt that their employer had used deceit and lies in order to convince them to take the job offer in Argentina. Maria remembers that the lady offered to "pay us cash, that she will pay us of course, there [in Argentina] you earn a little bit better than here [in Bolivia] that she was going to bring us back after one year, that if we wanted to come back, she would bring us back". She felt deceived: "Here she told us that she would treat us really well, that the work wasn't hard, all that. But it was exactly the opposite".

Isabel's parents had signed a contract in front of a lawyer. The lady had offered to teach her to work in textiles and to pay her a good wage. However, Isabel was unhappy with the situation she was in once she arrived in Buenos Aires.

She treated us badly and threw us out. Maria must have told you the same. Maria also ran away from that workshop. [...] She ran away first, then I ran away with my sister because she was treating us badly, because the food wasn't what it was supposed to be. The food was very heavy, like here in Bolivia, pasta, an egg, something like that. For that reason we run away. In addition to the bad treatment, Isabel was cheated when the employer offered to do the paperwork to regularize her stay in Argentina, making her pay 700 pesos when the actual cost was about 150 pesos. Debt bondage was also involved, resulting in severe curtailment of the girls' freedom. Maria explains that on Sundays they used to do:

"Nothing more than stay in our room, wash the clothes, our clothes. Because they wouldn't even let us go out. [...] Yes, because they had paid [for things] here, the paperwork, the fares, all and they were afraid that we would go, like that, without paying that back. She owed the employer US$360, had a monthly wage of US$200, but was forced to work for no pay for three months. Isabel also owed the employer US$200, for which she worked for the first month without pay. Maria and Isabel ended up running away from the workshop while their employer was away on holiday. While signing a contract is usually suggested as a protective practice, in the case of these girls the contract was used in order to keep them in the workshop. Isabel recalls: "We had to run away because he wouldn't let us since we were working under a contract. We signed a paper, so when the owner came here [to Cochabamba] on holiday, we had to run away."

There is also some evidence that other, more organized ways of finding cheap migrant workers are also operating, especially in the south of Bolivia for work in agriculture. Juan explains:

> I've heard commentaries. That here the currency in comparison with over there it's low, you see? And with that [that is the excuse they use]. Let's say, "I pay you Bs$500 per month"; Bs$500 is US$100 and they take them and there you don't earn only US$100, you should earn at least US$300 or US$400, for sure. And that's how they take them "I will pay you Bs$500, let's go". They take them, with passport and they make them work hard and they only give them US$100. Miriam's and Juan's experiences, both of whom travelled with family members, are very different as they were generally less disappointed with the whole migration process.

WORKING CONDITIONS

Juan and Miriam talk in a "matter-of-fact" way about their work in Argentina. Juan worked hard, especially if his age and ten- to 13-hour work day are taken into con-sideration. Although both Juan and Miriam found the work hard, they did not seem resentful of the working conditions or of what they found once they got to Argentina. As Juan said, I think the work is the same [between Bolivia and Argentina] [...]. One makes sacrifices because of wanting to earn more, if not they work better, I don't know, I would-n't find much of a difference, because the work is the same, I don't know. If one wants to earn more, one works more, if not, no.

Miriam's jobs in the agricultural sector were very similar. She worked piece- rate, earning between 15 pesos and 24 pesos a day, depending on how many boxes she could fill. The work, the work is hard, for my age at least, it's hard. I used to suffer working. I couldn't stand the heat. The heat here is one thing; over there it's another thing altogether! I suffered because I couldn't get used to it. Rather than perceiving very long days and the hard work as exploitative, most migrants perceive exploitation in terms of the injustices they are sometimes subjected to, for example, when they are not paid for their work. Miriam was working for her aunts picking strawberries for some time, but, despite being promised a wage, she did not get paid. In her view, her aunts took advantage of her and in the end she had to leave them without having gained anything.

Maria's and Isabel's experiences were very different. They were both disillusioned with what they found on their arrival in Buenos Aires. They knew very little about what Argentina was like and what to expect on their arrival. Maria said, "Really, I didn't imagine anything. [...] Nothing, nothing. As I say, it was a surprise. I barely had three days, with the formalities. I didn't know anything about Argentina. [...] Nobody had ever spoken to me about Argentina". The working conditions in the textile workshops were also hard to bear. "We were working from 8 a.m. to 8 p.m., but it was, how can I say, with machines". They had a 30-minute break and only Sundays off. She was earning 200 pesos, the equivalent to US$200, which was the bare minimum for the type of work and that period of time.

Isabel's wage was also very low for the general standard in Buenos Aires at the time. She was earning 250 pesos. Isabel's working conditions improved once she returned to the workshop after escaping. She was being paid piece-rate, which she considered better and was upgraded from being a helper to working on her own machine. Her wage increased to 450 pesos per month and she stayed for almost five years.

Consequences

As far as child trafficking is concerned, it is generally assumed that the consequences will be negative. The authors of an ILO report for example argue that "The loss of future productivity and earning power through low educational levels, ill health and potentially premature death is also felt at the country and regional level". Looking at these four life accounts as a whole, however, allows for the possibility to see the processes of change and the way these teenagers overcame their initial problems. Education is one thorny issue when it comes to assessing the pros and cons of children's engagement in paid employment, including their employment abroad as it is often argued that this has negative long-term consequences for their education. This does not seem to be the case in the four cases presented here. Juan and Maria are now finishing high school and considering continuing their studies at a university. Isabel and Miriam did not continue with their studies but for reasons quite separated from their decision to migrate.

Miriam was 15 when she started migrating and was still studying at the time but by then she had already understood that continuing with her education would be difficult. Isabel was also age 15 when she left for Argentina. She attributes the fact that she did not continue with her studies to her migration. I think that if I had not gone [to Argentina], I would have continued to study, I would have had a profession and I would be much better off than I am now. I went for the work, for the work, because my father is a miner, he could not pay for us to study. If I had stayed, I would have had some studies, now I would have been in a much better position. I only went there to earn a little bit, I learnt to sew, but also as I am now close to my parents, I more or less manage. Because Miriam and Isabel left school precisely when they migrated abroad, it would be easy to see migration as the main cause for cutting their studies short. However, a closer examination of their situation seems to suggest that they would not have been able to continue with their studies anyway, because of the family situations. In both cases, their families lacked the financial resources to enable them to continue studying.

Isabel went to Argentina following her father's accident. In her case, it would have been very difficult for her to achieve a "profession", as she says, if her family was in such a difficult financial situation. Despite the fact that she blames migration for not having a brighter future, had she stayed in Bolivia, she would probably have had to take on an income-generating activity to help support herself and her family. Moreover, it could be quite possible that in Juan's and Maria's case it was migration itself that enabled them to finish high school and consider a higher education, either through the money they were able to save while working abroad or by their families recognition of their contribution and desire to now return the "contribution" in the form of supporting them through higher education.

In all four cases the teenagers have not suffered any particularly difficult set- backs due to migration/trafficking and have made a smooth transition from being "victims of trafficking" to becoming independent adult migrants. Juan is currently living with his sister, finishing high school and helping out in the family store. Maria is now back in Bolivia, living with her parents, finishing high school and considering higher education. Isabel has also returned to Bolivia; she has her own family and is expecting her second child. Miriam is for now living in Buenos Aires with her partner and caring for her young baby. All four were able to overcome the initial difficulties they experienced while working abroad, either for their families or for others, finding more satisfactory employment opportunities and either (temporarily) settling in Buenos Aires or returning to Bolivia. Their lives are not significantly different from those of others who started migrating as young adults and who were not trafficked.

It could well be the case that they were able to do so because of the nature of child trafficking in this particular context. The traffickers were their parents, relatives, or strangers, but in comparison with child trafficking in, for example, the cocoa or sex business, child trafficking was in this case undertaken on a comparatively smaller scale and with smaller returns for the traffickers involved. When this is a family's subsistence activity, it is probably the case that most of the earnings were re-invested in the household while in the case of the textile workshop the earnings might be higher but still much lower than those of the criminal networks that control other child trafficking rings.

DISCUSSION OF POLICY IMPLICATIONS

It is clear that the four cases examined here present problems that are quite different in nature. Some might even question whether they can be considered cases of child trafficking. A quick look at the framework presented by the Protocol clarifies their position. The Protocol states "Exploitation shall include, at a minimum, the exploitation of the prostitution of others or other forms of sexual exploitation, forced labour or services, slavery or practices similar to slavery, servitude or the removal of organs". The debt bondage combined with the curtailment of the teen-agers' freedom clearly places Maria's and Isabel's experience within the scope of the Trafficking Protocol. They faced restricted freedom of movement by not being allowed outside the workshop, even on their day off; they were not given food deemed "decent" or "sufficient"; the wages were the bare minimum for that time and place with terrible working conditions, including overcrowded workshops with insufficient light and/or ventilation which made many workers suffer from fluff contamination, worsening eye sight, and serious back and shoulder pain; the sleeping quarters were often inadequate, with textile workshop workers often crammed into very small rooms, separated by sex, forcing various workers to take shifts sleeping on the same bed; the work hours were long, up to 12 hours with one 30-minute break is common; and they were recruited by a person who was purposefully deceiving them in order to convince them to accept the offer of employment abroad. There is little doubt that their situation could be categorized as cases of child trafficking.

The cases of Miriam and Juan are somewhat more complicated. Their work abroad contravened the Bolivian Children's and Adolescents' Code (Article 128) which prohibits taking any person younger than age 18 abroad for any type of work, unless they seek previous permission by the Judge of the Minors, which was not the case. Moreover, Juan was under the legal age of 14 for undertaking any type of employment, paid or unpaid, which is set by the Bolivian Children's and Adolescents' Code as well as the Argentine Employment Contracts Act (No.20.744) (UN, 2002, 2004). Both Miriam's and Juan's cases can, therefore, be classified as cases of child trafficking under the Inter-American Convention on

International Traffic in Minors on the grounds that they were taken abroad for unlawful employment.

Having established that all four cases can be classified as child trafficking, the questions that begs to be asked is whether this has actually added anything to our understanding of the main issues in question. In other words, how useful is it to treat these cases and many other similar ones, as cases of child trafficking? Whose interests are served if these teenagers are treated as victims of child trafficking? Some might argue that it is not useful to invoke the UN Trafficking Protocol or the Inter-American Convention on Trafficking of Minors given the relatively low levels of human rights abuses experienced by the teenagers taken into account here. However, the UN Convention on the Rights of the Child established that there is no hierarchy of human rights. Moreover, the policy implication derived from these four cases of trafficking can also be applied to other cases of more "severe" curtailment of the child migrants' human rights.

CHILD TRAFFICKING AND CHILD LABOUR

Child trafficking and the application of the relevant international instruments are intimately related with issues of child labour and in many ways, they suffer the same predicaments. International and national NGOs draw attention to issues of human rights abuses by representing the experiences of, in this case, teenage migrant workers as extreme victims of trafficking. This is the case in one of the documents published by Save the Children, which only focuses on extreme cases of child trafficking and makes no distinction between very young children and older teenagers. UNICEF argues against framing child trafficking within a child labour discourse:

> The research reveals a widespread perception of child trafficking solely as a child labour phenomenon. But trafficking violates the rights of children long before their actual labour begins. First, there is the separation of a child from his or her

home. Then there is the time spent in the so-called "care" of the traffickers while the child is transported to the eventual workplace a process that presents its own dangers and abuses. Then, there is the illegal reception or sale of the child and, ultimately, the child's final destination.

The experiences of the teenagers reviewed do not seem to find resonance with this portrayal of child trafficking. Moreover, an approach to child trafficking that distances itself from the issues related to child labour denies teenagers agency and in many cases curtails their already limited options by victimizing them rather than empowering them. In similarity with the problems experienced by working children as a result of the imposition of a universal child labour discourse the child trafficking discourse also needs to take into account cultural diversity and the contexts within which certain practices take place in order to avoid curtailing the already limited choices of migrant workers, including teenage migrant workers. Without wanting to argue against the usefulness of the Trafficking Protocol per se, the analysis of the case studies suggests that it might be useful to distinguish between immediate anti-trafficking initiatives that provide support to victims of trafficking and long-term initiatives that tackle the root causes of trafficking.

As it was shown, all four cases were trafficked to Argentina because a need for migrating existed – rooted in poverty, lack of opportunities, and gender-based discrimination as well as a demand for cheap migrant labour in a context of decreasing opportunities for legal labour migration. As long as this need remains, trafficking is unlikely to be eliminated. Moreover, other context- specific customs also influence these processes. The culturally specific understanding of adulthood is very closely linked to the various forms of child labour. Therefore, while there is an internationally agreed cut-off age used for defining legal child labour, set at age 15 by the ILO Minimum Age Convention (No. 138), it is useful to keep in mind that the concept of adulthood and appropriate age for engaging in paid or unpaid work is culture specific and, therefore, the people involved in what is legally or officially considered child trafficking might not consider themselves or be considered by others as children.

In Bolivia, the girls' fifteenth birthday is celebrated in grand style by those who can afford it and is given much more weight than the passing to the legal adult-hood at age 18. This seems to suggest that girls at this point are no longer considered girls, but have marked their entry into womanhood. Boys, in contrast, often need to wait until they are 18 and have completed the military service before they are considered men. As the case studies illustrated, the girls were deemed old enough not only to work but to leave home and work abroad on their own once they turned 15. Similar results are available in relation to child trafficking in Bangladesh, where most parents consider the ages between 12 and 15 as appropriate for employment-related migration. In these particular contexts, where it is culturally acceptable for teenagers to work or to migrate in search of work, it will be more difficult to apply inter-nationally agreed legislation or raise awareness about child trafficking in a way that would include all people young than age 18 as children. Other, more context-specific responses are, therefore, required in order to ensure that young people's opportunities and welfare are not curtailed.

Border controls and migration policies

Anti-trafficking initiatives often fail to target the root causes of child trafficking but rather focus on law enforcement and firmer border controls. The latest Trafficking in Persons Report published by the US State Department, for example, mentions in relation to Bolivia that "Senior government officials in 2003 expressed a commitment to undertake anti-trafficking measures, such as tightening immigration controls". For the case of Bolivia and Argentina any initiative focusing on border control is bound to be confronted by the institutionalized corruption of the law enforcement agents. This is illustrated by their low score in the rankings produced by Transparency International: Argentina scored 2.5 and Bolivia 2.2 where ten is deemed highly clean and 0 highly corrupt according to the perceptions of business people, academics, and risk analysts.

Migrants are mostly affected by bottom-level corruption, especially of the border police. Border officials often require "visas" from Bolivians entering Argentina as tourists, for which they charge about US$80, despite the fact that there is no such legal requirement. As associate members to the MERCOSUR agreement, Bolivians have the right to enter Argentina as long as they can provide proof of identity in the form of an identity card. The "tourist visa" they receive on the border usually grants them a 15-day stay; if they overstay, they are then required to pay an "exit fine" of US$50. In addition to asking for money for the "tourist visa", the border guards often ask to see proof that they have sufficient money to maintain themselves, generally in the form of US$1000. Most Bolivians have to borrow this money and they do so from agencies operating in the border towns, generally associated with the travel and transport agencies, which charge an exorbitant 10 per cent interest for what is usually a loan of a few hours.

Several reports, as well as the primary data collected, also confirm that border police (especially those guarding land border crossings) are prone to abuse their authority and are easily bribed. The implications for child trafficking are obvious. This is one of the first areas that needs to be investigated in any initiatives that aims to diminish child trafficking in the Southern Cone. However, even if border police were freed from corruption, tighter immigration controls would not necessarily ease child trafficking. In fact, they might be instrumental in further increasing trafficking of both adults and children. As Macklin argues, "Immigration law only partly controls who will come in and who will stay out. To some extent, it merely determines which entrants will be labelled legal and which will be labelled illegal". This is as true for adult migrants as it is for teenage migrant workers.

Illegality or the lack of formal, legal residency papers, is one recurring problem in the migrants' life accounts. For example, Miriam's stay was never regularized. This put her at a disadvantage in her working relationships with her employers, who refused to increase her wage. They also used her irregular status as a bargaining tool for keeping her in their employment, by making her believe that she would be unable to find alternative employment should she decide to leave them. In fact, tighter immigration policies are partly to blame for placing migrants in a vulnerable situation by forcing them in a situation of illegality. Govern-ments should acknowledge the existence of a demand for migrant workers in specific economic sectors and ensure these workers' rights will be protected by granting them work permits. Therefore, one way of decreasing trafficking will be to lower the barriers to legal migration.

The purpose of this paper was to overview child trafficking for labour exploitation in Bolivia and in Latin America more generally. It situated child trafficking within the broader migratory movements within the region and discussed some of its implications. The literature reviewed as well as the primary data show that child trafficking does take place. However, the case studies also reveal that the concept of "child trafficking" itself might not be the most appropriate one for either describing or tackling a phenomenon that is essentially teenage labour migration. The cultural barriers to a blank application of anti-trafficking policies, such as the culturally specific perception of adulthood and the fact that teenage girls are often considered young adults when they are 15 years old also raise issues in relation to the globalized application of standardized childhood concepts. The cases confirm that they were considered old enough to leave home and seek employment abroad.

The life stories examined in this paper have shown that the "victims of child trafficking" have through time developed into "normal" adult labour migrants. The push factors that led the teenagers to consider migration as a possibility correspond to the same factors that lead other people within the same communities to seek work abroad lack of employment opportunities, favourable exchange rates, personal crisis, and gender-based discrimination. The characteristics of the teenagers involved specifically, their age as well as the mechanisms involved, such as deceit and debt bondage, turn their migration into child trafficking. With time, however, their experience can again be categorized as "labour migration". The experience of "child trafficking", therefore, becomes only a phase within the larger and longer process of a person's geographical movements. Treating these teenage migrants as "victims of child trafficking" will do little to improve their situation. Banning them from seeking work abroad might actually place them in a worse situation by decreasing their already- limited opportunities to sustain themselves and their families or by forcing them to undertake the journeys abroad outside of the scope of legal protection thereby placing them at greater risk of exploitation and abuse.

Following this argument, it would be easy to conclude that interventions into child trafficking are of very little use. Clearly, interventions that tackle adult as well as child trafficking are necessary, especially in terms of providing information about the migrants' human and labour rights and sources of support as well as setting up the provision of immediate support in the form of, for example, secure accommodation and shelter to people who have been victims of physical, psychological or sexual abuse. The establishment of anti-trafficking programmes does not a priori secure the protection of migrants' human rights, especially in view of the fact that many such programmes still criminalize victims of trafficking on the basis of their irregular migration status and puts them at increasing risk by deporting them to their country of origin. These projects that offer immediate support to victims of trafficking are also no substitute for long- term interventions that aim to tackle the root causes of trafficking, such as poverty, inequality, gender-based discrimination and increasingly restrictive migration policies the structures that allow human rights violations to take place.

A SITUATION ANALYSIS ON PROSTITUTION OF BOYS

Sexual abuse and commercial exploitation of children have been emerged as a concerned and discussing matter globally. Different researches and consultations demons-trated although there have been a number of studies on child sexual abuse and exploitation like prostitution, pornography, trafficking for sexual purpose etc., it is not possible to be acquainted with in-depth expose of forms of sexual abuse. In addition, the empirical evidence also shows that men and women and sometimes children themselves exploit children sexually in different ways, for different purposes and in various contexts, which are remained extremely hidden and are mostly reluctant to disclose or regarded as slight look up its intensity and actions against CAS and CSEC in most cases by governmental and non-governmental actors. It is obvious that sexual abuse, especially commercial forms of sexual abuse of children is disturbingly hidden in society, which creating obstructs to address in effective manner. It is estimated that there are approximately 10,000 to 29,000 victims of CSEC in Bangladesh. 100,000 to 150,000 women are involved in floating and brothel based sex work.

A daily national paper named Sangbad, Bangladesh reported on 20th December 2005 that each month 100 children and above 50 women are trafficked from the country. A survey of International Organization of Mig-ration (IOM) revealed that each year 20 thousands women and children are being trafficked from Bangladesh. The survey report of Mass Line Medial Center has revealed that the incidences of trafficking are occurring higher across the bordering areas of North and South Western Parts of Bangladesh (reported by Daily Shangbad on 3rd July 2006). It is also reported that most of trafficking of women and children are occurring for sexual purposes as hidden strate-gies corrupting the government and community people. The situation is the production of various factors affecting the population in various ways.

The increased polarisation of wealth, diverse and un-equal development conditions between rural and urban setups, recurrent natural disaster and gradual decline in the economic situation in the country are breaking the surviving conditions of the people. Conflict in family and the despoliation and dislocation of families make the children vulnerable breaking psychosocial care and protection towards them. Marginalization, economic hardship and injustice resort the children to hazardous forms of works, such as sex work as a means of survival. Their survival strategy renders them vulnerable to all forms of exploitation and abuse. The entrapment of children for all forms of exploitation takes them on a course from one part to another in or outside the country. In the country, the issue of sexual abuse and exploitation of children, especially commercial sexual exploitation of children is disclosed as committing violence only on girls and women. But the extent and diversity of sexual abuse and exploitation on boys are overlooked seriously.

A situational analysis on the prostitution of boys in Bangladesh, conducted by ECPAT International and INCIDIN Bangladesh in 2004, indicated that young boys living on the street, migrant boys and boys working as child labourers are especially vulnerable to sexual exploitation. The research notes that the issues of male to male sex and the taboos surrounding it have led to silence and indifference towards sexual crimes against boys. The study also reveals that for many men their first sexual experience with another male was forced. The same study estimated that the average age of entry into prostitution was around 12 years old, with many boys having been sexually exploited at a much younger age, some as early as 8 years old. But the study was conducted covering the areas of the two divisional cities named Dhaka and Chittagong. The empirical and programmatic evidences have revealed that the prostitution of boys is organized in a network with separate languages within them in all spheres of the country. As the prostitution of boys is mostly unrecognized and unaccepted socially, culturally and in legal framework of the country, its dynamics and extant is remained as hidden hampering its intervention. In addition, as the victims of prostitution of boys suffer acute social exclusion and mostly reluctant to acquaint them with public spheres, so the prostitution of boys is considered as an inconsequential issue remaining as hidden in public arenas. The socio-cultural and political aspects hamper the government and development agencies to address the issue of prostitution of boys.

RATIONALE AND IMPORTANCE OF THE STUDY

The empirical evidence stated that the boys who are engaged in restaurants works, hotel boys, boys engaged in transport sector and street working boys are the victims of prostitution or at risk like situation of being forced in sexual interaction by older penetrator. Another thing is that the boys who are engaged in goods smuggling as carrier in extreme border belt region are at risk of sexual abuse and exploitation by cross border undocumented migration and trafficking. Different published report has put the number of street children in Bangladesh at approximately two million, most of them are observed in the divisional cities of the country. The sexual abuse and exploitation of the children is rampant. Rajshahi city is a divisional city where about 108144 numbers of children are in street situation, which is the third largest quantity of street children after Dhaka and Chittagong.

Those children are working as labourer, hotel boy, petty business, shop helper, begging, vendor, workshop helper, restaurant helper, mechanic helper, tokai, etc. It reported that children are coerced into massaging adults and are forced to engage in sexual activities in market places, parks, railway stations and boat and bus terminals. In this perspective, it is aimed to assess the vulnerability of the boy children in different settings along with finding out the causes and extent of sexual abuse and prostitution of boys. It is another issue to address the community response in cultural dimension on the prostitution of boys with determining the community care system for the victims of sexual abuse and exploitation and who are at risk. Because, due to socio-cultural perspective, very conservative societal value system and strict social taboo, the issue of the prostitution of boys is largely unaccepted, remained unbelief, reluctant, unreported and unrecognized in the community.

On the other hand, boys involved in prostitution are passing their lives in traumatic and stigmatic situation and even death. It is noted that through the study, it has addressed the issue of prostitution of boys among the civil society and community as a social problem. It has explored the situation of prostitution of boys in Rajshahi for getting a clear picture concerning this issue. Besides, the objectives of the study are helpful to determine and develop the community care system.

As national and international agenda, it will address the national level advocacy to legal framework of the national plan of action for sexually abused and exploited boy children, including trafficking. It will be effective documents to take up the basic strategic document for policy dialogue with the governmental officials to bring about institutional changes in favour of the sexually exploited boys.

The study was aimed to explore a qualitative analysis addressing the situation of prostitution of boys and assessing the vulnerability of boys relating to sexual abuse and exploitation. It has covered the areas of Rajshahi city and land port areas of Chapai Nawabgonj District, which purposely intends to explore the situation of vulnerabilities of prostitution of boys in socio-cultural settings. The study is an analytical framework exploring the extent and dynamic of sexual abuse and exploitation of boys. It is also aim to determine the community cares towards the victims of sexual abuse and exploitation and boys who are at risk like situation to be victimized to such violations. A numbers of research methods have been brought into play to scrutinize the study findings and reach its purposes.

The study has been conducted covering a numbers of areas of Rajshahi city (divisional city of the northern region of Bangladesh situated at border belt area of Bangladesh and India) and land port areas of Chapai Nawabgonj district, 60 Km. away from the Rajshahi city. In the Rajshahi city, the data collection areas include (a) Railway Station, (b) Bus stand, (c) Riverbank of Padma and its adjacent slums, (d) Shaheb Bazar Areas. The land port areas of Chapai Nawab-gonj district included different spots in the area. The study was basically the qualitative analysis but presented as quantitative where it is possible. Both primary and secondary sources of information have been used to induce the consistence of the study relating to vulnerability. The primary data have been collected through field based data collection techniques. The secondary data have covered the research studies and reports on sexual abuse and exploitation and also the documents of international, regional and national instruments.

The primary data was collected using rapid assessment techniques, which includes (a) In-depth Interviews by Semi-structure Schedule, (b) Focus Group Discussion (FGD), (c) Observation and (d) Tea Stall and Informal Discussions. The data were collected by conducting meeting or session with some selected NGOs. Apart from the primary collection of data, the research team reviewed different published documents on the issue of CSA, CSEC and prostitution of boys.

(a.) *In-depth interviews by semi-structure schedule*: The data have been collected by in-depth interviews with the boys who are sexual abused and exploited, prostitutes of boys and the boys who are in street situation but has experience of sexual abuse. The in-depth interview was conducted with 110 numbers of victims of boys (75 in Rajshahi city and 35 in land port areas) with predetermined semi-structure schedule. In-depth interview was also conducted with the exploiters, who are mainly known as Penetrators or Panthi. Through the in-depth interview with the respondents, it has been assessed the vulnerability of boys, worst forms of child rights violations, and assess nature and dynamics and determine the situation of sexual abuse and exploitation of boys.

(b.) *Focus Group Discussion (FGD)*: FGDs were conducted with the boys, who are sexually abused and exploited, peer and experiential youth, to assess the nature and dynamics and situation of sexual abuse and exploitation of boy children. Through the FGD, it is also assess the community perspective and response towards SAEC. FGDs were conducted with a predetermined schedule

(c.) *Observation*: Field visit was conducted to observe the real sights of boys working, sleeping and moving in street situation aiming to find out vulnerable situation affecting the children in abuse, exploitation and trafficking. Observation technique of data collection was viewed to watch behavioral approach of the boy victims and exploiters in the context of street situation.

(d.) *Tea Stall Discussions*: Tea stall discussions were conducted with different stakeholders to address the community response and belief of the issues of sexual abuse and exploitation of boys and the boys engaged in sex selling markets

(e.) *Informal Discussions*: Informal discussions were conducted with the stakeholders, especially care givers, duty bearers to determine the protective and preventive methods to combat sexual abuse, exploitation and trafficking of boys.

The study is a situation analysis on the prostitution of boys assessing the vulnerability of boys who are exposed to sexual abuse and sex selling objects and targeted by exploiters. It has also focussed on exploitation of boys committed solely by homosexual men in Kothi-Panthi framework. It is clear that the issue of the prostitution of boys is a serious one that has yet received the adequate attention by the government and development actors. However, it is so critical to address the prostitution of boys in the persistent realistic socio-cultural framework exploring the nature and dynamics of boys in prostitution understandable because of defining the prostitution in gender identity. For the study purposes, so it needs to define prostitution of boys and the key words related to prostitution of boys.

Every boy and girl under the age of eighteen years, a period of childhood accorded special consideration in human rights terms (UNHR Art 16b), characterized as a period of evolving capabilities and of vulnerabilities relative to those of adults.5 Under article 1 of the United Nations Convention on the Rights of the Child, 1989 a child is defined as every human being below the age of 18 years unless, under the law applicable to the child, majority is attained earlier.

VIOLENCE AGAINST CHILDREN (VAC)

There is no universally accepted definition of violence against children (VAC). But it is regarded that VAC includes a wide range of behaviors against children beyond their best interests and affecting them physically, mentally and sexually.

It is generally taking place between a child and an older person. The behaviors erotically arouse the older person, generally without consideration for the reactions or choices of the child and without consideration for the effects of the behavior upon a child. Different reports and studies entail violence as:

- All forms of physical, mental and sexual violence, injury and abuse harming children's body and mind, neglect or bad treatment, maltreatment or exploitation, inclu-ding sexual abuse and exploitation (child pros-titution, child pornography), trafficking of children for the pur-pose of trade and sale.
- A definition proposed by the Advisory Panel for the UN study on Violence against Children is as:
- Violence includes all forms of physical/mental (psychological/psychosocial) and sexual violence to children in the form of abuse, neglect, exploitation, as act of commission or omission of direct or indirect forms, that endanger or harm the child's dignity, physical, psychological, or social status, or development.
- VAC may be committed by individuals, single or collectively, who by their characteristics such as age, status, knowledge, structural forms of community are in a positicn of differential powering situation that are falling a child into vulnerable situations leaving them out from enjoying their rights.

CHILD ABUSE

Child abuse is any form of violence against children. The concept varies from country to country and society to society according to its magnitude and intensity. Every child, despite its individual differences and uniqueness is to be considered of equal intrinsic worth, and hence it should be entitled to equal social, economic, civil and political rights, so that the child can be fully protected and enjoy its basic needs for its survival and development, realize its inherent potential and share equally in life, liberty and happiness. In this context, child abuse has been defined by following and considering the different literature. And as a general guide point of view, child abuse is defined as any act of commission or omission that endangers or impairs a child's physical and psychological health and development. Such act is judged on the basis of a combination of community standards and professional expertise to be damaging.

CHILD SEXUAL ABUSE

Child sexual abuse is the sexual exploitation or victimization of a child by an adult adolescent or older child. Sexual Abuse of a child can be defined as 'contacts or interactions between a child and older or more knowledgeable child or adult, such as a stranger, sibling or parents, where the child is being used as an object of gratification for the abuser's sexual desires or needs. These actions are carried out by force, threats, bribes, trickery or pressure. Sexually abusive activities do not necessary involve bodily contact between abuser and the child. Abusive activities could include exhibitionism or voyeurism, such as an adult watching child undressed or encouraging or forcing children to engage in sexual activities with one another, while the abuser observes or films such activities.

The involvement of a child in a sexual activity to which he or she is unable to give informed consent (and may not fully comprehend) or for which the child is not developmentally prepared and cannot give the consent or which violates the laws or social taboos of society. Here, child sexual abuse refers to a range of activities: touching and fondling a child's genitals with or without penetration, forcible intercourse with penetration of child's vagina or anus by a penis or other object (rape and sodomy respectively) regardless of ejaculation. It includes exposing children to adult sexual activity or pornographic moves and photographs, making lewd comments about the child's body, having children pose, undress or perform in a sexual fashion on film or in person or peeping into bathrooms or bed rooms to spy on a child (voyeurism). The definition also includes fondling of breasts, oral sex and penetration of a child with or without the child's consent by an adult who is in some position of trust or power.

The sum and substance, child sexual abuse includes a range of behaviors, including vaginal, anal or oral penetration, fondling, exhibitionism, prostitution and photographing a child for pornography.

SEXUAL EXPLOITATION OF CHILDREN

The Declaration from the First World Congress against Commercial Sexual Exploitation of Children defines commercial sexual exploitation as "Sexual abuse by the adult and remuneration in cash or kind to the child or a third person or persons". The child is treated as a sexual object and as a commercial object. The commercial sexual exploitation of children constitutes a form of coercion and violence against children, amounts to forced labour and a contemporary form of slavery.

The UNICEF definition further links child sexual abuse to sexual exploitation:

> Child sexual abuse becomes sexual exploitation when a second party benefits through a profit or through a quid pro quo through sexual activity involving a child. This may include prostitution, brothel and street-based sexual exploitation, trafficking for sexual purposes and child pornography.
>
> The commercial sexual exploitation of children consists of criminal practices that demean and threaten the physical and psychosocial integrity of children. The Declaration and Agenda for Action against Commercial Sexual Exploitation of Children is a groundbreaking instrument that defines the commercial sexual exploitation of child as:
>
> "A fundamental violation of children's rights. It comprises sexual abuse by the adult and remuneration in cash or kind to the child or a third person or

persons. The child is treated as a sexual object and as a commercial object. The commercial sexual exploitation of children constitutes a form of coercion and violence against children, and amounts to forced labour and a contemporary form of slavery."

The primary, interrelated forms of commercial sexual exploitation of children often referred to as CSEC are prostitution of children, child pornography and trafficking of children for sexual purposes. Other forms include child sex tourism, and in some cases, child marriage. Children can also be commercially exploited in other, less obvious ways, such as through domestic servitude or bonded labour. In these cases, a child is contracted to provide work but the employer believes that the child can also be used for sexual purposes.

PROSTITUTION OF CHILDREN

Prostitution is an arrangement of sexual intercourse, based on commercial basis where generally the male part-ners pay for the gratification received. Women or children though gratify the sexual hunger of the males are usually deprived of their personal dignity and social respect, in the society. Thus the definition cannot be complete in a single dimension. Thus prostitution is defined by Farely with many inhuman acts in addition to buying sex, such as rape, battering, verbal abuse, violence, childhood sexual abuse, means of maintaining male domination of women, etc. The international Encyclopedia of Social Sciences defines prostitution as the "granting of sexual access on a relatively indiscriminate basis for a payment either in money or in goods, depending on the complexity of the local economic system payment is acknowledged to be for a specific sexual performance".

The prostitution of children occurs when someone benefits from a commercial transaction in which a child is made available for sexual purposes. Children may be controlled by an intermediary who manages or oversees the transaction, or by an exploiter, who negotiates directly with a child. Children are also involved in prostitution when they engaged in sex in return for basic needs such as food, shelter or safety, or for favors such as higher grades at school or extra pocket money to purchase consumer goods. These acts may occur in many different locations such as brothers bars, clubs, homes, hotels or on the street. Gradually, the practice of prostitution take various forms and arrange-ments which include places of availability, rate, glamour, and associated persons, pimps, shelter and connection with law enforcing agency. Khan and Arefeen (1998) identified several ways. The types of prostitution were broadly categorized under four main groups brothel prostitution, hotel prostitution, prostitution carried on in rented houses by small groups of girls, and floating/street/slum prostitutes. The prostitutes in Bangladesh are generally categorized into street prostitute, home based prostitute, brothel prostitute and hotel based prostitute.

The key issue is not that children make a choice to engage in prostitution in order to survive or to buy consumer goods, but that they are pushed by circumstances, social structures and individual agents inro situations in which adults take advantage of their vulnerability and sexually exploit and abuse them. The term 'child prostitute' or 'child sex worker' implies that a child has somehow chosen to make it a profession. This is wrong: it is adults who create 'child prostitution' through their demand for children as sexual objects, their misuse of power and their desire for profit, and as such children are victims of abuse. Commercial sexual exploitation of children through prostitution is a global problem and is closely connected to child pornography and the trafficking of children for sexual purposes.

The Optional Protocol to the Convention on the Rights of the Child on the sale of children, child prostitution and child pornography, Article 2(b) define child prostitution as . . . the use of a child in sexual activities for remuneration or any other form of consideration.

SEXUAL ABUSE AND PROSTITUTION OF BOYS

Prostitution of women and children that is girl children is practiced in the situation of public knowledge and realization in realistic manner and it is recognized in some cases in the society. But sexual abuse and prostitution of boys is realized but regarded as unrecognized and occurring as hidden manner in the society because of social taboos, norms and value systems, which make concrete to define it in a broad range of sexual abuse, exploitation and traf-ficking. However, sexual abuse of boys is regarded as homo-sexual act by another male counterpart, older or more know-ledgeable in sexuality and the homosexuality is hidden and mostly unrecognized because of social taboo and stigma. Different researches have found that many boys forced to prostitution described themselves as heterosexual and said they only solicited to earn money. Indeed, other studies have shown that one of the most distinctive attitudes of juveniles involved in prostitution is that many do not consider sex with an adult male homosexual activity. However, more recent research has found that most adolescent boys involved in prostitution identify themselves as homosexuals.

ECPAT International's research on Situational Analysis on Prostitution of Boys in India (Hyderabad) has outlined several categories of boys involved in prostitution:

Situational Prostitution: Boys who are forced to prostitution only under certain circumstances or occasions. Habitual Prostitution: Boys spending most of their time engaged in street life of which prostitution is usually an integral part. Occupational Prostitution: Boys who view prostitution as a means of income and regard themselves as professionals.

BOYS IN PROSTITUTION

Child sexual abuse (CSA) and child sexual exploitation (CSE) are endorsed as the most neglected forms of child abuse. The other form of child abuse- Commercial Sexual Exploitation of Children (CSEC) appears to be more menacing affecting the lives of the children. A portion of these children are victimized to adult sex gratification engaging in well organized networks of exploitation, some of which are also engaged in the money laundering activities, sale of illegal drugs and other criminal activities. Commercial sexual exploitation of children and child sexual abuse are suggested often as gender related violence emerging the girl children's care and protection. Girls are considered to be at greater risk of commercial sexual exploitation than boys revealing the most prevalent forms of violence that affect girls throughout childhood and adolescence. It is because of double discrimination and vulnerability on them, (a) suffering for their gender identity and (b) their socio-cultural-economic status.

Sexual abuse and exploitation have been found amongst boys. Boys are also clearly at risk of commercial sexual exploitation and sexual abuse. Most available estimates for commercial sexual exploitation of children and child trafficking for sexual purposes in many countries worldwide entail typically gender based feminine explanation. Very few researches have raised the issues of prostitution of boys as widespread problems, where it is requiring alarming proportions of measures. While most available estimates for commercial sexual exploitation of children and child trafficking in many countries worldwide are outdated, various national studies make clear that the problems of commercial sexual exploitation of children and child sexual abuse are widespread, and are acquiring alarming propor-tions. Boys in prostitution are the victimization of sexual abuse. Many of them have been left out from homes where they have been sexually or physically abused. The section of the study tends to present the nature of sexual abuse and exploitation of boys exploring its dynamics and extends where and how it occurs or who commits it or whether the child or youth consents.

Boys have been subjected to sexual abuse in particular manner. Boy children are subjected to sexual abused being subordinated and dominated by family members, relatives, neighbours, strangers in street situation and others who are older and living together for many purposes. The re-search findings have revealed that the boys who are engaged in prostitution are the victims of sexual abuse and exploi-tation which occurs in a numbers of ways by an older child, adolescents, adults and women taking advantage of a younger child or youth for sexual purposes. Such abuse and exploitation are perpetrated on children of all ages, from infancy to adolescence.

Age of Boys in Prostitution

The study findings has revealed the mean age of the boys in prostitution as 15.56 and median as 15.00. The age wise findings of the study demonstrated as follows where 61 per cent of boys are of 12 – 15 age group, 28 in 16 – 18 and 11 % of 19 year old are engaged in regular sexual performance.

Age interval	Frequency	%
12 – 15	11	61
16 – 18	5	28
19	2	11
Total	18	100

Days/years of engagement in prostitution:

Out of the 18 boys, 50 per cent boys have been engaging in prostitution for 2 – 4 years, and 28 per cent for 5 – 7 years, and the 22 per cent boys have been engaging in prostitution for above 8 years.

Years	Frequency	%
2 – 4	9	50
5 – 7	5	28
8+	4	22
Total	18	100

Intensity of prostitution of boys

The findings have revealed that 44.44 per cent boys who are 12 – 15 years old have been engaging in prostitution for 2 – 4 years and 16.67 percent boys of same years have been engaging in prostitution for 5 – 7 years. On the whole, 61.11 per cent of boys of age 12 – 15 years old are engaged in prostitution from 2 to 7 years. 27.78 per cent boys of 16 – 18 years have been engaging in prostitution from 2 to above 8 years, among those 5.56 and 5.56 per cent are engaged in such work for 2 – 4 and 5 – 7 years and 16.67 per cent boys are engaged in prostitution for 8 or above 8 years. Another

5.56 and 5.56 per cent of 19 years are engaged in such work for 5 – 7 and 8 or above 8 years. It is noted that mean median of age of the boys are 15.56 and 15 and mean and media of years engaged in prostitution for is 4.89 and 4.50 respectively. That means the boys have been engaged in prostitution at the early adolescence periods.

Experience of Sexual Abuse and Exploitation

The research findings have revealed the first experi-ences of sexually abuse of the boys are occurred in the years when they were in the position of the begging of their adolescence. Out of the 18 respondents, 13 boys responded that they were abused at the 8/9 years old and it was occurred forcefully. The boys were sexually abused by room-mates, relatives, strangers, friends or friends who are older, neighbours etc.

The victims' case analyses have revealed that offenders sexually abuse the boys in a process making a good relation and showing love and affection to them and tend them in remuneration process in turn of permanent sexual gratification. Most of the abusers are male in these cases. Moreover, the case of sexual abuse takes place in the context of an ongoing relationship between the abused and the abuser. The strangers are the offenders in just of sexual abuse against children on street, market place, Bazaar, parks, station or vehicle stands etc. The children are also sexually abused by non-relatives which include boyfriends, roommates, acquaintances, teacher etc. Boy sexual abused can be found in all classes and cultural communities. The power relation between abused and abusers tend the children with physical or mental impairments to more vulnerable to sexual abuse. Children are sexually abused and exploited by family members, neighbours including by others known to them or by a stranger, which are involuntary.

Dynamics of Sexual Abuse and Exploitation of Boys

Sexual abuse and exploitation of boys are found either as hidden or non-hidden agenda in the whole spheres of the community. The findings have revealed that sexual abuse toward boys in the framework occurs in several numbers. This cannot be magnitude in quantitative. But the findings have revealed that the boy children are victimized to extreme forms (worst form) by the perpetrators while they are placed in street situation. Through the focus group discussion it has been come out that a boy is sexually abused in home rather while he come out of home, he is sexually exploited. Here the argument is that the boys come in the urban setup in migration process and got a free space of moving for surviving. Their needs of surviving tend them to engage in sex selling market. It has been revealed that the offence of sexual abuse on boys is unobvious rather the victims or sexual abused are reluc-tant to disclose to offence of sexual abuse because of age, powerlessness, dependency of livings, fear to be trap-ped in societal norms and value systems and conflicting conditions within themselves.

Modes of Sexual Abuse and Sexual Exploitation of Boys

The sexual abuse and exploitation of boys involve a range of behaviours which is classified in two categories in the study - (a) Contact and (b) Non-contact sexual abuse of boys. The non-contact sexual abuse may include a range of approaches naming a) making sexual comments, (b) expo-sing intimate body parts, (c) exposing child to pornography, (d) voyeurism, (e) having a sexual fixation on a child or youth's clothing or body parts, (f) luring,(g) making sexually related phone calls and h) engaging in sexually related correspondence through the media. Contact sexual abuse may involve making the children engaged in such acts which include touching (fondling) or digital or object penetration of intimate body parts. In the study process it has been revealed that boys are especial vulnerable to be sexually abused and exploited in Kothi-Panti framework. Kothi has high demand to Panti in sexual interaction in exchange of money, false love and affection, gifts or even by force. The study finding have revealed the following forms of sexual exploitation of boys:

(a.) making children in sexual intercourse by love and affection,

(b.) fondling and touching sexual organ making illegal and

trickery sexual relationship in exchange of gifts, love, affection,

(c.) penetrating with different organs, anal

(d.) making the children dependent on the abuser, engaging the children in sexual interaction forcefully,

(e.) making anal penetration while the children are sick

(f.) Anal penetration, and

(g.) Attempt to penetration in the chance of loneliness of the children.

According to the speech of victims (Kothi), the abusers act alone and intend to do sexual act with early aged boys. While contracting sex, the offenders use a number of tactics to gain access to children ensuring their victim's silence. These tactics include the use of false love and affection, threats, physical force, bribery and other forms of physical and psychological coercion. The boys are sexually abused in sex selling market in organized group or network. In this case, the perpetrators are the same sex as the victims (Kothi) recommend that the perpetrators (Panthi) are male. One offender intends to do sex with more than one child are more likely to be male. Most of the sexual abuses have been taking place in the context of an ongoing relationship between the Kothi and Panthi. The long-term relationship within Kothi and Panti give the penetrators opportunity to more exploit the child's desires. The findings have revealed that typically there is a power differential between the Kothi and Panthi. The Panthi are older and are likely to be more knowledgeable about sexual activity. They spend a lot of time to get of chances of befriending and grooming the Kothi. They use threats, physical force, bribery, trickery or other forms of psychological coercion or appearances, stimulus to gain access to, and make them compliant.

Abused and Abuser in Power Relation in the Society

It is the perpetrators who initiate the sexual activity and the perpetrators are responsible for the abuse no matter what the child does. This long-term relationship gives the offender opportunity to exploit the child's desires and fears. Incestuous perpetrators as for example may give his child special privileges or gifts to obtain his or her cooperation and silence. Children always want to tell about their abuse so that it can be stopped, but they are often afraid that they will not be believed or protected, or they are afraid of what might happen if they do tell. It is normal for children to delay telling about their abuse for a year or more after it occurs. They may talk about the abuse more readily if another victim discloses abuse by the same offender or if they are asked direct questions about the possibility of abuse. Especially in cases of incest, when the abuser is a close family member, children may not reveal their sexual victimization until they become adults. Many never tell even then. The abusers enforce secrecy and create in the child a fear of destroying the privacy and otherwise intact sense of security provided by the family.

It is so hard to displace the signs of sexual abuse because of the victim's age and developmental stage, gender, family's non-interest functioning of abused and exploited and its support. It is also community's ambiguous interests to support to sexual abuse and exploitation of boys. There may show a range of signs, but many of these signs are responses to other types of abuse such as psychological or physical abuse. The physical signs include behavioural problems, sleeping problems, eating problems and skin and substance injured. There may be physical evidence of trauma to their oral and anal areas. Emotional signs include becoming quiet and depressed, preoccupied, hyperactive or anxious behavioural problems such as physical aggression, running away, suicidal behaviour, substance injured. Developmental signs include lags in their cognitive development and intellectual performances. The findings have revealed that perpetrators or abusers use various tactics to gain access to, isolate, manipulate and control children to abuse the children in view of his/her gratification.

Typically, it is a power differential between the abuser and abused or victim. The findings of the study that all of the abusers or perpetrators are older than the victims or abused and they are well-informed and powered to sexual activity. They spend a lot of time or chances of befriending and grooming their victims. They use threats, physical force, bribery, trickery or other forms of psychological coercion or appearances, stimulus to gain access to, and make their victims compliant. It is repeated acts to abuse the children by the way of befriending, intimating and grooming. The acts are more serious consecutively, simultaneously and intrusively over time of the victims' development stage. The acts are not magnified in quantitative. At the time of data collection it has been revealed that the offence of sexual abuse is unobvious rather the victims or sexual abused children are reluctant to disclose to offence of sexual abuse because of the following interrelated causes relating to power structure.

Children including physical or mental disabilities are especially vulnerable to sexual abuse, as the children are not able to give informed consent to sexual activity because they cannot fully understand adult-child sexual contact or predict the consequences. On the other hand, the abusers are able to take special advantage to abuse a boy child in the gender specific socialization process of the community. They easily manage to isolate the child by manipulating the people and situations in socio-cultural aspects. In the study process, it has been revealed that the boys of early age are in such a position to be sexually abused by the Panthi, where the offence is looked as slight or sight and being unrecognized under existing social norms and value system. In addition, the society is not in a position of deep concern of the matter.

VULNERABILITY OF CHILDREN

WORST FORMS OF CHILD RIGHTS VIOLATIONS

Children in Bangladesh have been the victims of various types of violence. The violence occurs within the family, society and in state structure. A few of incidences of violence come to the public knowledge or are taken place in the mass media. Most of the incidents of violence and abuse of children are not even exposed to their surrounding society where it occurs. Because of the scarcity of information, it is even stands beyond the knowledge of assessments of its vulnerability. On the other hand, most of the worst forms of violence against children are severely unreported and covered under the shape of public know-ledge. Sometimes it is highly reluctant to disclose collapsing its dynamic and consequent forms. Thus, it becomes difficult to describe an actual situation of violence against children as well as the vulnerability on children lives.

Whether reported or not, the vulnerability of children is a difficult question in socioeconomic, cultural and political spheres of the community. However, it is highly sensitive and unreported matter as it touches on power relation between children and adults, socio-cultural and political values and customs, social stigma, etc. As unreported matter of violence against children, especially sexual abuse and exploitation it is difficult to measure its extent and magnitude. Along with lack of systematic data and information, the reluctance of its recognition in the community have collapsed to display its extent, causes and conse-quences and further demoralized the community and even the state to take preventive and protective actions against such crimes. On the other hand, stereotyping social status and value system demonstrate the violence of sexual abuse and exploitation perpetuated only on girl children. But the incidences of violence of sexual abuse and exploitation on boys are remained as hidden under the societal disclose and value system. In this section of the study, it was intended to explore the deep rooted vulnerability of the boy children and the factors affecting the vulnerability in socioeconomic, cultural and political spheres.

VIOLENCE AGAINST CHILDREN AND VULNERABILITY

There is growing number of boy children who are abused, exploited, neglected and experienced violence at family, schools and other institutions, community and na-tional level. The rights of the children are largely violated in their socioeconomic, cultural and political setups. Despite of the types of physical violence such as killing, rape, sexual abuse, kidnapping, trafficking and acid burn, the boy children who are sexually abused and affected by social, economic, cognitive and psychological vulnerability suffer from mental repression and trauma every day and every spheres of their lives. Patriarchal values and power structures that result in different socialization processes of the children lead to them adopting different coping mechanisms and manifesting the impact of abuse and trauma in different ways on them. They are likely to experi-ence low self-esteem and poor psychosocial care and sup-port. So, the children are growing up experiencing unsafe and insecure living condition and stereotyping their socio-cultural practices.

Child sexual abuse is the sexual exploitation of a child by an adult, adolescent or older child. The sexual activity does not necessarily involve force; children are often bribed or verbally coerced into sexual acts. The difference in age and sexual knowledge between a child and an older person makes informed consent to sexual activity impossible. "Abusers" come from all social classes and groups and can be either male or female, but statistically men comprise the vast majority of those who sexually abuse children. Abusers may be parents, teachers, employers or religious leaders, members of criminal gangs and networks or people from law enforcement agencies. Sexual abuse is an abuse of power and trust, and the situation of powerless abused children entails suffering in silence and secrecy and the added weight of a heavy burden of shame and guilt. Sexual abuse can lead to social exclusion and a whole range of psychosocial problems.

Many victims and families of victims are reluctant to report abuse due to the stigma attached. They also fear reporting their case, because the entire justice system is rife with entry points for further victimisation. Poverty makes children vulnerable, but that fact does not imply that economically disadvantaged people are more likely to commit sexual offences than people from affluent socio-economic groups or that illiterate people are more immoral than a professor, a police officer or a politician. The point is that sexual abuse is more prevalent where poverty and denial results in weaker regulations on child protection issues. Little control over basic life situations deprives people of means for self-protection.

Poverty, age, sex, employment opportunities and geographical location therefore make children more vulnerable to illegal migration resulting to trafficking for sexual purposes The phenomenon of child sexual abuse in relation to trafficking exists in every country, culture and transcends all socio-economic groups. Poverty increased by natural catastrophes appears to make children more vulnerable to sexual abuse and exploitation. The children who are particularly vulnerable to sexual abuse, exploitation and trafficking include those groups of children who are in conflict situation for surviving, child workers, street children, children with disabilities, those living in dysfunctional families, in prisons and institutions, children who are alone, children living illegally in a country or who belong to a minority group etc.

The children's residence has demonstrated the experience of residential transformation of the children rendering them in vulnerable situation. The vulnerability has rendered them to migrate resulting in different socialization process of them with adopting different coping mechanisms and manifesting the impact of abuse and trauma in different ways. Out of total 110 responded children, 75 children are living in the Rajshahi city and 35 children are living land port areas, most of whom are migrated from different setups for surviving.

Backdrop information revealed that 74% children come from rural setup, 17% from other urban setups except Rajshahi metropolitan city and land port areas and the rest 7% and 2% children responded that they are the inhabitants of Rajshahi city and land port areas. It means that above 90% percent children are the victims of urbanization that is in the rapid urbanization process the children are intended to migration either with family or alone.

As development stage, age is the main factor of a child in assessing the vulnerability. No age is safe age. Children are always vulnerable. The age group of 10-14 years came across as the period during which the highest number of abuses occurs. It is mentionable that the vulnerability of children, the evidence of occurring abuse towards children varies from child to child when they grow up. The study has demonstrated that most of the victims are in the age range 7-14 years old. Among them, 20% and 40.91% children are in the age range 7-9 and 10-14. And the rest 36.36% children are in the age group 15-18. The study findings have revealed that most of the children have been victimized to sexual abuse at early adolescent period which has the impact on their development and their socialization process.

Family Backdrop Creating Vulnerability

The vulnerable conditions of the family drop the children in vulnerable situation. Where children work and pass their lives in street situation, the father often works as either a rickshaw puller or day labourer etc. and the mother as a domestic help. Poverty pervades in every sphere of their lives leading to domestic conflict, tension and ulti-mately results in cruel treatment of children. The mother, being over burdened with work, can loose interest in her children and neglect them. 56% per cent of people of Bangladesh are landless. They either work on the land of others on a contact basis, or become floating labour moving from place to place. Without a stable income the children become a burden to parents and must find work for their own survival.

The family vulnerability of the child respondent includes poverty, large family, illiteracy or lack of education, lack of health care, lack of recreation, lack of take care and behavioural approach, discrimination, family conflict, separation, death of father or mother, dependency, domination etc. The vulnerability causes the family ignore and unconscious in care and protection towards children. The economic hardship is caused by having a large population and large member of real families. This has created various kinds of social problems creating the vulnerability of children.

Family Size

The family size of the children has revealed that 48 % children's families are consisted of 5-6 members and 20% of 7 and above 7 members, and 26% children's families are consisted of 3-4 members. The family size of the children means that the large family size renders the children in abusive, vulnerable and hazardous situations whether in street situation or working condition or in families or in community. Among respondents, 57.27% children have parents. In specific, 20.91% children have only mothers and 16.36% have only fathers. The rest 3% children have no father and mother and 3% children do not know about their parents. 54 respondents who have parents have informed that their mothers are housewives and never do outside work. Mothers of 12 respondents work as maid-servants in others households and messes. One's mother collects firewood and mother of another prepared Pitha (cake) for selling.

Regarding fathers, out of 68 in number, 21 were rickshaw or rickshaw-van pullers, 15 were day labourers, 12 were small businessmen, 2 fish seller and 2 butchers. Fathers of 8 respondents were older and workless, where fathers of the rest 8 children were barber, driver, farmer, night guard, porter, sweeper and beggars. Mothers of floating children without fathers, in maximum cases, worked as maidservants in messes and households.

About 57 per cent out of the total children would go to school and the rest about 43 per cent would not go to school. The finding regarding schooling has pointed out that the attendances in school of the children who would go to school were not at regular basis. After a certain period each children has been compelled to drop out from school. About 37 per cent of 57 children have been dropped out after 1 year of schooling, 24 per cent of those children have studied from 2 to 5 years and the rest 39 per cent children have studied in school above 5 years.

Vulnerability in Urbanization and Migration Process

Urbanization in Bangladesh has led to a phenomenon termed as urban poverty. The urban poor can be rightfully defined as people who cannot afford to meet basic need requirements with their own incomes. Basic need include food or nutrition, clothing, primary health care, education and shelter. There are specific socio-economic and anthro-pological criterions for fulfilment of the above basic needs. Considering the multi-variant definition, urban poor are identified not only as income poor but also capabilities poor. The study findings have revealed that the vulnerability of child victims in urbanization process for surviving. The Rajshahi City is headquarter of the Rajshahi division of Bangladesh comprising the North -Western districts within west of the Jamuna River and north of the mighty Padma River. With the growth of urbanization and expansion of communication system, the population mobility is increasing throughout the city.

Rajshahi City is the fourth largest Metropolitan City of Bangladesh. The rapid growth of urbanization is also clearly visible in this city. Overnight the number of people living in this city turned up twice by just 10 years, which was 5 lacks at the beginning of the 90th decade of the last century. The stream of floating people is increasing noticeably in this city. The stream of poor rural people is towards the city due to river erosion, poverty, droughts, unemployment and landlessness, seasonal unemployment etc. Those are the mean time causing manifold socio-economic problems including the problem of slums. In this condition, a huge number of street and working children are entering in the metropolitan city of Rajshahi. The Rajshahi city, fourth largest and divisional city of Bangladesh, is situated at the bank of Padma. Through the urbanization process, the urban slum has been developed at the bank of Padma demonstrating the vulnerability to crime, smuggling, and physical insecurity, skewed distribution of the delivery of basic services, subsequent health problems, sexual abuse and exploitation. From the modern-day enslavement of trafficking victims to the exploitation of domestic workers, child migrants face hazards that testify to a lack of adequate opportunities to migrate safely and legally. The silted up river bank has caused of flood and river bank erosion in the region during the rainy season compelling the people to migration for their lives and livelihood in the urban setups. It has created easy access of cross border undocumented/illegal and irregular migration devastating the vulnerability of trafficking of women and children and HIV/AiDS.

Environmental factor influencing either rural-urban or cross-border migration has been emerged as another matter increasing vulnerability. Migration occurs within an environmental context as detecting a migratory response to environmentally risk indicators that persist in the face of a wide array of socioeconomic controls for labor force opportunity, climate, and demographic structure. The geographical setup, the contiguous land mass, long porous borders and development conditions in the areas have also created a scope of cross border migration of children as a natural phenomenon. India is sharing its long land borders with the districts of Rajshahi and Chapai Nawabgonj. These areas have become transit areas for undocumented/illegal migrants increasing the intensity of trafficking of children. The land port of Shibgoanj of the districts Chapai Nawabgonj is located far 40 Kilometres from Chapai Nawabgonj Town. The port has created opportunities of employment of many people including children. The area is densely populated and child labour prone zone. There observed boy child labours higher than girls in the region.

The most of the children are working as labour of goods transportation/bearer, hotel boy, smuggler, sweeper etc. and passing their lives in street situation. It is the place of living of the drivers of bus and trucks creating a space of floating, hotel based and home based prostitution. In the area, it has tended the children to migrate across border in search of better livelihood options by the truck drivers. The children also cross the spike fence around the border belts under risk like situation. The findings have revealed that the incidences of human trafficking have escalated con-siderably. The children's decisions to migrate are often taken under conditions of distress and disparity thus heightening their vulnerability to various forms of exploitation including trafficking, forced labour and bonded labour. Additionally, the lacks of knowledge, information and of opportunities for safe migration, are the contributing factors to fall the children into the trap of abuse and exploitation. The children are the victims of force labour, unpaid labourers, slaves and domestic workers in some cases and in other cases they are surviving as commercial sex worker, beggar, servants etc. They are exposed to cross the border under the risk like situation and to various abuses such as drug, sexual, physical torture and finally they are frustrated in vulnerable situation.

It has been explored that vast majority of the children interviewed for the present study are engaged in some kind of works from which they derive some income. It has been identified as many as nine different kinds of remunerative works which include Domestic servant/ maid, Luggage bearer, Sex worker, garbage Scavenger, Day labourer, Vagabond, Factory labourer, Fuel wood vendor, Laundry-worker, Rickshaw peddler, Restaurant worker, Taxi helper, Smuggler, Shoe-maker, Mobile vendor, Book binder, Hair cutter etc.

The child migrants are working as garbage collectors tempo helpers, tailors, domestic workers, shop assistants; vegetable, fruit, flower and fish sellers, hotel boys, van drivers, etc. The study has revealed that children have come from rural areas and passing their lives in the setups as street and working. In the regard of working the study revealed that 23 per cent children work per day up to 4 hours and above 50 per cent children continuously work per day from 4 to 8 hours and 23 per cent and 3 per cent children continuously work from 8 to 12 and above 12 hours respectively. Smuggling of various goods is an open secret matter in the regions because of its geographical setups. These goods include drugs and from raw materials to sari or cosmetics, cattle etc. Besides, there has been communi-cation and relations between street children and prostitutes. 10 respondents acknowledging the relation among them 6 are boys and the rest 4 are girls. They are only 10 to 12 years old. For hunger, the street female children have stepped forward the way of darkness, prostitution.

Society Created Vulnerability

Some children are more vulnerable due to factors that isolate and marginalize them in their homes and communities, such as poverty, disability, racism and other forms of discrimination. In particular the undermining of traditional beliefs, values, family and community structures have contributed to sexual abuse. Social attitudes towards the sexual abuse of boys are not well accepted, where the boys engaged in sex selling market makes the question as difficult to well explore its extent and dynamics. The nature and dynamics of sexual abuse and exploitation of boys are made the community known in small scale and somewhere else regarding as bad and sinful acts. The societal norms and value systems lead to denial of it to address it in the community at large. The existing culture treats it as a sense of guilty and trying to keep the offence of sexual abuse of boys in secret. Traditional/social customs and attitudes toward children are also contradictory.

The social and cultural created honor and respective behaviour towards community people and honored and respected individual beyond the community makes opportunity to abuse the children, where disclose of the offence tends to reluctant and untrustworthy. It is the community created deception, false hope, gifts, making a relationship of trust, making love affairs, belief etc. that are approached by them to intend the children to carry out such offence. The dynamics of socialization as well as society's collective history of denial of child sexual abuse contribute to build such environments in which opportunities for abuse occur. As an individual within community, the developmental age and gender of the child also contribute to risk. The socioeconomic perspectives have revealed that the children of urban slum have been sexually abused more than other. The slum of urban community contains all types of extreme forms of sexual abuse. It is the place where most prevalent natures of sexual abuse exist.

State and Civil Society Created Vulnerability

Bangladesh is one of the first signatories and ratified countries of the Convention on the Rights of the Child (CRC) in 1990. As a primary duty bearer the government of Bangladesh has four types of obligations, which include (a) respecting people's rights, (b) to protect people's rights, (c) to facilitate people's rights and (d) to provide people's rights. According to the obligations, the government has the main responsibility for bringing about the realization of children's rights and are accountable both the international community and to all people living within its border. The government's commitment to protecting and upholding the rights of children has been demonstrated by its early ratification of the UN Convention on the Rights of the Child and, in September 2000, of the Optional Protocol to the CRC on the sale of children, child prostitution and child pornography. In March 2001, the government made a further pledge to protect child from sexual exploitation and trafficking through its ratification of ILO Convention 182 on the Worst Forms of Child Labour. The government of Bangladesh has reflected its commitments by developing National Plan of Action for Children 1997-2002 and National Plan of Action against sexual abuse and exploitation of children including trafficking. The government formulated a National Plan of Action (NPA 2005-10) seeks to achieve the Millennium Development Goals (MDG) through implementing the PRSP and to implement CRC. NPA is a multi-dimensional action plan that covers various aspects of child survival, child development and child protection.

Though the government's commitments and interests have been reflected by ratifying the international conventions and by developing its different national laws and policy in different time periods with the children, the reflection is yet to discourse and confine a unique definition of age under its different laws and policy relating to UN CRC. Some ambiguities are still remaining in different ways because of unwillingness and improper initiatives of government and other duty bearers in a sustainable platform. These are vastly deteriorating the child protection. In addition, the child protection is being deteriorated because of lack of awareness about children's rights and its programming approaches by the government, development and civil society actors. The low level of birth registration is another major constraint to protect the child rights.

The UN CRC's Optional Protocol on the sale of children, child prostitution and child pornography supplements the Convention by providing States with detailed requirements to end the sexual exploitation and abuse of children. It also protects children from being sold for non-sexual purposes—such as other forms of forced labour, illegal adoption and organ donation. The protection of a child as victim as well as witness has been mentioned under the Optional Protocol as a part of the protection of child rights and ensuring the best interest of a child. There is no specific law on the protection of child victim and child witness in Bangladesh. On the other hand, the existing laws and ratifying conventions of international agencies are not properly implemented and vastly affected by religious and dogmatized social taboos. The existing legislation fully fail to protect the victims of boys relating to sexual abuse and exploitation because of societal attitudes, more importantly social taboo and stigmatized situation vitally ignores its legal process.

Another positive and protective action and com-mitment of GoB has been reflected in implementation of the act Prevention of Repression against Women and Children 2000. The act deals with punishment to the accused of violence towards women and children - acid throwing, trafficking, abduction of any one and collecting ransom, rape, sexual violence and harassment, dowry related violence, violence like deterioration or deformation of any part of a body of an child etc. perpetuated against women and children. It is reflected in Section 10 (1) of the act that 'if a man intentionally touches the sexual organ or any other organ of a female or female child by this male organ or any other organ to meet his sexual need, it shall be a sexual abuse and shall be punished with punishments. The punishment may extend to ten years and shall not be less than three years. It also includes fine. Basically, the section rigorously ignores to define the sexual abuse of boys by an individual hampering the relevant punishment. However, Article 2 (k) of the legislation confined the children's age to 14 years and the Article 9 defines that if a child of above 14 years old engaged a woman in sexual intercourse forcefully and without consent of the woman, it will be regarded as rape and the child will be accused with punishment. So, it lacks to define the sexual abuse of boys by an individual and protect the accused from punishment. On the other, the child is being to accused and placed in safe custody. As a result, the legislation fails to protect the children from abuse and to take punishable actions to the accused. Because, under the law, the boys, sexually abused fail to get justice in the case of being raped.

Vulnerability of Sexual Violence

The abused are too young developmentally, cognitively or emotionally to articulate what happened to them. Their feelings of powerlessness have trapped them in such circumstances where they are threatened to act such inhumane acts or forced to be enacted in sex against their willing. Their feelings of powerlessness increase their dependency on adults increasing their reluctance to disclose of such inhuman act. Their dependency on adults and society increase the fear of social norms and values. The social existing norms, values and care system socialize the children to be dependent on adults and to be stigmatized stereotyping those they cannot say. They are also afraid of the perpetrator's reprisals or other negative consequences of telling others. They intend to protect them. They feel conflicted and suffer confusion or shame. They indent to consider the abuse as fault.

There is little evidence that many children deliberately make false allegations or misinterpret appropriate adult-child contact as sexual abuse. In few recorded cases children appear to have made false allegations. It has usually been the result of manipulation by an adult. False denials of sexual abuse (saying it did not happen when it did) and recanting a disclosure of abuse (denying that it happened after having told someone about being abused) are much more common than false reports. Children sometimes recant truthful allegations of abuse. This is not surprising because the child naturally fears the impact that a disclosure will have on the family, or fears that he or she will not be believed. As well, the child may recant in fearful recognition of the fact that the offending adult has so much more power. Non-offending family members may also experience negative consequences when a child or sibling is sexually abused or exploited. These consequences may vary by factors such as the nature of their relationship with and dependency on the perpetrator. For example, they may feel shame, anger and guilt about their failure to protect the child.

The children who were sexually abused may suffer from depression, anxiety and suicidal thoughts and behaviour etc. The initial effects is the psychological reactions, which include fear, anger, hostility, guilt and shame, low self-esteem, anxiety, early overt sexual behaviour, and behavioural disturbances (such as running away and truancy).Those who experienced both emotional abuse and multiple acts of sexual abuse are the most likely to have poor mental health. Sexual abuse toward children revealed to be a single act, or repeated acts. These acts are more serious, consecutive, simultaneous and intrusive over time. The result of sexual abuse renders the abused or victims to lifetime negative effects, to be traumatized, stigmatized and socially disgraced. The victims of sexually abused are engaged in sex selling practices by the process of repeated acts of sexual abuse.

Consequences and Impact of Sexual Abuse and Exploitation

Children who are sexually abused are vulnerable to physical, developmental emotional and stigmatized problems. They are also prone to sexually transmitted diseases including HIV/AIDS. Being sexually abused has immediate impacts on the children's experiences of childhood and their personal development. Children who are sexually abused may experience disruptions in their developing view of themselves and the world, which can result in significant emotional and behavioural changes. They may try to cope with the abuse by acting in a secretive manner and behaving in a helpless way. They may delay disclosure or disclose in conflicting and unconvincing ways. Their sense of personal integrity, safety and security is violated. They experience shame and guilt. Opportunities to play, learn and have healthy social interactions with others are extremely hampered.

The impact of sexual abuse has far-reaching effects that

may not be apparent until later in the individual's life. Some research suggests that child sexual abuse experiences may (among other factors) also contribute to a young person's later experiences of sexual exploitation. Many young people who are sexually exploited ran away or were abandoned at an early age from home environments that frequently included physical, sexual and emotional abuse. Long-term psychological effects of child sexual abuse often last until adulthood. Adult survivors of child sexual abuse may exhibit depression, anxiety, sleep disorders, dissociation, and low self-esteem.

Most of the researches on child sexual abuse have highlighted the vulnerability of children to sexual abused, especially sexual abuse and exploitation of girl children relating to the protection of street children. The studies have been demonstrated and manifested on sexual abuse and exploitation of girls in general in different ways. The focused attention and action to address the commercial sexual exploitation of boys is still lacking. The practice of abuse and exploiting boys sexually thrives in many countries, and takes place in locales including streets, markets, bus terminals, hotels, restaurants, religious places, etc. Very few studies which are conducted by a limited agencies show that a number of boys are engaged in prostitution and have been victims of sexual exploitation. The studies indicate that this phenomenon is largely unreported, under-reported or misreported and highly ignored and reluctant by the community. The chapter has focused to express the belief of community on boys in prostitution. Through the working process it is also to articulate the prostitution of boys finding out its nature and dynamics in socio-cultural perspectives.

It also focuses the different types of difficulties faced in the community. Some cultures, such as in India, may have a history of child sexual exploitation ('prostitution') in the temples. Others may have no history as such, but in extreme poverty the child's body is seen as one of the few available ways of making money. Different cultures will also have different beliefs about virginity, chastity, homosexuality, rape and the general value of children. In Thailand and Burma, for example, commercial sexual exploitation (non-consensual 'prostitution') may be seen by some to be an honourable activity, a way of paying back to parents what they have given to the child. These religious and cultural viewpoints must be understood adequately to gain an accurate picture of the situation. Rape of women and children is seen by some to be a weapon of war. Many sub-cultures, including Christian, have an 'ostrich head in the sand' mentality and deny that abuse exists. Churches cannot afford to ignore the facts that amongst their members are those who perpetuate sexual abuse against children. By not facing up to the problems in their community, churches risk exposing children to further abuse.

In the perspective of Bangladesh, the people have been socialized through religion, cultural belief, taboos, gender stereotype socialization process and other social mechanisms to accept sexual subordination and sexual operation of male on female or female on male. Social structures generate the conditions of gender specific socialization process creating belief of sexual operation as only male to female. And it is the belief of power structure between male and female. The socialization process of the country renders the community to be uninformed on the sexual abuse perpetrated on boys. In addition, lack of knowledge and lack of willing to disclose the nature and dimension of sexual abuse of children are the main factors of the many factors rendering more susceptible of the consequent of sexual abuse. The boy children who are abused of touching or fondling or kissing of sexual portions of body are considered as highly negligence or joke or funny than girl in its cultural context. Also individuals of the family and community are unwilling to make it out as sexual offence on boy. The findings have revealed that the boys at early age have been the victims of sexual abuse through appreciation but not regarded as sexual offence as because of the victims' reluctance and lack of knowledge on it and its consequences. On the other hand, the community people uncared attention and perceptions have hidden it to disclose and their reluctance to recognize it as sexual offence.

The children are highly subordinated and dominated by

adults, which have made vulnerable to be victimized to sexual abuse, where they are powerless to protect and disclose it's a guilty. They do not either disclose the incidence towards their parents or prevent those because of shame and insecurity in their life, social taboo, ideologies, values, norms, burdens and lack of source of making reliable of such attitudes. It is also that their poverty tempts them to get additional income source by selling their sex, which is another cause to reluctant of such offence. However, the disclosing of such sexual offence makes them more vulnerable to further abuse by family and their community making the question of their gender identity. It also causes of question of family's anxiety to consider their children as homosexual identity. The gender specific socialization process makes it as burden to disclose the offence and it is overlooked by the family keeping their anxiety in surreptitious because of social disgrace. The cultural and gender identity make it easy to isolate the sexual offence towards boys.

Although child sexual abuse and exploitation has occurred throughout history, it was not publicly recognized as a societal issue in its cultural and political contexts. However, although there have been a number of studies on child sexual abuse and exploitation, it is not possible to address the extent of the problems in the community and so it is remained as hidden and overlooked by the community where the actions against sexual exploitation of boys have made a question to interventions. The findings manifested that many people have inverse conceptions about the prostitution of boys, how it happen in what manner as it is viewed as an issue of homosexuality and solely related to child sex tourism. Many reported that boys in prostitution in the region are limited to home based sexual interaction in Kothi – Panthi framework. Other reported that boy children are sexually abused by forcefully by the strangers or neighbours. On the other hand, the forensic reports revealed that in last year numbers of boys are raped by male. In this regard relevant cases have been filed up in their respective Thana.

The community response highlighted that boys are used as sexual objects and targeted by exploiters and the exploitation of boys is not exclusively limited to homosexual men. As the cases are under-reported and overlooked or out of area of interest in the community, the magnitude of the problem is deeply rooted in hidden framework tending to the risk of cross border trafficking. The community response articulated to the sexual abuse and exploitation of boys by women where the women and adolescent girls tempt the boys for their sexual gratification. The community response clearly demonstrated the unequal knowledge and power relations affect the vulnerability of children. It has been reflected that children are mostly vulnerable to sexual abuse and exploitation in the myths of community and stereotype gender constructions.

Many reported gender segregation to be a factor intending the vulnerability of children to sexual abuse and exploitation. It creates the beliefs of community to restrict male-female relationship perceiving the risks for girls to sexual abuse and exploitation. Boys in these situations appear to become vulnerable to sexual abuse and exploitation (SAE) as they can be easily accessed and targeted by the exploiters crossing the gender barrier, where the sexual abuse and exploitation of boys may be remained invisible and overlooked by the community. The community reflected that both girls and boys are victimized to sexual abuse and exploitation, where the nature of risks and the types of abuse differ. Where the sexual violence against girls is a form of gender based violence centring the power relation between male and female, sexual violence against boys is more typically and particularly considered as the conflict situation as a method of intimidation. The social and cultural norms, customs and value system of the community render it difficult for boys to speak out about their experiences and the community to recognize that boys are engaged in prostitution. The cultural norms and beliefs resort the boys in recurrent sexual abuse and in turn in prostitution in the hide of public knowledge. The children are victimized to sexual abuse as helpless victims. Their lives, choices and opportunities are directly and indirectly affected to a great extent by the social, economical and political realities in which they live. The section of the study includes the social, economic, cultural and political aspects of prostitution of boys through analyzing the factors behind the prostitution of boys.

The study findings have revealed that all the children are vulnerable to sexual abuse, but some are at more at risk than others, who are sexually exploited. The children of economic vulnerable and marginalized families are the victim of sexually abuse and exploitation. They are victimized in street situation and in a position of dependency on others. Children without parental care, orphans, unaccompanied and separated living on their own are the victim of sexual abuse and exploitation. The children in foster families and institution face the abusive and exploitative situation sexually in their daily lives. Mentally and physically disabled children are another segment of population who are the victims of sexually abused, especially of sexually exploitation. Children are confined to community's cultural practices where their interest and participation are highly overlooked. Their rights are deeply and directly overlooked and distracted by the adults while their reveal tends to hurt the honour and status of abuser or exploiter.

Sexual abuse and commercial exploitation of boys have been emerged as a concerned and discussing matter reflecting its vulnerability, but society is static to take the issue in consideration and to address it in effective manner. Rather the society itself mostly intends to keep the issue in hidden because of social dogma, taboo system and stigmatized situation. As hidden agenda, sexual abuse and exploitation of boys is spreading its vulnerability affecting the lives of a large number of children. Due to socio-cultural perspective, very conservative societal value system and strict social taboo, the issue of the prostitution of boys is largely unaccepted, remained as unbelief and the community itself are fundamentally reluctant to reported and recognized as human rights violation of boys. It is noted that the community are fully unaware about boys involved in prostitution are passing their lives in traumatic and stigmatic situation keeping themselves in darkness society.

However, sexual abuse of boys is regarded as homosexual act by another male counterpart, older or more knowledgeable in sexuality and the homosexuality is hidden and mostly unrecognized because of social taboo and stigma. The community has rare beliefs of the prevalence of sexual abuse and prostitution of boys, which should have concrete definition in a broad range of sexual abuse, exploitation and trafficking but should make it realize in the community. Commercial Sexual Exploitation of boys appears to be more menacing affecting their lives. A portion of these children are victimized to adult sex gratification engaging in well organized networks of exploitation, some of which are also engaged in the money laundering activities, sale of illegal drugs and other criminal activities. In the community, commercial sexual exploitation of children and child sexual abuse are suggested often as gender related violence emerging the girl children's care and protection by the development actors. Where it is highlighted, girls are considered to be at greater risk of sexual violence and engaging in prostitution. Boys are victimized to the most prevalent forms of violence throughout childhood and adolescence under their deteriorated socio-cultural-economic status.

Boys of all ages, from infancy to adolescence have been subjected to sexual abuse in particular manner. The boys who are engaged in prostitution are the victims of sexual abuse and exploitation which occurs in a numbers of ways by an older child, adolescents, adults and women taking advantage of a younger child or youth to fulfil their sexual desires. The boys have been engaged in prostitution at the early adolescence periods. The mean and median of age of the boys engaged in prostitution are 15.56 and 15 and mean and media of years engaging in prostitution for is 4.89 and 4.50 respectively. The first experiences of sexually abuse of the boys are occurred in the years of 8/9 and it was occurred forcefully. The strangers are the offenders just sexually abuse the children on street, market place, Bazaar, parks, station or vehicle stands etc. The non-relatives include boyfriends, roommates, acquaintances, teacher etc.

Sexual abuse is the worst forms of child rights violations which break the grips of power and trust, create extreme forms of vulnerability and add weight of a heavy burden of shame and guilty. Sexual abuse leads to social exclusion and a whole range of psychosocial problems. Traditional/social customs and attitudes toward children are also contradictory. The nature and dynamics of sexual abuse and exploitation of boys are made the community known in small scale and somewhere else regarding as bad and sinful acts. The societal norms and value systems lead to denial of it to address it in the community at large. The existing culture treats it as a sense of guilty and trying to keep the offence of sexual abuse of boys in secret. In addi-tion, the social and cultural created honor and respective behaviour towards community people and honored and respected individual beyond the community makes opportunity to abuse the children, where disclose of the offence tends to reluctant and untrustworthy.

It is the community created deception, false hope, gifts, making a relationship of trust, making love affairs, belief etc. that are approached by them to intend the children to carry out such offence. The dynamics of socialization as well as society's collective history of denial of child sexual abuse contribute to build such environments, in which, the opportunities for abuse occur. As an individual within community, the developmental age and gender of the child also contribute to risk under the socio-cultural practices and taboo system. There is no specific law on the protection of child victim and child witness in Bangladesh. The existing legislation fully fail to protect the victims of boys relating to sexual abuse and exploitation because of societal attitudes, more importantly social taboo and stigmatized situation vitally ignores its legal process.

The government's commitments and interests reflected in ratifying the international conventions and by developing its different national laws and policy in different time periods with the children failed to protect the children and properly implemented, which are vastly affected by religious and dogmatized social taboos. The reflection is yet to discourse and confine a unique definition of age under its different laws and policy relating to UN CRC. Some ambiguities are still remaining in different ways because of unwillingness and improper initiatives of government and other duty bearers in a sustainable platform. These are vastly deteriorating the child protection. In addition, the child protection is being deteriorated because of lack of awareness about children's rights and its programming approaches by the government, development and civil society actors. The low level of birth registration is another major constraint to protect the child rights.

It is important to recognize that various factors (push-pull) precipitate boy's involvement in commercial sexual exploitation. Firstly there is demand of boys in sex selling markets in Kothi-Panthi paradigm. On the other hand, in power relation younger boys are precipitated to sexual abuse by older (men and women). Here, the children are in a position to be used as a commodity of buying and selling, which is resulted from the demand of sexual desires by adults. Secondly there is supply resulting from the availability of vulnerability children for sex work, who are vitally affected by family poverty. Boys seeking work in advanced urban setup are particular vulnerable to prostitution. But the prostitution of boys is remaining as hidden and unreported agenda under the social unconsciousness, dogma, stigmatization, weak safeguard and protection. So, sexual abuse and exploitation of boys need to be better explored for design of strategies and intervention. It needs for more updated information, the prevalence, dynamics and extent of sexual abuse of boys and its adverse effects on mental and physical effect and development. A range of action needs to be emerged to address the root causes of sexual abuse and exploitation by governmental and non-governmental actors. These include the protection of children against abuse at home, the provision of skill training and non-exploitative work opportunities and parenting care and support towards children. The stakeholders and duty bearers need to be involved in both preventive and protective approaches to curb the vulnerability of sexual abuse and exploitation of boys. Particular attentions need to be emphasized in strategic approaches.

Community as a whole are directly interact with the children. As a significant part of prevention of sexual abuse, exploitation and trafficking of children, there is a serious need to generalize the community with the issue of sexual abuse of boys. It is to provide in-depth and conceptual information about the sexual abuse and exploitation of boys. In particular, it is to address the prevalence of the sexual abuse and exploitation of boys. In this regard, the community people should know the roots of sexual abuse of boys. The main objectives of community mobilization should be sensitization of the mass people to improve the mass public opinion and responsiveness towards children and sexual abuse and exploitation of boys. It is also to reduce the social problems and conservativeness to break the social taboos. Special attention should give on those who are affected by pervasive poverty (surviving poverty and knowledge poverty).

However, it is a question of sustainability of community mobilization, that is, the community mobilization should be sustainable. In this regard, it is responded to institutionalize the community mobilization, which will be intervened by governmental, non-governmental and media agencies. The people need to be educated in a process of social education system, activeness and responsiveness, realization of vulnerability towards children's mental and physical development. Specific groups such as the community people, governmental and non-governmental actors, law enforcing agencies, police, security guards, night staff of public install, especially bus and train station, port areas, need to be mobilized and sensitized about sexual abuse and exploitation of boys and CRC.

There is very little knowledge among the community people on the effect and impact of sexual abuse on children. It is to give special attention to uphold capacity amongst certain societal groups, who are affected by poverty and surviving with risk like situation to be victimized to sexual exploitation and trafficking. Youth and adults, parents, teachers, community leaders, health practice soner, employers, police, lawyers, members of local governmental administration and the general publics as well are the important target groups who need to be promoted by capacity building. It is the improvement of their opinions and responsiveness towards victims of boys of sexual abuse and exploitation. It is not enough simply to capacity building of the adults and youths on the issues relating to CRC, those must be realized in practice. So their capacity building should be aimed to accelerate the awareness raising actions and initiatives to protect the rights of children and sexual abuse and exploitation of boys. Similarly, the victims and who are at risk situation to subordination, abuse and exploitation need to be developed as self-help strategies so that they can reclaim their rights in real –life situation by consummating their capacity. Through the capacity build-ing strategies, it needs to develop their knowledge on the followings to appropriate measures of sexual abuse and exploitation of boys.

(a.) Its dynamic forms and vulnerability,

(b.) Its negative impact on physical and mental effect and evelopment,

(c.) Parenting care and supports,

(d.) National and international laws and policy on Protection of Children's Rights (PoCR), and

(e.) Preventive strategies.

It is to give the opportunities of stakeholders, especially the young people to develop positive attributes and skills that would have a positive impact on the lives of vulnerable and victims of sexual abuse and exploitation of boys. By strengthening their capacity, effectiveness and responsiveness and bringing up their participation, it is to build the opportunity to identify the problems that affect the lives of vulnerable segments of population. Their participations most importantly will induce valuable solution of the problems of sexual abuse and exploitation and the development of relevant policies, programmes and activities. The stakeholders' involvement needs to work to curb demand of the sexually exploited children in sex selling markets. The hotel workers and shop owners need to be reached and engaged to interrupt sexual violence, abuse and exploitation.

Furthermore, all of the stakeholders are not a homogenous group rather they differ accordingly by age, maturity and socio cultural and economic backdrops and their familial and social status. So the participation of children and young people are disproportionately hampered by the social norms and value system. At the social levels the participation children and young people are purposively hampered, which ultimately impedes their ability to advocate for their rights. It is so rare where they have been able to influence or get opportunity to provide their cordial innovations rather they are barred by complicated social infrastructures. So, it is important to break down the existing social practices and develop appropriate policies to ensure the innovative creation and opportunities for the children and young people's meaningful participation. Their participation in decision making process will induce appropriate measures of protection of violence in a policy framework.

Both the society and state are in a position of affecting the socio-cultural norms, beliefs and attitudes, where both of them have to move forward to address the issue of prostitution of boys. The community itself is confined under the grip of the value system, social taboo and stigma. On the other hand, the state lacks the implementation of National Plan of Action for the children addressing the issue of prostitution of boys. The existing legislation fully fail to protect the victims of boys relating to sexual abuse and exploitation because of societal attitudes, more importantly social taboo and stigmatized situation vitally ignores its legal process. So, it makes a question about the management of cases relating to boys sexual abuse and exploitation and the sexual violence of boys. So, it needs to develop a strategic approach to advocate the civil society and law enforcing agencies, where the effective management of case filled up will be addressed within minimum cares and standards.

To address the issue in legal framework and policy, it emerges to conduct 'two ways advocacy system', one with community's mass people and another with governmental and non-governmental actors. Here, the programming approaches of advocacy should be the strategy of addressing issues in community to induce their effective responses to develop policy and ensure the minimum care and protection of victims of boys affected by sexual abuse and exploitation. The governmental actors, especially law enforcing agencies (LEA) can play a vital role to take protective action against such offence with effective management and handling the case of such offence under prosecution and reflecting its prevalence and vulnerability. The most important advocacy issues should include as follows:

- The legal protection of their rights removing the contradiction of defining the children and legal process, provisions, instruments for the boys victims of sexual abuse to see justice. It takes into consideration of male to male or female to male sexual abuse and rape in legal process to provide justice to the boy victims of sexually abused and exploited.
- Sexually abuse has impact on physical, developmental emotional and stigmatized problems of the victims, and high risk of STD and HIV/AIDS, but the community is fully unaware about the matter, which should be addressed with quality and appropriate healthcare and support services.
- Education and information related materials addressing STDs/HIV/AIDS by electronic and non-electronic media is approached a gender based intervention rather it should include the vulnerability of boys' sexual abuse and exploitation.
- The governmental and non-governmental actors' approach to addressing the issues in Child Rights Programming approach.
- Realization of NPA formulated by government for its proper implementation.

To address the issue of prostitution, community based interventions needs to be partnership and networking based approach with the CBOs to enforce the issue in most organized and effective manner. The networking and partnership will be heavily strong approach to address the issues in collective manner and to address the community responsiveness and activeness towards the issues of prostitution of boys. The partnership and networking with national and international development actors will make platform to address the issue in policy development frame-work, which will create a mandate for the state agencies in realization of sexual abuse and exploitation of boys, take up the national plan of action as programmatic strategy and bring about institutional changes.

The government formulated a National Plan of Action seeks to achieve the Millennium Development Goals (MDG) through implementing the PRSP and to implement CRC. NPA is a multi-dimensional action plan that covers various aspects of child survival, child development and child protection. But, the existing legislation and policy developed by the government fully fail to develhop and protect the victims of boys relating to sexual abuse and exploitation because of societal attitudes, more importantly social taboo and stigmatized situation vitally ignores its legal process. So, it needs to proper monitoring addressing the issues of boys in prostitution which will be reflected by proper supervision at national levels. Some ambiguities are still remaining in different ways because of unwillingness and improper initiatives of government and other duty bearers in a sustainable platform, where it need proper evaluation revealing the gaps of implementation of NPA.

Bibliography

Adepoju, Aderanti (2005) "Review of Research and Data on Human Trafficking in Sub-Saharan Africa." *International Migration* 43:75-98.

Aghatise, Esohe (2004) "Trafficking for Prostitution in Italy: Possible Effects of Government Proposals for Legalization of Brothels." *Violence Against Women* 10 1126-1155.

Allred, Keith J. (2006) "Peacekeepers and Prostitutes: How Deployed Forces Fuel the Demand for Trafficked Women and New Hope for Stopping It". *Armed Forces and Society* 33:5

Andrees, Beate and Mariska N. J. van der Linden (2005) "Designing Trafficking Research from a Labour Market Perspective: The ILO Experience". *International Migration* 43:55-73.

Andrews, Sara, K. Winter (2004) "U.S. Domestic Prosecution of the American International Sex Tourist: Efforts to Protect Children from Sexual Exploitation". *Journal of Criminal Law & Criminology* 94 (2):415-453.

Arnold, Christina and Andrea M. Bertone (2002) "Addressing the Sex Trade in Thailand: Some Lessons Learned from NGOs, Part I". *Gender Issues* 26-53.

Bastia, Tanja (2005) "Child Trafficking or Teenage Migration? Bolivian Migrants in Argentina". *International Migration* 43:54-87.

Belser, Patrick (2005) "Forced Labour and Human Trafficking: Estimating the Profits," Geneva: International Labour Office.

Bennett, John W. (1996) Applied and Action Anthropology. Ideological and Conceptual Aspects. *Current Anthropology* 36: S23-S53.

Bruckert, Christine and Collette Parent (2002) *Trafficking in Human beings and Organized Crime: A Literature Review.* Research and Evaluation Branch. Royal Canadian Mounted Police.

Bump, Micah N. and Julianne Duncan(2003) Conference on Identifying and Serving Child Victims of Trafficking. *International Migration* 41(5): pp. 201-218.

Bump, Micah N., Julianne Duncan, El¿bieta M. GoŸdziak, and Margaret MacDonnell 2005 2nd Conference on Identifying and Serving Child Victims of Trafficking. *International Migration* 43 (1/2): pp. 343-363.

Burke, Alicia., Stafania Ducci and Giuseppina Madd-aluno 2005 *Trafficking in Minors for Commercial Sexual Exploitation: Costa Rica.* Torino. UNICRI.

Cadet, Jean-Robert (1998) *Restavec: From Haitian Slave Child to Middle-Class American.* Autin: University of Texas Press.

Caldwell, Bruce K. and Indrani, Pieris et al. (1999) Sexual Regimes and Sexual Networking: The Risk of an HIV/AIDS Epidemic in Bangladesh. *Social Science and Medicine* 48(8): 1103-16.

Caliber Associates (2003) *Needs Assessment for Service providers and Trafficking Victims.* Fairfax, VA: Caliber Associates.

Chapkis, Wendy (2003) "Trafficking, Migration, and the Law: Protecting Innocents, Punishing Immigrants." *Gender and Society* 17:923-937.

Chase, Elaine and June Statham (2005) "Commercial and Sexual Exploitation of Children and Young People in the UK – A Review". *Child Abuse Review* 14:4-25.

Chuang, Janie (1998) "Redirecting the Debate Over Trafficking in Women: Definitions, Paradigms, and Contexts". *Harvard Human Rights Journal* 65.

Claramunt, Maria Cecilia (2002) Commercial sexual Exploitation of Minors: Costa Rica. Geneva: ILO.

Cole, Jeffrey, Sally S. Booth (2007) *Dirty Work: Immigrants in Domestic Service, Agriculture, and Prostitution in Sicily*: Lexington Books

Constable, Nicole (1996) "Jealousy, Chastity, and Abuse: Chinese Maids and Foreign Helpers in Hong Kong". *Modern China* 22:448-479.

Coonan, Terry and Thompson Robin (2005) "Ancient Evil, Modern Face: The Fight Against Human Trafficking." *Georgetown Journal of International Affairs* 6:43.

Curtol, F.; Decarli, S.; Di Nicola, A.; Savona, E. U. (2004) "Victims of Human Trafficking in Italy: A Judicial Perspective." *International Review of Victimology* 11:111-141.

Finger, Carla (2003) "Brazil pledges to eliminate sexual exploitation of children". *Lancet* 361:1196.

Government Accountability Office (GAO) (2006) Human Trafficking: Better Data, Strategy and Reporting Needed to Enhance U.S. Antitrafficking Efforts Abroad.

Goode, Erich (1997) *Deviant behavior*. Upper Saddle River, NJ: Prentice Hall.

Hennink, Monique; Simkhada, Padam (2004) "Sex Trafficking in Nepal: Context and Process". *Asian and Pacific Migration Journal* 13:305-338.

James, Allison (2007) Giving Voice to Children's Voices: Practices and Problem, Pitfalls and Potentials. *American Anthropologist* 109(2): 261-272.

(2003) Journeys of Jeopardy: A Review of Research on Trafficking in Women and Children in Europe. International Organization for Migration. (Migration Series, No. 11). 2002. 69p

Kempandoo, Kamala with Jyoti Sanghera and Bandana Pattanaik (2005) *Trafficking and prostitution reconsidered: new perspectives on migration, sex work and human rights*. Boulder, CO: Paradigm Publishers.

Petros, M. (2005) "The costs of human smuggling and trafficking." *Global Migration Perspectives*, 31.

Pochagina, Olga 2007 Trafficking in Women and Children in Present-Day china. *Far Eastern Affairs* 35(1): 82.

Scheper-Hughes, Nancy (1995) The primacy of the ethical: propositions for a militant anthropology. *Current Anthropology* 36(3): 409-440.

Sheldon, Zhang X, Ko-Lin Chin, Jody Miller (2007) Women's participation in Chinese transnational human smuggling. A gendered market perspective. *Criminology* 54(3): 699.

Shigekane, Rachel. (2007) "Rehabilitation and Comm-unity Integration of Trafficking Survivors in the United States." *Human Rights Quarterly* 29:112.

Tyldum, Guri. and Anette Brunovskis (2005) Describing the Unobserved: Methodological Challenges in Empirical Studies on Human Trafficking. *International Migration* 43(1/2): 17-34.

Weitzer, Ronald (2005) Flawed theory and method in studies of prostitution. *Violence against Women* 11(7): 934-949.

Williams, Suzanne and Rachel Masika (2002) Editorial. *In* Rachel Masika (Ed.), *Gender, Trafficking and Slavery*. Oxfam Focus on Gender. Pp. 2-9.

Index

V

W